*'A joy to read.'*

'What a thoroughly engaging memoir this is. Apart from anything else it is so well written. It is a joy to read. From beginning to end the prose is that of a true professional. It has a spare clarity, a directness and economy acquired in a long career of journalism and an ongoing engagement with words. We learn so much about the now lost world when newspapers dominated the media landscape and there were large newsrooms and hot type printers.

'The focus is on Elliot's career in provincial Queensland, more specifically in Bundaberg where he learnt his trade and Townsville where he edited the *Daily Bulletin*. This regional focus enhances the book's importance. There is a shortage of studies which outline the way that national themes played out in the country's major provincial cities.

'Elliot's time in Townsville saw the final years of the confrontation between the Communist Party and the DLP and of even greater significance the fundamental transformation of the country's attitude to race. He was also a sympathetic and perceptive witness to the milieu which gave rise to the Mabo case which changed Australia for ever.'

*Henry Reynolds*
*Professor Reynolds is a leading Australian historian and author who*
*pioneered the history of European/Aboriginal relations while living*
*and working in Townsville at James Cook University.*

**'Let his musings remind us of what we are losing before it is entirely lost.'**

'As famous mastheads die, sadly defeated by 'disruptive technology' I feel a deep sadness for the decline of classic journalism. Perhaps something vibrant will replace it but, at the moment, this ancient practitioner can only regret its passing, the by-lines that, one by one, become fading memories. A recent example, the death of that valiant Queenslander, my old friend Evan Whitton.

'So, it is a great pleasure to celebrate the fact that Elliot Hannay is still alive and kicking. Elliot's autobiographical musings are a joy to read, full of insight and humour. His long and ongoing career will, I'm sure, attract the attention of the Media Hall of Fame. More importantly, it should attract a wide readership. Let his writings remind us of what we are losing before it is entirely lost.'

*Phillip Adams*
*Phillip Adams AO, FAHA is an Australian humanist, journalist, broadcaster, columnist and farmer. His first by-line appeared in the Communist Guardian 65 years ago. He is one of Australia's Living National Treasures who was expelled from the Boy Scouts at the age of 13 and resigned from the Communist Party at the age of 18.*

# THE COLT WITH NO REGRETS

Hard copy, hot metal and the power
of the written word

A memoir

## Elliot Hannay

Published by:
Wilkinson Publishing Pty Ltd
ACN 006 042 173
Level 4, 2 Collins St Melbourne, Victoria, Australia 3000
Ph: +61 3 9654 5446
www.wilkinsonpublishing.com.au

Planned date of publication: 05-2020
Title: The Colt with No Regrets
ISBN(s): 9781925927030: Printed — Paperback

A catalogue record for this
book is available from the
National Library of Australia

Printed and bound in Australia by Ligare Pty Ltd.

*'Not to know what happened before you were born
is to remain forever a child.'*

Marcus Tullius Cicero, Roman statesman 106-43 BC.

———————————

This book is dedicated to the memory of AAP,
Australia's trusted national newsagency for 85 years
and the 500 journalists now losing their jobs. Another
blow to professional journalism and an opening for
the excesses of dodgy web sites and fake news.

# CONTENTS

# INTRODUCTION

This is a timeless story about growing up. It's the personal journey of a 16-year-old boy starting work in a country town when reporters toiled with hard copy and hot metal and tough old editors taught cadets their craft with a mixture of instruction and reprimand that would be branded today as workplace harassment of the highest order.

It's also about finding love and sharing life with an amazing partner who can still catch the Colt's breath with her cheeky smile or the casual flick of a greying lock of hair after all these years.

The people are real, the events did happen, and the dialogue and detail are as honest as unreliable memories can recreate.

My first editor threatened to kick my arse all the way down the stairs if I ever misquoted anyone, and that warning resonated with me when extensive dialogue started to appear on the pages. There are no diaries or tattered reporter's notebooks to support these sections, only the intrusive voices of my old colleagues which are still loud and clear to this day.

Much of this story focuses on the role newspapers played in cities and towns in the so-called 'Golden Age' of Australian journalism. Many metropolitan journalists and editors who later became gold-plated, started off in the bush.

Its central theme is a young man's growing friendship with an eccentric gay Englishman who found sanctuary among hard-nosed, cynical journalists and tough war-veteran printers, in an era when intolerance was far more common than inclusion.

While dredging through memories and old newspaper files from 60 years ago, and then reading today's headlines and watching television, I am reminded of a wonderful quote from Faulkner: *'We may be through with the past, but the past ain't through with us!'*

It is not an author's role to apologise for or warn about passages from the past that might be offensive to some of today's more sensitive readers. However, I am reminded of a quote by Mark Twain who said: *'Under certain circumstances, urgent circumstances, desperate circumstances, profanity provides a relief denied even to prayer.'*

Urgent and desperate circumstances were just part of the job, even on a country newspaper and I quickly concluded that my chosen career path was populated by many naturally gifted swearers, who were also decent, intelligent, literate and articulate. Words that, in polite company, would jolt and even offend, could be partnered with normal speech, and with the appropriate timing, produce surprisingly expressive passages.

Aboriginal and Torres Strait Islander readers are also advised that this work contains the names of deceased elders and activists.

I don't think we did things better all those years ago, but I'm certain we did them well. I do, however, regret that many papers across Australia are now edited remotely and most of the presses are also located 'somewhere else'. It is obviously more cost efficient, but how do young reporters today 'learn stuff', without working and drinking with printers — the 'boys out the back'?

Today's young journalists in training, particularly in universities, probably don't know that a spotted dog has a much better sense of smell than other breeds, or that Jesus was in the building trades when he was a young bloke.

It is also hard to shed some of the lessons and doctrines that were drummed into me in my formative years. So, I'm still allowed to shake the Sunday tabloids in anger at smart-arsed puns for headings that don't really make sense or switch off the television when vision of a bloody fluffy cat being rescued from the top of lamp-post in Prague intrudes into the precious time allocated for our national news broadcasts.

I can imagine my first boss and mentor, Mort Nash, being fast-forwarded by a time warp and seeing how television has become a major source of our daily news. 'Jesus wept Colt... what has happened? Why are baby fucking pandas so important in the scheme of things now days?'

*Elliot Hannay*

# FOREWORDS

*Striking a nerve with the truths of journalism*

I had not heard from Elliot Hannay, my old editor at the *Townsville Daily Bulletin*, for more than 35 years, until an email in July 2014 congratulating me on the 50th anniversary of the launch of *The Australian* newspaper. That email address came in handy two years later when in retirement after 14 years as editor in chief of 'The Oz' I began working on my memoir, *Making Headlines*.

I wanted to check a story from the '*Bully*' published in the late 1970s or early '80s for a chapter explaining my longstanding interest in Aboriginal affairs. I ran the details past three former fellow *Bulletin* journalists I had worked with, but they couldn't remember it.

The story concerned the firebombing by off duty soldiers of Aboriginal people living by the banks of Ross River under the bridge connecting the north and south sides of the city. I emailed Elliot and he remembered the yarn well. He sent the details quickly. It's the sort of story no committed newspaper editor forgets publishing. It took courage for Elliot to campaign against such outrages in the very parochial — and at the time racially divided — port city of North Queensland.

When my book came out Elliot was quick with his assessment and soon took the opportunity of our renewed contact to send me early drafts of his own memoir, *The Colt with No Regrets*. He earns the nickname Colt in the early chapters dealing with life as a cadet journalist at the Bundaberg *NewsMail*.

These stories struck a nerve with me. Many are whimsical and speak of the truths of journalism from the days of hot metal printing. Days when the public bar was a training ground for young reporters, journalists spoke to their sources daily and drank with them often. Reporters rang police direct and there were no police media departments to hide the truth from reporters and their readers or protect the police force and its political masters from scrutiny.

Today's young journalists, with their digital recorders and university degrees, their twitter feeds and their social activism, are a world away from the life of the Colt in 1958, his editor 'appointed by God' Mort Nash and his sub-editor mentor Myles Carruthers, who the Colt realises only late in the piece is indeed gay.

This is the newspaper world I grew up in. Many of us knew old gay subs from England hiding out in the colonies and drinking gin after work when most of the reporting staff and all of the comps and printers were downing schooners. These were the keepers of good grammar and in most papers the great sticklers for accuracy.

The Colt brings a sympathetic eye to his tales of Myles's travails in an industry that opened its doors to such characters long before they were accepted in other fields. In the era of legalised gay marriage readers will find reinforcement for their vote in Elliot's evocative stories.

He brings a similar tone to his courtship of a sea nymph on the beaches of central Queensland's Coral Sea. He remains devoted to his wife, the novelist Barbara Hannay, in their Atherton Tableland writers' hideaway.

The Colt also touches as an editor in mid-life and later as a political adviser on many of the big issues still driving journalism today.

Not only did Elliot know of racism in provincial Australia, as editor of the Bully he once met representative from the Ku Klux Klan in his office and handled their approach deftly as they warned about a dangerous activist gardener at the city's James Cook University, one Eddie Mabo. Later there is an excellent chapter on a young State politician later to become a federal independent, Bob Katter. Elliot has also written a book with Katter, and here describes how progressive the young Bob was a State Minister for Aboriginal Affairs.

The Colt discusses his first trip to China as a working journalist and the already fraught tensions over Chinese occupation of islands in the South China Sea, probably the hottest issue on the planet.

A couple of chapters on a $3 million writ from investor Eddie Kornhauser and Sydney crime identity Abe Saffron tell a tale of intrigue over Queensland's second casino licence. The story is full of pre-Fitzgerald Inquiry police corruption and even has links to the casino investments of a future US President: Donald Trump.

Elliot has written a highly entertaining and amusing book that includes something for everyone, but especially for journalists interested in their craft and some of the big social and political issues still driving it.

*Chris Mitchell AO.*
*Chris Mitchell received an Order of Australia Medal on*
*Australia Day 2019 for distinguished services to print media*
*and Indigenous education programs.*

## *Sharing a writer's life*

Don't become a journalist.

This is the advice my father gave me in the mid-1960s when I was still in high school and contemplating my future career possibilities. Dad knew that English was my best subject and that I loved writing, but he was quite firm. Journalism was no career for a young lady. Journalists spent all their time in pubs.

Obedient daughter that I was, I became an English teacher instead — and, of course, not too many years later, I married a journalist. And, inevitably, my father was right. In those days, as you will soon discover when you read the Colt's story, journalists did spend rather a lot of time in pubs. That's where the police were, after all — and the best news stories.

After I developed my own writing career as a successful novelist, some of our friends joked about whether Elliot had appeared in one of my romantic novels, at least in the fictional form of a tall, rugged Australian character. Now, in a happy turn of circumstances, I find that I've appeared as a real-life character in his memoir.

I'm the girl who'd just left home and was feeling adventurous in a bikini 50 years ago when I caught the Colt's attention on a midnight swim in the Coral Sea. Later in the story I appear as a young wife and mother whose editor husband seemed intent on provoking very dangerous people — including corrupt police and gangsters from Kings Cross.

I must admit it's now far more relaxing to share the Colt's life as a writer in our 'senior years' than it was when deadlines, broken shifts, work on public holidays, and sudden postings to new locations were part of our family life.

So, what's it like when two writers live together for almost fifty years?

I think it helps that Elliot and I have always written in very different styles and genres, so there's been no sense of competition. Elliot was a professional journalist working in either newspapers or television and radio, while my writing was merely a hobby. I attended evening classes in creative writing, but although I wrote one or two short stories which found homes in women's magazines, mostly I was scribbling adventure stories in exercise books for our kids or penning simpler stories (usually about princesses) for them to illustrate, which I then turned into homemade books by stitching the spines on my sewing machine.

During those early years, when we moved around a fair bit and I was busy with the children, Elliot shared very little about his work when he came home at the end of the day. I guess with eager children greeting him at the door, he welcomed the chance to leave the workday issues behind him. So, in many ways, this memoir was a revelation to me — especially stories from Elliot's days as a newspaper editor, including his meeting with the Ku Klux Klan.

For me, it was in the mid-nineties that the need to write my own stories returned with ever increasing urgency. By then, my father had been diagnosed with a terminal illness and one of the last gifts he gave me was a collection of the world's greatest love stories. At this point, I was using whatever time I could scrounge, mostly on weekends or in the school holidays, to write my romance stories and Elliot became my most enthusiastic cheer squad.

I might not have persevered through years of rejections if my wonderful husband hadn't kept assuring me that I really could write and that my stories were great. Sadly, my Dad died before my first book was accepted for publication.

And so, in the past twenty years, since I've also become a professional writer, Elliot's and my mutual love of words and storytelling has become a feature of our daily lives. We are each other's all important 'first reader'. He's a wonderfully enthusiastic and encouraging critic and also a great brainstorming partner.

In return, I've been able to use my years of working with editors and revising my novels to help Elliot refine his manuscript into a work of non-fiction narrative, rather than a collection of anecdotes. However, it's his story and his unique voice and I must confess that my favourite section is the trauma and humour of his early years as a cadet journalist on a small country newspaper. Elliot had told me bits and pieces of the time before we met, but I loved the way he's shared it here, showing us a naïve young fellow fresh out of today's equivalent of Year 10 and entering a man's world

Having learned the need for 'emotional punch' in my own novels, I see this as a coming of age story that will resonate across generations.

*Barbara Hannay*
*Barbara Hannay writes women's fiction with over 12 million books sold worldwide. Her stories set in Australia have been translated into 26 languages. She has won the coveted Rita Award from Romance Writers of America and has been short-listed five times. Two of Barbara's books have won the Australian Romance Writers' book of the year award and one of these has been optioned for a film in the UK, USA and Canada.*

# PROLOGUE

*A double brandy on a double brandy*

Myles Harrington Carruthers stepped off a slow train from Brisbane with no luggage and wandered into The Imperial an hour before closing.

I wasn't anywhere near legal drinking age, but I was there when it happened. But it was okay. I was into my second year working at the paper next door, and I had been given the nod.

I had been taken in one day by Tommy and Mervyn and received the nod from Mother Moore, the widow publican.

'Always wear a coat and tie when you're with us, Colt. Stand up straight so you look older than you are, make sure you start with a dash of sarsaparilla in the first beer and stay off the rum until you're twenty-one… and for God's sake loosen that tie, pull the knot over to one side so you look like you're taking a well-earned break and not about to attend a bloody funeral.'

My entry to this world of men also got the nod from the plain-clothes who never seemed to pay for their drinks. Detective Sergeant Neil Harvey looked like a grey goshawk watching a duckling in a chook pen on the first day I walked into the bar.

He looked at Mother Moore who gave him the nod, then turned to Tommy and Mervyn and they all exchanged nods. He ignored me. I badly wanted to give someone the nod.

By the time Myles Carruthers hit town, I thought I was a competent nodder, but modified my modus operandi after Tommy pulled me up short. 'Stop it, Colt, you're nodding to every poor bastard who walks through the door. You look like a bloody parrot in a cage.'

So, I didn't nod at Myles Carruthers when he stepped through The Imperial's old batwing doors, letting a chilly westerly sweep through the bar.

He was pale, pink and skinny and he looked crook. I was young, and he seemed old. He had a nylon Hawaiian print shirt stuck into light brown corduroy shorts that were soiled around the pockets. Dirty white short socks and what looked like plastic slippers.

Myles was dressed like an English remittance man in sultry Singapore, but it was a cold Bundaberg winter's night. Later, his fellow drinkers would suggest that he'd consumed so much alcohol that his blood chemistry had changed, and it acted as an effective anti-freeze.

In the four years he was with us, I never saw him wear a jacket and can only recall the shirts changing. The corduroy shorts, unwashed socks and plastic shoes, took on the appearance of permanent attire.

His arrival in the pub that night became the stuff of legends in later years. I vividly remember him ordering a double brandy on a double brandy in a plummy, almost stuttering English accent that silenced the noisy bar.

That's when I first saw his trademark pub theatre. The glass raised high into the air for inspection against the hard-overhead lights, like an Amsterdam diamond cutter appraising the largest stone he'd ever seen. The other hand, with the little finger sticking up in the air, sweeping back his long greyish-blonde hair.

Then, just as you were preparing for the bar to erupt with derision, Myles, with the timing of a Shakespearean actor, would put glass to mouth and with a sudden tilt of his head backwards, drain four shots of Chateau Tanunda brandy in a split second.

We all realised in that first hour of his first night with us, that Myles was in the grip of the grog. He could repeat the quadruple brandy theatre until he ran out of cash or credit.

Like the worst of alcoholics, Myles had a huge capacity for drink and it soon became obvious that beer, even Aussie beer, was but well water to the demon inside him.

He told me much later that he was greatly relieved that first night when he saw soot-blackened cane cutters drinking beer with five-ounce over-proof rum chasers. They were so black from working in the burnt sugarcane that Myles first thought they must have been coal miners, but it was their capacity to quaff strong spirit that really impressed him.

'A civilised society cannot be maintained by beer alone, old boy. Spirit drinkers are a sign of civilisation. Distilling is a gift from God, passed to us through the ancient monks. It is all about the search for purity and essence, just like a good tabloid sub being able to condense four hundred words of purple prose into a beautiful intro, supported by two meaningful and informative paragraphs.'

Yes, Myles was one of us, a newspaperman, and a hard copy journo.

Others in town came to describe him as a con man, a bullshit artist, a queer and a bad influence, but I believe he was the closest I ever came to having a real English gentleman as a friend.

He was certainly a welcome voice of encouragement in an era when young journalists were trained with much more reprimand than praise. A year after his grand entry Myles, who was holding court in the pub, decided that he'd seen enough of my rounds copy to publicly announce I was, 'one of the chosen few.'

I was old enough to realise such an unexpected ego-boost had probably been planned, and now it would be difficult for me to resist when the usually cash-strapped Englishman later bit me for ten shillings.

But, it was official. I had been professionally anointed by an eccentric, alcoholic, war-wounded retired major of the Irish Guards who sometimes alluded to degrees from both Oxford and Cambridge. Myles had decreed that I would survive this painful period of my training and do what journalists are supposed to do — right wrongs, expose injustice and help create a better world.

My problem was that our tough old editor, Mort Nash, had warned me that 'working journalists' who covered the rounds, council meetings and court cases, would never have time to write copy like that. I would just have to wait and see what the future held for me.

I'd had a shaky start to my cadetship and was still gripped by the fear of failure, so I felt it was more important to keep my job and learn the journalists' craft rather than be influenced by Myles' unexpected praise. I'd been told often enough that this newspaper game was a tough one, and editors were quick to weed out cadets who didn't perform, even in their second and third years.

A career that didn't involve processing words into print seemed unthinkable. I suppose it was because I'd been strangely drawn to the power of the written word at such an early age — at primary school.

# PART ONE
# THE COLT

## CHAPTER 1.

# The Colt discovers the wonder of words

*Bundaberg West State Primary School 1950. A shell-shocked teacher and 70 kids in a crowded classroom.*

I was a skinny, wheezy, eight-year-old, desperately trying to find something at school that I might be good at.

Mr. Sheppard was trying to manage a double class of over 70 smelly kids, because our normal teacher, Mr. Lobegeiger, had started crying at the school Anzac Day parade a few days before and hadn't been seen since.

On that day, two of the boys, Noel and Donny, had got the giggles when we were supposed to be quiet. It was pretty strange standing out in the sun, with everyone, even the teachers, looking at their feet. We heard later that someone had farted and that set Noel and Donny off.

Mr. Lobegeiger, who never used the ruler on anyone, started belting the boys with both his hands, really hard. Two of the other teachers, including Mr. Sheppard, had rushed in and stopped him because he was crying his eyes out, sobbing, just like Noel and his little mate who were copping the biggest hiding the school had ever seen.

They sort of carried Mr. Lobegeiger off, with one of his arms over each of their shoulders, just like the wounded soldiers from the war books in the library.

We weren't sure if he was ever coming back. Some of the older kids said a teacher wasn't allowed to cry in front of pupils — it was against the law or something. They didn't do anything to Noel or Donny.

Mr. Lobegeiger had told us earlier that we wouldn't be doing poetry until next year, so it came as a surprise when Mr. Sheppard told us it would be on that week.

'Just go home and learn some poetry, anything you like, it only needs to be one verse. Everyone will have to recite their piece the day after tomorrow.'

The fact that Mr. Sheppard could stand near the door or move close to the open casements and take deep breaths of fresh air entering the stifling classroom, was probably the real reason for the move from his cramped desk which was almost surrounded by extra pupils.

We all stank at school in those days, particularly in a hot place like Bundy. No such thing as air-conditioning. Sweaty, barefoot kids, either charging madly all around the schoolyard, or packed into small rooms, shoulder to shoulder. For some strange reason the big kids, the ten and eleven-year-olds, stank even more than us.

I was worried. We were moving on to poetry already in Grade Three? I didn't know a 'real poem', but I knew someone who did. Uncle Bill, one of Mum's brothers was staying with us and he could quote Shakespeare. He had stayed in the army, still had his uniform and was making maps or something.

Uncle Bill had brought me a green cloth cap with a red anchor on it. You could fold the side flaps down over your ears. He said it was a Jap marine cap and it wasn't really too big for me — it was like a kid's cap.

I'd been wearing it to play war down the street with Cliffy Dullaway and John Bylsma, when an old man on a bike called me over and told me to hand it over. He seemed angry for some reason and said it wasn't the sort of thing I should be wearing.

He was scary and only had one arm. His face was thin and bony, and it looked like his eyes had sunk back into his head. He stuffed the Jap cap in his back pocket and rode off. His bike wobbled a lot. I had never seen him before, so we couldn't do much about getting the cap back.

Uncle Bill was happy to help with my verse of poetry but didn't think Shakespeare was what Mr. Sheppard had in mind. So, he recited part of 'The Man from Snowy River'.

*There was movement at the station for the word had passed around*
*That the colt from Old Regret had got away*
*And had joined the wild bush horses... he was worth a thousand pound.*

It was wonderful and sounded like a cross between a prayer and a hymn. When he said that the horse 'was worth a thousand pound', his voice changed, and he said it softly, like it was something amazing or he was sharing a secret.

Mum said his family nickname was 'Rowdy' because he was the quietest of her six brothers. But Uncle Bill changed into something completely different when he recited poetry. He looked different and sounded different.

When I asked him about it, he said that my mum's lot, the Sorrensens, were Danish, but they had Irish as well, from their mum, who was a Finnegan. That was the reason he could make poetry sound so good.

He also told me that the Finnegans didn't believe in ghosts, but all of them could tell if one had been around.

I thought he would write the verse out for me, but he said I had to learn it in my head. I repeated each line after him and then he sent me off to practise on my own.

He got me to run it through for him late the next afternoon and was so pleased he clapped his hands at the end. He couldn't stop grinning and I was so relieved.

He said it was possibly an improvement on the original and he was sure my teacher would enjoy it as well.

When it was my turn the next day to stand up in the packed classroom, I was full of confidence.

'Hannay, what have you got?'

'The Man from Snowy River, Mr. Sheppard.'

'Okay, take us down the mountain then.'

Before I started, I told Mr. Sheppard and the class that I'd learned it by heart from my uncle and I didn't have to read it from a piece of paper or a poetry book.

I took a deep breath and tried to think I was part Irish — Uncle Bill said it always helped him.

'There was movement at the station for the word had passed around that the colt with no regrets had passed away...'

I was beaming with pride when I finished the verse. The important bit, about the thousand pounds, came out like a whisper.

Mr. Sheppard was a kindly man. My Dad said he was 'a returned man' whatever that was. He seemed very happy with my effort and he actually praised me in front of the class.

'That rendition would have brought a smile to the face of Banjo Patterson himself... possibly even a tear.'

Then he added: 'You ever wonder why the gifted Mr. Patterson called it The Man from Snowy River and not the Colt with no Regrets?'

'No, Mr. Sheppard.'

'Well I suggest you find a printed version of it my boy and read it carefully, word for word. You may be enlightened. But for today we will assume your colt has not passed away… he may have some regrets but he's running free… out there with the wild bush horses.'

I just kept smiling. I realised just how wonderful words could be. It was the best day I had ever had at school.

## CHAPTER 2.

# The newsroom is a dark and fearful place

*The News Mail 1958. In the days of hard-copy and hot-metal journalism, fear of failure ran high in the six-month probation period for children starting their four-year cadetships.*

The newsroom of the Bundaberg *News Mail* was on the top floor, just one flight up a dark stairwell with a dusty, web-shrouded lightbulb to provide some flickering illumination during the night shifts. I was 16, just out of school and physically fit but, for some strange reason, I felt sick in my stomach when I finished the climb. The brightness and fresh air of freedom in the outside world slowly dimmed with each heavy step I took towards the start of work in my third week.

At the top of the stairs, there was a piece of furniture that looked like a pulpit, or a lectern, just outside the editor's office. Sitting on it, with grandeur like that of the Holy Bible or the Koran, was the duty book which listed the tasks for each reporter or sub on shift that day. For a cadet on six months' probation, it was not a welcoming sight, but a dark sentinel that needed to be approached with caution, because you never knew what strange or disturbing duties might be listed for you.

So many of the jobs in producing a daily newspaper seemed to be far beyond my life experience or schooling. It was obvious that reporters, sub-editors and printers spoke a second language at work, and I wasn't just illiterate — I was dumb-struck.

I had even been given a new workplace nickname, The Colt. I realised it was probably a send-up, seeing I was skinny as a rake, pushing six feet four and still growing. Tommy, the sub who had christened me, was at least friendly, but this was also adding to my confusion when instructions or orders were being shouted at me in a name I was slow to recognise.

Would I be up to the task? What new unachievable challenge did the fearsome editor, Mort Nash, have in store for me today? I approached the big ornate leather-bound duty book and there it was, the page wide open — my initials, 'EH', with the stark notation, 'see me.'

Shit, not again. I was about to be carpeted by the boss. The last time this happened was only a week ago, and I'd burst into tears. I wasn't one of those kids who cried all the time. When I broke my left arm at the combined primary schools' sports, and even when I dislocated my shoulder at high school, there had been no tears.

I don't know why I had lost it. The tears just welled up. I was embarrassed and angry with myself, but I couldn't help it.

I'd copped a painful caning or two at school from old Piggy Bourke and held up okay, but Mr. Nash made you suffer. You had to stand up through it all and it seemed to go on for hours.

Now, I was about to cop it again. Obviously, I'd made some serious stuff-up, and I was so clueless that I couldn't tell what it was. But I was smart enough to realise that I couldn't go on this way for another six months of probation, and it seemed that my dream of a grading at the end of four years was just that — a stupid bloody fantasy of the mind.

Ok, so the job interview had gone well, but things were different now that I was actually on the job. I was getting my arse kicked so regularly I concluded that I only got the cadetship because no one else applied.

Now I was gripped with the fear of failure and my goal at the moment was to avoid the shame of being the first *News Mail* cadet reporter to be sacked before completing their six months' probation period.

My worst fears were realised when I plucked up the courage, knocked on the editor's door and heard his first words.

'Listen carefully, Colt, I'm not happy… not bloody happy at all. Didn't you learn a thing when I got stuck into you last week for wandering around like a stunned mullet? This isn't American bloody baseball where you get three strikes. This is the newspaper game and you only get one crack at it.'

The squat, round-shouldered man blew cigarette smoke up into my face before stubbing the ash into a scab-encrusted glue bottle on his disorganised desk. I stood stiff and straight as one of the Queen's guards. I had obviously stuffed something up big time and he was about to sack me.

'You okay, Colt? You look crook.'

I knew from last time that the boss expected a response to every question. If I said, 'Yes Sir', or 'No Sir' he'd snap at me about not being at school or in the bloody army. So, I was prepared this time.

'Yes, Mr. Nash.'

'Yes, I am crook in the guts and about to throw up all over your desk, or, yes, I am okay thanks, Mr. Nash?'

Why didn't he just get it over with? Couldn't he just say something verging on being nice to ease the pain when he sacked me? Like telling me that not everyone is suited to journalism and that I could probably look forward to a successful career digging ditches or emptying dunny tins? I had to tough this out, so I needed to stop showing just how scared I was.

'Yes, I am okay thanks, Mr. Nash… couldn't be better.'

He looked at me a bit strangely. 'Right then…those swimming results you brought in last night were a mess. One big error supported by disjointed copy that was all over the place like a madman's shit. It shouldn't be that hard… age division, freestyle, backstroke whatever, the distance and the time.'

'Yes, Mr. Nash.'

'Well, one of the times you had listed was almost an Olympic record and you expect our readers to believe it was swum by some pimply 12-year-old? It doesn't get much bloody worse than this, I can tell you. We will have to publish a correction tomorrow and that means all of us, not just you, gets dipped in professional shit in the eyes of our readers.'

How would I explain this to my parents and my mates? I had only lasted three weeks before I made one of the worst mistakes in sports' reporting and got the boot. It wasn't a stuff-up in covering the Olympics, but in Mort Nash's eyes it was just as bad.

I couldn't bear this any longer so, I asked the question.

'Am I being sacked, Mr. Nash?'

He looked genuinely shocked.

'Sacked? You don't know the difference between getting the sack and being counselled in your craft? When I sack you, son, you will have a sore arse from where my boot connected with your backside as I pointed you down the bloody stairs.'

So, I still had a job, but the way Mr Nash was sounding off convinced me I was still on very shaky ground. Tommy, the sub, had warned me that anything could happen during my cadetship and he'd even joked that the definition of an optimist was a cadet bringing a cut lunch to work on the mistaken belief that he would still be on the payroll by lunch time.

'Yes, Mr. Nash.' I wasn't sure what counselling entailed, but it was better than being fired.

'So, for Christ sake, listen to what I'm about to dish up, because I don't want valuable lost time with my contacts in The Imperial to be totally wasted.'

It was about to start. I looked longingly as the spare chair beside me, but I knew I wouldn't be allowed to sit down.

And then, there was the terrible smoke haze in the boss's office which was hard for someone like me who had just graduated from being an asthmatic kid, to a young bloke with a weak chest. I knew better than to wave the smoke away from my face, or to have a coughing fit in front of him — that would have been fatal.

The boss always had a cigarette in his mouth but managed to talk at a great rate at the same time. He smoked with total commitment to the task and with an amazing determination to suck each smoke right down to the butt.

This was only achieved through strange, upper body contortions, when he twisted his head sideways in an apparent attempt to avoid the last of the hot, glowing ash which ended up so close to his hairy nostrils.

This amazing display of a dedicated smoker trying to distance himself from the last of his cigarette also required his right shoulder to be twisted under his chin, which made his back arch up, like the Hunchback of Notre Dame.

As a non-smoker, I was so fascinated that I sometimes stopped listening to what he was saying — which was very dangerous.

Now he was staring straight at me, with a new Capstan smouldering on the side of his mouth.

'You paying attention?'

'Yes, Mr Nash.'

He held up a large roll of white perforated tele-printer tape. To me they were just a lot of holes and they only became words after they were run through the printer.

'You learnt to read these yet, the dot codes, so you have some idea of what's likely to come out the other end of the printer?'

'No, Mr. Nash. I know how to cut copy paper, do the carbons and file the exchange papers.'

I paused. Shit, that didn't sound like much.

'I can read the temperatures and do the humidity calculations at the post office.'

'Well bugger me… you've been here over a week and that's all you've managed to pick up? How old are you again?'

'Sixteen.' I was desperately looking for excuses but immediately regretted suggesting that I was too young to be blamed for my mistakes.

'You seem a lot younger, Colt. Even if you are tall in the saddle. Talk about a long streak of pelican shit. What are you, six three or a bit more?'

'About that, Mr. Nash.' Here we go again. Just because I was taller than usual it didn't mean that my IQ was supposed to rise at the same time as my height. If I couldn't claim my lack of years as an excuse, then the boss shouldn't try to suggest that someone over six foot should be a lot smarter than I was.

'Well, you've got some real growing up to do. And I don't mean you need to get any taller, you understand?'

I nodded anyway.

'You've got to be a lot sharper. I want good, clean, hard copy. Ask questions, check everything. Learn about times, so you'll know a fast one from a slow one and not make mistakes like that in the first place... and if a junior at the Kokoda Pool ever does an Olympic time, we'll put your story on the front page, I promise, okay?'

I nodded and relaxed a bit. I preferred it when the boss became facetious. It felt better than being verbally abused by him.

'Now I've got to correct it in tomorrow's paper... I'm not happy. It's not only you... it should not have got through the subs. What condition was Tommy in when you came back last night?

I had to be careful here. Tommy was pretty pissed by the time I got back from the night carnival, but he was still working away subbing copy when I dropped mine on his desk and took off. He was the one bloke who seemed to be trying to help me. 'He was normal, Mr. Nash'.

'Normal? So, he was half cut but you're not game to say it?'

I shrugged.

'Well, well. Only been here a couple of weeks, but already covering for poor old Tommy. Take a tip son, stick up for your mates by all means, but don't spend too much time strutting on the moral high ground. That's where they crucified Christ... remember?'

'Tommy usually tells me when I've made a mistake.'

'Most of the time, yes. But you've got bloody eyes, haven't you? You must know what happens when he's been on the turps. He'll let anything through around midnight if he's been sucking on the Tanunda bottle.'

I nodded.

The boss opened the copy of today's paper on his desk, flipped to page three, turned it around so I could read it and stabbed a finger and the headings.

'This is what Tommy can do better than most. Headings that all fit perfectly and make sense, and tightly subbed copy with clear intent. But we all know he also has a problem, so I don't want you to disrespect him. He's a brilliant sub up to ten at night… copy book stuff. They reckon the Bible is the only text that can't be improved by subbing, but no one has ever given Tommy a crack at Genesis early on a shift on a non-race day.'

I decided to have a good read of Genesis when I got home, to see what this was all about.

'If Tommy is pissed and hard-pressed around deadlines, you could give him five-hundred made-up words about the mayor rooting owls and there's a good chance he'd correct the spelling, grammar and punctuation, mark it up in eight point, give it a double column thirty-point Bodoni heading, and spike it for the printers.'

The boss was staring at me with a strange look. What was I supposed to do, laugh or look serious? I knew about hypotheticals but what if it was a test to see if I also knew anything about people actually having sex with owls? I was out of my depth and sweating.

'Listen carefully then. It's not just about avoiding errors getting into print. I don't want you making mistakes in the first place that might get past any of our subs and into the hands of the proof-readers to gloat over. Newspaper errors are like turds on the desert sand, they last forever…you understand?'

'Yes, Mr. Nash.'

'Okay, what else do you know?'

'I know I shouldn't make mistakes or expect the subs to pick them up… and you don't like having to publish corrections.'

'Look, I don't expect you to have a wise head on your shoulders just yet, but you need to grow up a bit faster and pick up on things. And you also need to be 'in-the-know' in this game. You know what I mean by, 'in-the-know'?

'Yes, Mr. Nash. A good reporter must be well informed.'

'Well informed my arse. People can be well informed and still know bugger-all about what's really going on. A good reporter should know who's up who and who's paying the rent. It's all about who's doing what, and who they're doing it to. You get to know that in in a place like this and you'll be more than well informed, believe me.'

Some of this was hard to absorb. Only a couple of years earlier I was being told that a Boy Scout must be clean in thought, word and deed. Now, as a cadet journalist, I had to learn about sleazy, adult stuff.

'But we don't print stories like that, do we?'

'Of course, we don't. Remember what I said about not all the facts being newsworthy or printable, but I want all my staff to know what's crawling under every mossy rock in this town?'

'Thanks, Mr. Nash. So, if the mayor was really having sex with owls, you'd want your reporters to know all about it, in case it was ever linked to something in the future?'

He suddenly slapped his hand on the desk and made copy paper fly.

'Chapter and bloody verse Colt... the whole box and dice. I'd want to know what sort of owls, how many, how old they were, male or female, when, where and why.'

I must have looked pleased with myself.

'Well, don't start polishing your Walkley Award for Journalism just yet, you've still got some pretty dry gullies to cross. Your interview revealed some sports or hobbies that could be regarded as adventurous and might require a tougher hide, or wiser head, than you seem to have.'

I didn't know what to say. What did this have to do with my training — apart from being another obvious shortcoming?

'Rifle shooting, even archery and skindiving… fairly mainstream… but taxidermy and falconry? It seems you've been seeking things out that are a bit different. If you have a choice you are more interested in the ones that have a challenge?'

I wasn't sure whether to shrug or nod. I decided to nod, because it was a lot easier than trying to explain the amazing feeling I had the first time I fitted an arrow to a proper bow, pulled it back to the side of my mouth and felt the fletching touch my cheek — it was as if I had done it all before, in a dream, or even in another life.

'Okay, son, I should have realised this before. Your sort of background has its good points in this game, but blokes like you can also stray the other way and become too bloody dreamy. Just now, you're showing all the signs of wandering off into fucking fantasy land and the only cure is a regular dose of newsroom reality. I'll bet London to a brick that you don't know what an intrusion is.'

I looked at my shoes.

'It's what reporters do to get a story. Foot in the door stuff. Going where angels or Anzacs fear to tread, fronting up at a funeral and being prepared to ask questions… doing your job of work and finding out if the accident victim was killed outright or had any last words…doing whatever it takes.'

He was staring straight at me. I just nodded.

'So, the local soldier who was accidentally shot by one of his mates in Malaya …. are you up for it? Find out if she's expecting and when he was last home on leave…was it six months, nine months or a year ago. Dates are important if there's a pregnancy involved. Ask how she feels about the trigger-happy mate who shot him?'

I just stood there. At first, I thought it was some sort of sick joke or a send up for the new cadet, then realised the boss was deadly serious. Earlier he'd seemed worried that I might be sick on his office desk. Now my head was spinning and my stomach churning.

'If I give you the keys to the van around teatime, can you go out and talk to the family … ask them for a photo of their boy to help break the ice and then work in the questions?'

I choked on my reply for a moment, then blurted it out. 'No, Mr. Nash… I'm sorry, but I couldn't possibly do that.'

'What do you bloody mean you can't?' He really did look angry now.

'I'm too young to drive.'

He relaxed a bit — but only a little.

'Well, make sure the tyres on your bike are pumped up… you need to be ready for this sort of thing. This reporting game is not all tea and bikkies and you'll have to toughen up as well as smarten up, or you might not make the grade.'

He waved me out of the office and returned to shuffling piles of copy paper on his desk.

I walked back into the newsroom. At least I wasn't crying this time — not on the outside anyway. But how the hell was I supposed to have known that growing up quickly was a requirement for this job or that letting your imagination run wild could ruin your chances for a career in journalism? After this session I wasn't sure whether I could handle a job that involved causing even more grief to families who were about to bury their dead children.

Two days later I was on my bike, riding over the Burnett River Bridge to interview the family of a famous rugby league player who had died suddenly — my first intrusion.

Mourners were crowded on the veranda of the North Bundaberg home when I nervously introduced myself and asked if the family had any preferred photographs that they would like us to run with the obituary. It all happened quickly and with good grace. They even trusted me with the famous player's scrapbook, which I promised to return the next day.

The men offered me a beer, but the ladies fussed me into the kitchen for a 'nice cup of tea'. I didn't feel like an intruder at all.

# CHAPTER 3.

# Grime, smoke, copy paper, ink and glue

*This is not a normal office job. Gathering and printing the daily news is rushed, noisy, stressful and confusing because they don't teach you any of this stuff at school.*

The newsroom, which most of us referred to as 'the editorial', but which Percy, our senior reporter insisted was actually the 'literary department', wasn't a very welcoming place.

It had cold old brick walls that had been thinly painted a dirty cream and it always seemed to be grimy, even though a pensioner named Jim came in very early to sweep up the paper mess and dump all the cigarette ash. Only the pressmen, or those who worked very late, ever saw much of old Jim.

The editor's office was tucked away to one side at the top of the stairs and it was the only room that had a door.

The rest of us worked around two large desks. There was one telephone on a small silky oak table, and a long bench against one of the walls with annual bound copies of the newspaper going back at least twenty years. It was my job to spike clean copies of the paper each day — one for cutting and daily reference, the other to be guarded jealously for future binding.

The subs' desk was the biggest and dominated the main area of the newsroom. It was a grand piece of furniture, a magnificent dark red cedar table that could probably have seated ten or more elegant diners in the Victorian era. But it was a functional desk and had several finely fitted draws with ornate brass handles.

The basic grandeur of the desk couldn't be hidden, but the subs did their best to camouflage or deface it with several big bottles of glue with sticky pigs-bristle brushes either plunged deep into the glue or left stuck to the tops by their wooden handles. There were islands on the desktop created by the subs' 'cut and paste' tools of trade — loose razor blades, several pairs of old tailor's scissors, blotting pads and paper, ink bottles, spare pens, biros and lead pencils, both blue and red.

Prominent amongst the subs' treasured detritus were glass or metal ash trays of various size and quality including a large ornate silver hub cap from a vintage Rolls Royce. Everyone smoked, except me.

Parts of the table looked like a forest of porcupine or echidna quills. Each sub seemed to need at least three copy paper spikes. The apprentice printers out the back made them up from old tobacco tins which they filled with molten printer's metal and then inserted a metal spike cut from a bicycle wheel spoke, which was much stiffer and tempered than wire. This was then sharpened on a grindstone to a point so keen it would easily spike a dozen or more sheets of copy paper in one hit.

I later found out that it could also penetrate straight through a sub's hand should he be hard pressed spiking copy near deadline, or possibly had stayed too long in The Imperial at smoko.

To place a typewriter on the sub's desk was sacrilege. It was below the dignity of a sub to touch the reporters' tool, particularly if a major re-write was needed. They would simply throw the offending copy back at the guilty reporter who'd produced 'dirty copy'.

The typewriters on the reporters' desk were big noisy machines, Underwoods, with black enamelled frames and brass keys worn to a polished gold colour. When speed touch-typists like Percy and Tommy attacked them, they rattled with each keystroke and zinged loudly with each carriage return.

To manually return the carriage to the next line required a lever to be pushed from an extended position on the right, back to the far left. The Underwoods' workings were so robust that this was best achieved by striking the lever forcefully with the right hand. With Tommy, it was like swatting flies. Percy's method was more like a savage right hook. There was so much vibration that the big solid desk shook, and the typewriters actually started to walk. Some moved backwards, others tracked sideways.

Percy's favourite typewriter crabbed to the left, so he simply slid his chair along the floor with his feet while seated and followed it down the desk. When working on a lengthy court story he could end up down my end, blowing smoke in my face and telling me to stop crowding him. Percy seemed old to me and his dark hair was flecked with grey. He could be a bit severe at times and didn't smile anywhere near as much as Tommy.

Tommy mainly subbed, but the editor often used him on rounds and council meetings as well — it all depended on the boss' assessment of his drinking habits at the time. Tommy's Underwood preferred to go backwards, so he didn't have the option to move or crawl up onto the table to keep track of it. Every ten carriage returns would see the little bloke hold on to the carriage lever and drag the whole machine back in the one movement.

This would all be achieved without losing a beat, the short sheets of copy paper being ripped off and new ones rolled in — words flowing like water, words all spelt correctly, the right amount of words, not two or three words when one would do, words that informed, not embellished, words that formed phrases, and punctuation that left the reader in no doubt about the meaning of the text, or how it should be read.

All this happened on the reporters table, which by custom and tradition, had to be a few inches shorter than the subs' desk. It wasn't a round table, but Percy was certainly our King Arthur and his chair was slightly bigger than the others. He was the senior reporter, the one and only A Grader on the staff. The grading system was nominally an industrial classification that determined rates of pay under the Journalists Award. But it also defined professional status.

The graded journalists had priority on all things, including access to the worktable and its typewriters. This included the *News Mail*'s woman journalist Janice, who was afforded the space appropriate for her grading, no more, no less. The number of typewriters didn't match the number of staff because all of us were never on the same shift at once, but for some strange reason I always seemed to be giving my typewriter, and my space at the desk, to a reporter who outranked me or someone who had copy that was far more urgent than mine.

The whole place was all about priorities.

The sub's desk was given top priority in the allocation of light. There were two huge light globes under shades that looked like white enamel washing-up dishes suspended by chains from the grimy ceiling. They reminded me of the lights they have hanging over billiard tables. These things threw intense white light straight down onto the subs table, but they also acted like radiators in both summer and winter.

It got so hot at the sub's table that coats and ties were taken off and shirt sleeves rolled up. The older hands, including Tommy, wore sleeve-garters just above their elbows. They looked like jazz or banjo players, or those gunshot gamblers in the movies. Tommy said garters allowed you to shorten your sleeves, so the cuffs wouldn't get soiled, but it looked to me like they just wanted to cool off.

Everyone at the sub's desk wore eyes-shades, some were green and made of celluloid, but Rod MacAlpine, who was a bit younger and only just made it into the war as a junior naval rating, wore a stiff canvas or fabric shade like some of the glamorous tennis players in the movies.

When the coats came off, you could see that old Percy, who questioned everything and didn't seem to trust anyone, wore a belt as well as braces and little Tommy had a light-weight waistcoat that had a special pocket wide enough for a standard shorthand notebook.

Anyone could walk up the stairs and get straight into the newsroom. The only counter in the building was down in the front office. There was a partition in the newsroom, but it was a more recent addition, to screen and, to a certain extent, silence the chattering tele-printer.

After a while, I realised that the excitement that went hand-in-hand with this strange working environment could counter some of the fear I felt. I just had to show that I'd be good enough to survive the probation period.

The Imperial Hotel next door functioned as an annex to the paper and newspaper people were its main customers at lunch time, morning and afternoon smokos and changes of shift.

There was even a private room with its own fridge, table and chairs, that was accessed through a locked door in the laneway. That was for the late shift workers who finished at two or three in the morning. They placed their orders early on the shift, got a key from Mother Moore and kept the noise down so they didn't wake the hotel guests in the early hours.

I sensed that it was during these breaks in the pub that all the good stories were being told, the best jokes shared and many of the town's darkest secrets revealed. There was never much chatter in the newsroom because everyone had a job to do and all the tasks had deadlines. It was much the same for the printers.

It was all happening next door, but I was 16 and excluded.

I was being sent out on some of the rounds every day and tried to recall things I had learned at school, anything that might help me with my confusing job. The only experience that seemed to have any practical application was two years' basic military training in in the Army Cadets.

Admittedly, knowing how to strip down a Bren-gun while blindfolded, how to react to an ambush in the jungle, or being able to shoot a four-inch group with a military rifle didn't help much when I was out on the shipping rounds. But, thanks to the cadets, I also knew how to listen to instructions as if my life depended on it. I was familiar with a chain of command, and I knew I would suffer horrible consequences if I stuffed up.

I quickly learned that you could never come back to the office from rounds with too much detail. It was drummed into me to make sure anyone who was named in the newspaper could not be confused with someone else. Percy said this was top priority for a 'working journalist'.

Fortunately, the detail was there, for all to see, on the ambulance records and in the police accident reports. Full name, age, marital status, occupation.

A housewife who got her hand scalded in the washing boiler, or a farmer who fell off a tractor and broke a leg, had their personal details publicly exposed in the next day's issue of the *News Mail*.

Percy said the details were very important, particularly in his court reports, because a person's reputation could be compromised if there were other people who had the same name as the convicted felon.

He also said that we had to publish everything that went through the courts, even so-called minor things like speeding or not indicating a turn, and, of course, drink driving. Exposing and even shaming the wrong-doers was part of the punishment. Percy seemed proud of his role in all this.

My training was on the job, or rather out on the streets. After years of classroom schooling I'd been looking forward to the sense of freedom that reporters seemed to have. In my last year at high school I would often run into Rod Gallegos downtown, after classes. He was always yarning with someone, not stuck in the office. He proudly told us he was 'on the rounds'.

When my turn came, I felt like a shag on a rock. In those early months, I was never given an assignment or even a lead for a story. I had a notebook and pencil and not a clue. I felt sick in the stomach almost every day, weighed down by responsibility and a constant fear of failure.

Rod was a year older than me, and a year ahead in his cadetship, but I felt it was more like ten years. I was a good head taller than him, but that didn't help, because Rod looked and acted like he was twenty-seven. I was gawky and reserved. Rod was compact and super-confident.

All legs and arms, and had trouble buying clothes that would fit. Even with Mum's best efforts in taking in shirts and slacks, they never seemed quite right. Rod, of course, was a snappy dresser and he even wore one of those trilby hats so popular with the senior reporters, racegoers and plain-clothes coppers. I tried one of them in the men's-room at Buss and Turners and, on my head, it looked stupid, as it made me seem even skinnier and taller.

Rod had even mastered wearing his tie in the style of the older men. Out in the street it was done up properly but, in the pub and at the work desk, it was loosened and pushed slightly to one side. The gap between tie and collar at the throat was about two fingers wide and the complicated Windsor slipknot helped achieve this cool, casual look with a skilful, sideways tug.

It never seemed to work for me. When I tried the loose look in the newsroom, Tommy said I looked like some poor bastard whose execution had been stuffed up by a drunk hangman.

Rod even drank in other pubs as well as The Imperial, under the noses of the coppers, that's how confident he was. I would often see him charming Mother Moore and the barmaids, cracking one of his carefully selected, appropriate jokes, beaming with his broad smile or studying racing form with Tommy.

The boss had a plan to move Rod into more sports reporting, particularly racing, so I started to inherit some of his rounds, mainly the State Government offices. The best-looking girl on the counter of the Department of Primary Industries was obviously miffed when I replaced the cheeky and charming Rod Gallegos.

# CHAPTER 4.

## The boys out the back

*Printers are smarter than journalists and hot metal*
*is actually really hot.*

'Out the back' was production. I'd been quickly walked through there on my first day to see the sacred home of the printers and their chapel. It was crowded and incredibly noisy with banks of massive, hot, clattering linotype machines spitting out type, the operators key-stroking words from slips of subbed copy-paper at astonishing speeds, their fingers flashing and swiping over the shiny metal keyboards.

This whole hectic scene was lit by hot, white, overhead lights and all the flat surfaces glistened with beautiful shiny black dust, a mixture of lead, antimony, tin and graphite.

Nobody seemed to worry about all the fumes and black dust, and nothing was wasted. At the end of the shift it was all swept up, the sparkling black dust, lead shavings and used type was thrown into a big electric furnace on the same open floor. It produced silvery ingots and whenever the lid was opened, spewed out acrid fumes that hovered between floor and ceiling like grey mist. I was told the printers got a glass of milk a day from the bosses, and that protected them from the dreaded lead poisoning.

The Father of the Printer's Chapel told me that my union didn't give a shit about workplace safety. 'Sorry, son, but you journos are up the creek on this one. You'll probably crawl away under a desk and die from lead poisoning before you've had your first root.'

My next serious contact with the boys out the back came when I was told to refill the subs' glue bottles. The sub-editors fancied themselves as being a professional cut above the hack reporters, so they jealously protected their professional status in front of other crafts or trades. They certainly never lowered their personal standards by refilling their own bottles.

They went through glue almost at the same rate as they drank beer next door. Armed with razor blades or scissors, the subs cut and slashed the reporters' stories as fast as the copy came off their noisy Underwood typewriters. They then reassembled all the pieces with generous brush splashes of obscene looking glue, convinced that their changes and wordsmithing had greatly improved the original works.

I suspected that in my first week I'd become the butt of a journalistic joke involving glue bottles that probably dated back to the first newspaper ever printed. One of the subs, Rod MacAlpine, who was in the war but was still young enough to be in the lifesavers , told me there was a ' lesson in life' if I looked closely at how dried out glue at the top of the bottle eventually blocked entry of the glue brush.

'Just remember Colt, that as you go through life you will never encounter anything so unique... it's the only hole known to man that gets smaller with use.'

I looked over at Tommy, who was subbing next to Rod, to give me a lead, but he had his head down and kept spiking copy. How was I supposed to react? Give a bawdy laugh as I would have done a few months ago with my mates at high school, or just nod knowingly like a young man who'd been given sage advice by an elder.

I was too insecure to do either and suspect that my lack of response had pissed Rod off. His joke, that I inwardly acknowledged as being both bawdy and clever, should have been shown the humorous respect it deserved but I had just stood there silently thinking of something to say which might indicate I was ready to enter the ranks of working men.

Rod waved me off dismissively. 'Loosen up for Christ's sake son. This is a newsroom not a minefield, you don't have to go around looking like you're about to shit razorblades all the time.'

For a moment I thought about laughing, but quickly decided Rod wasn't joking.

Now, only a few days later, Rod had instructed me to go and fill his glue bottle. There was no joke this time., he just told me to 'see Mervyn' out the back in production.

Mervyn, Mr Cooper to me, was the foreman compositor. I'd been introduced to him during my quick walk through on my first day. He wore khaki overalls and army boots. When he was flat out on the comp floor everyone gave him plenty of room. Mervyn and his team set up the pages, column after column of tightly packed individual slugs of type, laid out on a flat marble or granite bench. They worked on 'the stone' and were proud of it.

I entered production through an ancient red cedar door with ornate brass fittings and cautiously approached Mervyn who was inking a long galley of type with a hand roller. I was determined to be extra polite.

'Please, Mr. Cooper, can I have some more glue?'

He looked stunned.

'Well, root my boot…it's Oliver Twist his self.'

I must have looked as confused as I felt.

'I'm the foreman here son, the bloody boss. I'm not the fucking glue man.'

I turned to continue my search for the glue drum desperate to escape the embarrassment of my unintentional contact with Mervyn, the foreman compositor — not the 'fucking glue man'.

But Mervyn wanted to chat.

'Don't rush off son, just hold on a minute.' He patted me pater-
nally on the shoulder. 'You'll soon learn the ropes and I am really
glad that I've got someone from editorial here just now, because we
have a problem with a heading. Can you check it for me?'

'I'm not graded or qualified or anything like that yet Mr.
Cooper. I don't know if I…'

Mervyn just smiled and reached over to a linotype machine,
grabbing a slug of type as it emerged. He studied it for a few
moments, shifting it from one hand to the other.

'I think they've got a U here when it should be an O. Can you
check it?'

It was a trick as old as printing itself and here I was, the
ultimate trophy for a scorched hand, some kid from editorial
who was dumb enough to reach out and accept the friendly
offering. No one had told me that these blokes could handle hot
metal like ice cubes.

They juggled them from hand to toughened hand rather than
waiting for slugs to cool down. You just couldn't waste time if you
were working on 'the stone'.

I squealed like a weaner-pig and dropped the white-hot slug —
straight down the unlaced top of Mervyn's left boot. His yell hit
an even high note than mine and he started hopping madly on his
right leg, while trying to pull off the smoking boot.

There was no way even a veteran printer could endure a hot
slug of metal wedged between army boot leather and a soft tender
instep. Mervyn's burned foot meant that I at least got noticed on
the comps' floor in my first week.

His older mates joked about it, but I never did. I was very
pleased when he stopped limping a few days after the burnt foot

incident. Mervyn was a little man with a receding forehead but could be scary at times.

Mervyn and a much bigger, round-shouldered workmate, Bevan, had gone off to war but never joined the RSL. Mervyn had served in New Guinea and later in Borneo. Bevan had slogged through the North African desert and the Syrian campaign before being shipped home to push the Japs back from Kokoda and Shaggy Ridge.

We didn't get much detail, but like the other ex-servicemen in the production area they mainly told stories about each other, not themselves. It was a known fact that during the war Bevan had often quietly lead his patrol around mine fields. How he sensed where the mines were, hidden under the desert sand at night, no-one knew. Percy who knew everything about most people in town, had been told about it by Striker Blackburn, the local black-smith, who served with Bevan.

Little Mervyn also had other strange attributes that helped during the war. He could smell Japs in the jungle from a great distance.

I was too timid to question Mervyn, so I asked Bevan about it and he simply nodded, like it was nothing special. 'It's not mystical son, it's because all your senses, even some the doctors don't have a name for, are heightened by danger and Mervyn also has a snifter on him as good as a spotted dog.'

'A spotted dog?'

'Yes, Colt, a spotted bloody dog. Don't you know anything?'

My relationship with the men out the back had to be respectful, but it was also far more casual and comfortable than being in the newsroom with my superiors.

Men like Bevan and Mervyn were married, had kids, knew about sex, racehorses, spotted dogs and politics. Bevan even knew some words in French and Arabic. I was impressed by even a limited knowledge of foreign languages, but Bevan said it was only useful when they were single, and it could keep you out of the military stockade or, get you into a decent bordello.

'It's all relative, Colt. I knew the words for "you have beautiful eyes, show me your bed" and the other one was "we are Australians, surrender or die on the bayonet". So, it was useful back then when you were on leave, or if you were on the front line trying to put the shits up your enemy… but not much bloody use today, I can tell you son. Even if there was an Arab sheila in Bundy for me to flirt with, she'd be off limits for me now as a married man and unfortunately, we aren't allowed to bayonet Frenchmen anymore.'

I must have looked puzzled.

'Yes son, Frenchmen…The Vichy French in Syria and the Lebanon. We called them the Vicious French… right pack of bastards they were.'

'I thought they were on our side?'

'Not the bloody mob we encountered. The French Foreign Legion were the worst. Not a bit like Beau Guest from the movies and books. Germans, Italians, Japs and the bastard French — they were all grist for the mill when I was doing my bit with the Seventh Division.'

I shook my head.'I didn't know. They never told us that in school. In history lessons, I mean.'

Maybe the editor was right. If I listened and asked questions I might end up knowing stuff you don't learn at school, like which dogs have the keenest sense of smell. After all, these men were special — they had travelled. Bevan, who had a chest like a beer barrel, could sing songs from Gilbert and Sullivan and Mervyn had a bullet hole in his leg.

Mr. Nash asked me what I had learned in the first month and I told him I was learning lots of things from the printers as well as the editorial staff. He said my IQ would probably go through the roof in my first year at the *News Mail* if I kept listening to the boys out the back.

# CHAPTER 5.

# Women are better at this game than us

*'Just remember son, you'll be in serious fucking trouble*
*if you ever swear in front of Janice.'*

'Boss is looking for you Colt.'

My blood froze. I had just walked up the stairs with not much copy from the rounds and met Tommy at the top. I wanted to know more, but Tommy pushed past me in a hurry. The boss's door was shut, which was unusual because the editor normally kept it wide open, so he could see what was going on in the newsroom. I knocked gently and was sure my hands were shaking. There was no response.

I almost bolted but realised there was no way I could avoid another painful session. Whatever was in store, he'd come out sooner or later. I just prayed that the boss hadn't had another bad day at the races.

I turned the doorknob and looked in. The *News Mail*'s esteemed editor was sound asleep, sitting in his chair, both hands on the desk, still gripping his pen. His head was back and there were gargling noises coming from his open mouth.

I gently closed the door then knocked loudly several times. There was a loud grunt, so I opened the door again. He looked confused when I stepped in.

'Well, what do you want? I'm trying to write the bloody leader.'

'Tommy said you wanted to see me, Mr. Nash.'

'Tommy? Oh yes, I had a talk to him about you... earlier in the day.'

He stared at me like I was supposed to know what this was all about.

'Pull up that chair and sit down, Colt.'

Shit. This was it. He always kept us standing when he was giving anyone a serve, so, being politely invited to sit down could only mean he was about to soften the bad news.

'Just remember, son, that I am the only one in this building who's allowed to make your life miserable. It's part of my job to knock you into shape.'

I was too tongue-tied to even say the usual 'Yes, Mr. Nash'. I just nodded.

'You don't know what I'm bloody talking about, do you?'

I just shook my head but then realised that I should have nodded instead.

'I'm talking about Barry bloody Regan. You listen to me, not him.'

I suddenly got my voice back. 'Yes, Mr. Nash.' Barry was a graded reporter who had only recently arrived from Sydney. He was short and nuggetty, had a broken nose and very short hair. He looked tough and would often say mean things about other work-mates when they weren't around. Sometimes he would send me off on weird jobs like cashing his personal checks at various banks.

'I can't spend all my time fussing over you young blokes like a mother hen, so don't rely on me to get you knowing all the ropes. Ask the older reporters. I've told Percy, Tommy and Rod to keep an eye on you, but that doesn't include learning anything from that that fucking foul-mouthed Barry.'

I started to relax, the boss was pissed off with someone else for a change. I wasn't in his firing line this time.

'He's a smart arse and he's giving our Janice a hard time as well as you. I suspected it and Tommy confirmed it.'

I didn't know what to say.

'He resents girls like Janice being paid the same rates as men in our game. In her case he's pissed off that she's taking more home than he is. He's been giving her a hard time, deliberately dropping the F word in front of her as if that's the price she must pay for equal pay. I don't want you caught up in it.'

He lit up another cigarette.

'You know why Janice gets equal pay and women have done since the award was first set up bloody years ago?'

I must have looked blank.

'Because the founding fathers of journalism, even in their wildest dreams, never thought that women would be crazy enough to actually want to work with a mob like us. You mark my word; we'll eventually be swamped with sheilas. Look at Eve and Pandora. Women have always been equipped with more natural curiosity and instincts for news gathering than any of us.'

He leant closer to me as if he planned to share some dark secret.

'At the *Courier* and *Tele* in Brisbane, I can remember when they were only working on the social pages, or fashion and stuff like that. Now they are all over the place, including general news and the courts. If this keeps up, we will have some places where they outnumber the men.'

'So, it's a bad thing?'

'Christ, haven't you been listening. Jan is by far the best educated person in the newsroom. She's about to finish an Arts Degree by correspondence, she's reliable, doesn't spend half the day in the pub, she writes to house style and when a nice girl like her interviews a reluctant politician he will open up like a Mater nurse at confession.'

I nodded. I had only recently been introduced to Mater nurses by my mate Johnny Mikkelsen down at the Kokoda Pool. They were shift workers like us.

My mind started wandering to these interesting girls I had never met at school. Catholic girls in Speedo one-piece swimming togs — the ones with a piece of elastic stitched on between the shoulder straps at the back — to stop the top from ever slipping down. It was a most enjoyable vision, but I was quickly brought back to reality by the boss.

'Colt, you're wandering… do you want to learn more about our female work colleagues, or do you want to stare blankly into space?'

'No, Mr. Nash. I'm listening.' This was all very interesting.

'Just remember that girls like Jan, all of them, have memories like bloody African elephants…which is very handy for a reporter.'

'So, they are actually different from us?'

'Colt, you're probably too young to have experienced it, but believe me, women have a different system in their brains to remember things, and it's streets ahead of ours.

'Blokes have electrons or something, but in women it's also chemical. Very small little things from years ago… things that you've forgotten… will be thrown back at you in the finest painful detail.'

I felt safe enough to join in.

'So why aren't they paid the same as the men in the other jobs?'

'That's only half of it, son. Not only are they on lower wages, but as soon as they get married, they will lose their bloody jobs, that's what happens. All the government offices, the councils, the schools and most of the private businesses sack girls as soon as they get married.'

That didn't sound fair. I was full of questions, but the boss cut me off.

'Anyhow, back to Barry. You probably think he's a pretty tough bloke from Sydney, that's the impression he tries to give. I hear that he's been interfering with your work, under the guise of giving you his professional advice. Don't be awed by blokes like Barry who talk tough and swear all the time. There are much better benchmarks, even around here. You ever heard Bevan, the night foreman, swear in front of a woman or try to throw his weight around?'

'No, Mr. Nash.'

'Well, take it from me, Bevan's the hardest man you'll ever come across in your lifetime.'

I was surprised. 'But he doesn't look tough, like Barry, he just seems normal.'

'Normal, of course he's not bloody normal any more after what he's been through. Do you think it's normal for a decent, well-mannered family bloke like Bevan to know several different ways to kill a man with his bare hands? You think that's something useful for him to pass on to the apprentices out the back?'

'No, Mr. Nash.'

'Don't get me started on that subject.'

I started to realise that there were lots of things that could get the boss stirred up — it wasn't only me.

'Just remember any galah who swears in public or in front of a woman is lacking in intellect and vocabulary. And, I don't want you coming out of your time here with a limited vocabulary because of Mr. Barry Regan.'

I waited. I sensed he had more to say.

'Colt, there is no single secret to success in this game, but there is one thing in our profession you must remember… ask questions. Assume nothing and, when in doubt, leave out. By the way, what are we paying you as a first-year cadet?'

'Three pounds ten a week, Mr. Nash.'

He looked genuinely shocked.

'Jesus wept! Does your hand shake when you sign the bloody pay slip? The unions and the AJA have a lot to answer for. No wonder management is paranoid about costs. You alone must be eating up half the paper's profits each week.'

He looked me up and down and then shook his head. 'Do you realise, that not long ago I fought all the King's enemies for not much more than that? No overtime, no time books, just the silent thanks of a grateful nation and lots of happy memories to keep me awake at night.'

'I'll try to ask more questions, Mr. Nash. I want to earn my keep.'

'Okay. Don't get bloody philosophical on me.' He gestured towards the door. 'Just bugger off and get on with it.'

In the following weeks, I became much more aware of Janice and how good she really was at this job. She had short, dark hair, wore reading glasses, had turned twenty-one and didn't have a boy-friend. She wasn't beautiful, but she still looked good to me.

After Mr. Nash's lecture about women reporters and Barry's bad conduct in front of her, I also became a bit protective — even though Jan was older and never gave the impression she needed protection.

I became super-sensitive about bad language in the office, constantly checking to see if our female colleague was nearby if one of the boys let fly with a swear word. Strangely enough it didn't happen often. It was if the men could sense when Janice was in earshot and adjusted their language accordingly.

Barry, of course was the exception. He not only swore in front of Jan, but on occasions it seemed like he was swearing at her. I felt like saying something, but because Jan ignored him and just kept typing as if Barry wasn't even there, I did the same.

Ignoring Barry was a good strategy because it seemed to upset him even more.

Out on the rounds with Janice one day I asked if a graded journalist like her ever got bored with the un-interesting details we had to gather as part of the job. I was surprised by her reply.

'You have to remember that much of the copy on rounds that might not seem like news is important to many of our readers. Things like the temperature, rainfall, tides, ship movements, train times, fish prices. Get this down accurately, do the best job you can with the detail, and you'll be better equipped to handle the bigger stories when they do come along.'

The boss was right. Women journalists were probably smarter than us — they were certainly more incisive. What really struck me was that Janice had a different view of things than blokes like Percy and even Tommy. I could never imagine Percy saying that my shipping notes and rainfall figures were just as important to our readers as one of his big court stories.

# CHAPTER 6.

## Bloody murder and the big city crime reporters

I learned early on that journalists working in the country could not expect to become famous or win awards. There only seemed to be one big prize in journalism and it was called The Walkley Award.

I asked Percy about it and he just smiled.

'Unless we're unlucky enough to have a mass murderer come up here from Sydney or Melbourne and give quiet old Bundy half a dozen funerals overnight, our chances are sweet-fuck-all Colt.'

That made sense to me. Nothing like that ever happened in Bundy. It was all happening down in the big cities — down south where there were lots of murderers, crime bosses and corrupt politicians.

Then one night in May 1959 it did happen. A cane farmer and his wife were killed in their bed at night, brutally bashed with a piece of lead pipe and then shot with a twenty-two.

The Kalkie Murders were about to make Bundy famous.

A killer on the loose.

Queensland's top detective on the job.

Doors and windows were being locked on farms throughout the district.

Surely not a local? It must have been some crazy person from 'Down South'.

A Brisbane reporter from 'The Truth' suggested police were investigating whether it was a 'rum killing' — Bundy's famous over-proof rum could turn a normal man into a frenzied killer. To back this up it was also pointed that Bundaberg Rum had the sole contract to supply the Royal Navy with its famous rum issue to its fighting sailors.

This was too big for even Detective Senior Sergeant Neil Harvey to handle alone. The Police Minister sent up Inspector Bill Cronau and his offsider Bill Buchanan. According to Percy and the others, Cronau was famous and all the Brisbane reporters called Inspector Buchanan 'Buck'.

Inspector Cronau was a little man, like Tommy, while Buchanan was big and broad, like a front-row forward.

This was a national news story. Suddenly there were other reporters in town, including Ken Blanch from the *Telegraph* and he was just as famous as the detectives. Percy was pleased and said he was competing with a team of the best crime reporters in the country.

I didn't think Percy would let me tag along, but he actually insisted that I go with him to one of the afternoon briefings at the police station in Quay Street.

It was a small, crowded office and I was pressed hard up against the back wall — but I was still part of it all.

I was surprised that it wasn't different. I thought something like this, because it was so special, would be different.

But the reporters, even the ones who came up from the big Brisbane, Sydney and Melbourne papers, just listened, took notes and asked Inspector Cronau questions. It got a little rowdy when several tried to ask questions at the same time, but it was pretty much what I was being trained to do — just more exciting.

I was on the night shift two days later when Ronnie Lovett, a school mate who was also an apprentice lino-type operator, called me over. He was a couple of years older but lived in my neighbourhood. He had a girlfriend, and everyone knew they were going to be married.

Ronnie and his girlfriend were down near the beach on one of his nights off, when he disturbed a mob of hares in his car's headlights. This was very exciting news indeed. My Dad and one of Mum's uncles had introduced me to rabbit shooting with a spotlight when we visited Torrington in Northern New South Wales. I also loved the idea of the wild harvest where you brought great food home and didn't waste anything. According to Ronnie the hares were in plague proportions.

'Mate, there were dozens of them running all over the place. They would hop a little way off and then squat. They're down on the old Barolin rifle range reserve so the grass is nice and short. There's a farmer about a mile away who's also growing peanuts and the hares are getting stuck into them. What do you reckon?'

'It's too good to miss. You want me to bring my shotgun?'

'That's what I was thinking. I'll drive and spot them in the headlights and you can pot them with the shottie. You like roast hare?'

'Too right, mate. Mum soaks them in vinegar and salt water and it takes the stink out of them… the buck hares are a bit on the nose.'

He nodded. 'Okay, then… tomorrow night when we finish the late shift. We can run down there, clean some up and still get home to bed before the sun is up.'

It worked a treat. We had a great night and ended up with five hares. It didn't take long. The range was under thirty yards and I potted them in quick succession.

Then, the shit hit the fan when I turned up for work at six that night. Ronnie dashed into the newsroom, his face white and his hands shaking. 'We've got to talk mate… out the back… now.'

I was confused but followed him straight out to the production where my mate took me into a far corner.

'We're in deep trouble. The coppers are after us. Haven't you heard?'

I shook my head.

'I've just been setting the copy from Percy... the latest on the Kalkie murders and it's us mate... it's fucking us... we could be arrested at any time.'

I just stood there staring.

'They think it's us. Shots fired down near Kalkie late at night. People being terrorised. The boss detective is telling people to lock doors and windows. Percy even has a quote from someone at the rifle club saying it's okay to shoot back if you think your life or property is being threatened.'

I tried to stay calm, but I realised that the southern press team in town for the murder investigation would grab at this and we would get a run in all the big city editions. It didn't matter that Barolin was miles away from the murder scene. Shots in the night, that's all it took. I should have realised, but all I could think about at the time of our hunt was an exciting wild harvest of roast hare.

'It's okay, Ronnie... we didn't do anything wrong. You're allowed to shoot hares at night, and we were on an old rifle range anyway.'

'Come off the grass, mate, they don't give a rat's arse about that. We've got a team of the best detectives in Queensland after us. They'll find something to pin on us, even if it's not the murders. We'll be locked up and questioned for bloody sure.'

I was sure Ronnie was over-reacting. 'I'll tell Percy and he'll sort it out. It will be all right, you'll see. We were using a twelve-gauge shotgun and the killer used a twenty-two.'

My mate then turned on me and I was shocked.

'What do you mean "we" were using a twelve gauge? You were so caught up you didn't even offer me a bloody shot. You say one word about this, and I'll knock your bloody block off. I'm getting married in six weeks' time… no matter what.'

I wanted to argue, but Ronnie played club rugby league and was built like a Roman arch. Ronnie being upset was one thing, Ronnie being angry with you was something else.

'Okay, mate… Okay. Let's just leave it and see what happens.'

Ronnie and I suffered silently for two more days before Inspector Cronau and Butch Buchannan solved all our problems. They arrested a neighbouring farmer for the murders, and we were off the hook.

It was all rather sad in the end. The murder victims, and the bloke who was convicted and got a life sentence, all came from a close community of respected families.

Ronnie got married as planned and I kept him a clipping about our late-night gunfire from one of the national dailies and gave it to him at the reception. He seemed happy — even a bit proud.

# CHAPTER 7.

## The day the music died

*'Buddy Holly... is he the Peggy Sue bloke?'*

There was one story I was proud of. I didn't write or sub it, but I was still responsible for it being published in our paper. It was big news, but the night subs didn't seem to understand.

February 3, 1959. 'The Day the Music Died.'

Buddy Holly, Ritchie Valens and the Big Bopper all died in a light plane crash in an American cornfield.

I was putting the tapes through the tele-printer which converted lots of little holes into words on paper... and there is was. I tore the copy off and ran into the subs' room in near hysteria, yelling, 'Buddy Holly's dead... There's been a plane crash in America.'

Tommy looked up briefly under his green eye shade, decided no one was actually on fire, and went back to writing headings.

Rod reached over, took the copy from me and began to read.

I kept interrupting. 'This is horrible, Rod... everyone I know will be shocked.'

He didn't seem too impressed, sat back in his chair and looked at me.

'Listen to yourself, Colt. Horror... shock... drama... you think we've suddenly changed from broadsheet to bloody tabloid?'

'But, Rod, it's big news.'

'So, you're suddenly a copy taster now are you, in your first year? You decide whether this should get a run or not? Do you think you should put the book together tonight?'

'No, no … it's just that he's famous.'

'Okay, settle down. Is he the Peggy Sue bloke?'

'Yes, that's him … and the one about It's Raining in my Heart' … I tried to sing part of the verse, but my voice cracked.

'Jeez, Colt spare me the bloody vocals… I'll see if I can find a space for it… but the paper is tight tonight.' He looked back at the copy and started to sub it.

'It's spelled here as Holly, but that name can also have an "e" as well.' He was frowning.

'It came over the wire like that… I think that's on his records as well.'

'Just because it comes on the wire doesn't mean we don't have to check it. Try to contact one of your mates… break the sad news and get him to check the spelling on a record label.'

'I'll ring Johnny Mikkelsen down at Bargara… I know they have a phone.'

It made one of the early pages the next day, a single column. I'm not sure if this great tragedy, which historians later called '*the day the music died*', would have got a run in the *News Mail* if I hadn't stuck it under the sub's nose and pleaded the case for Buddy, Ritchie and The Big Bopper.

The older generation just didn't get it — rock and roll was here to stay.

A year later we published a story about the world-famous harmonica player, Larry Adler, who was on a tour of bush towns with the ABC.

Larry, who knew a thing or two about 'proper' music, publicly put the boot into rock and roll. Percy Grey reported that Mr Adler believed the new wave rock and roll was 'a parasitic form of music whose material offers practically no opportunity for the musician.'

The local radio station, 4BU Bundaberg banned rock and roll and was proud to boast that they were, like the churches, taking a stand against the moral decadence that was influencing today's young people.

In my last year at school my parents had even stopped my hopeless attempts at learning to play the guitar when I was caught doing side-ways pelvic thrusts and strumming away in a vain attempt to copy Elvis Presley.

They needn't have stopped my lessons because the musically inclined railwayman I was learning from was a big fan of country music and I probably would have travelled down that dusty road instead. He idolised the legendary Chad Morgan, also a local lad, who was hitting the big time and making lots of money with songs like *The Sheik from Scrubby Creek, Chasing Sorts in Childers, My Shotgun Wedding* and *The Day I gave Up Drinking*.

The most popular of his songs was *The Thrashing Machine*. Everyone in town, with obvious exception of my mum and dad and Mr. McCormack who ran Radio Station 4BU, knew it was really a very dirty song.

Chad sang about showing his girlfriend the workings of his thrashing machine — his 'vertical piston, dry thrashing machine' — in a machinery shed, on a farm at Childers.

Chad had also invented a unique vocal signature for many of his songs in which he howled like a dingo. Mervyn argued that it sounded more like a blue heeler cattle dog that had been left chained up to a tank stand and not fed for a couple of days. All the printers out the back liked Chad Morgan and sometimes the chorus from *Thrashing Machine* would break out, even when they were busy at work.

So, rock and roll was banned on the local radio station and preached against in the churches, but here I was singing a dirty song along with grownup men at work.

The songs on the Elvis Presley records were mostly sad and romantic and Buddy Holly was sometimes sad, but mainly happy, so I couldn't work out why they were banned on the radio, but Chad wasn't.

Much later, when The Beatles were honoured by the Queen for their contribution to British, music, art and culture, our editor wrote a scathing editorial about how the award had devalued the ancient Order of the British Empire.

# CHAPTER 8.

## Thinking about girls just adds to the confusion

*Timely advice about girls from an acknowledged expert.*

About this time, I started to work more closely with a colleague who was supposed to be the font of knowledge about a subject that was a mystery to me but was dominating my daytime thoughts and giving me disturbing dreams — girls and the distant possibility of sex. Ray Peek was one of our stringer photographers and I was working up courage to ask him questions about the opposite sex.

I was acutely aware that I lacked even the most basic physical contact with females, apart from the normal motherly hugs which I'd started to resist in late primary school. Being an only child, I didn't have an older sister who could bully me, but also give me the occasional cuddle when I need one. I had a pretty cousin two streets away and it had been innocent fun to have pillow fights and hose fights when we were young, but of course that was taboo once we became teenagers.

I couldn't even remember when I had the protective comfort of an embrace from my own father. He intruded into my happy life with Mum at the end of the war when I was three, and at the time he had terrified me. Mum had shown me a photo of this big man in his Air Force uniform to assure me there was another important person in our family, and he was called Daddy. But when I first saw him at our door, he was a gigantic stranger with scary yellow coloured skin from taking anti-malarial drugs for four years.

He wasn't the hugging type. He was more your 'run hard, tackle low' father who'd spent several of the best years of his life manning a 50-calibre machine-gun. I could never remember a bedtime story, or in the years of puberty, any advice about girls or what to do when I realised my little dick had a mind of its own. And now, here I was soon to turn seventeen and a bit more knowledgeable, but apart from the occasional 'pash', still totally lacking in serious form of physical contact with the opposite sex.

Seventeen was also the legal age for girls, which added to the confusion. They were allowed to 'consent', and we could 'do it' without ending up in the courts, but we would also shame our families and our souls would certainly rot in Hell. I wasn't very worried about the Hell bit but shaming my own or a girlfriend's families was out of the question.

I was probably more interested in just getting close to a friendly girl on a regular basis, maybe feeling how beautifully soft they were, or touching lips and tongue. Anything more that that was too daunting. I wasn't scared of girls; I was simply awe-struck.

I had to learn more about them, and I knew that Ray Peek was just the man to teach me. We didn't have a staff photographer but several from the commercial studios were on call. In my first few months I was teamed up with the best one in town.

My main job was to get the spelling of names correct because subs would never trust photographers to record anything accurately. Ray was about ten years older than me and very worldly bachelor but treated me like I was a 'proper reporter' and not a wet behind the ears kid.

He was also the first person who ever gave me an indication that there might be a softer side to 'my old man'.

On one of my earliest assignments he told me about taking photos at an Anzac Day charity concert at which my dad was the master of ceremonies. Dad was president of the Bundy RSL. I obviously hadn't been there.

'It was quite moving, mate, your father got a big round of applause when he broke down halfway through his piece about the debt we owe to the fallen. He is obviously a pretty tough bloke, but it really brought the message to the audience when he choked up.'

I didn't know what to say. I had never seen Dad cry — not even when my lovely old grandma, Victoria Maria, died. His own mother.

There was a lot that I didn't know about my parents, but I knew I was supposed to have been part of a large happy family because Mum had four miscarriages before I was born. I was angry about that when I suppose I should have felt sad for Mum.

She called Dad her 'knight in shining armour' and I found out later from one of my aunties that he had somehow saved her from a very nasty priest in Gayndah, when she was young. It seems Mum also spent a year away from home for reasons never discussed openly by her family. Most of the Sorrensen-Finnegans stopped being Catholics as a result, so it must have been bad.

So, I was happy to learn something new and personal about Dad from my workmate. Ray was also fun to be with, cheerful, witty, creative, and above all confident. I was too young to drive when I first started, so we used Ray and his car to get the news photos that the boss wanted. Generally, it was boring stuff for me, because the stories were being written, or had already been spiked, by the senior reporters.

But Ray was always coming up with detours of his own to photograph colourful characters he wanted to include in his professional portfolio. He had won several national portrait prizes.

They were usually elderly people with weather-beaten faces, old cattlemen or canecutters, timber-getters, trawler-men with Viking beards, and large happy ladies who still boiled the family bed sheets in outdoor wood-fired coppers and strung them up on rickety clothesline attached to chook pens.

Ray had a great rapport with his subjects and on most occasions, I just sat and listened to them chatting. In getting them to act naturally and relax, he asked much better questions than I could and got the most interesting answers.

The boss told me to learn from the older hands and I was very anxious to learn about girls from Ray who was rumoured to be a very popular ladies' man. I was sorely disappointed because he was also very discreet, and I never heard him talk about a conquest or his romantic techniques. He most certainly never mentioned a lady's name.

When I did nervously ask him for advice about girls I was surprised by his answer.

'You probably won't believe this, mate, but I strongly advise you to just concentrate on kissing. Pretend you have paralysis of the arms, so you don't start grabbing, and just take your time kissing. You're a skindiver so you should be able to stay with it longer than other blokes before having to come up for air. Most girls your age will be up for that… and the longer it lasts, the better they'll like it.'

I didn't know what to say. I just nodded. But there was more.

'The Good Lord adds to man's life span the hours spent in foreplay.'

I thought that referred to hours spent fishing, but I didn't say anything because it would have sounded crass. I liked Ray's version better.

# CHAPTER 9.

## Crook in the guts... like *The Sentimental Bloke*

*Tommy the sub explains the meaning of life.*

Cliffy Dullaway, my best mate from the age of four, had a mum who included me in the family as her third son. When Cliffy and I had turned sixteen she warned that we were about to experience 'growing pains'. My Mum and Dad never seemed to talk about what was involved with me growing up.

I was now having the strangest feelings and suspected I was in the grip of Mrs Dullaway's dreaded growing pains. Sometimes I became very sad when there was no reason not to be happy. I had never really worried about not having brothers and sisters, but in recent times I often felt so lonely it was almost painful. Even in my dreams I seemed to be searching — I kept opening doors that just led to more doors that had to be opened.

Before I started work, I had felt reasonably knowledgeable, at least amongst mates my own age. But now I just had this over-whelming feeling of inadequacy — there was so much about work and life that I didn't understand.

I was concentrating so much on these great unanswered questions in my life that my work started to suffer.

My mind would wander, just like it used to do during French lessons at school. I would find myself staring at the bright overhead lights in the newsroom in some sort of dream state, while the office phone was ringing loudly beside me.

Even patient Tommy started ripping it up me for regularly handing in copy with so many obvious errors. I didn't like to upset Tommy because he was very good at explaining things. Percy often criticised, but Tommy showed you how to do it.

Tommy was also quiet, but very funny in his own way. He used rhyming slang and it sounded natural when he referred to his 'cheese and kisses' and their 'billy-lids'.

'What's the bloody matter, Colt?' Tommy finally asked. 'You've been wandering around here lately like a moon-struck poddy calf.'

What could I say? I just shrugged.

'Are you having second thoughts about this job, or have you got a new girlfriend?'

How embarrassing. I didn't even know what my problem was, so what could I say? I realised I must have been acting like an absolute dill in front of my workmates. Tommy had probably been covering for me as well.

'No, Tommy, there's no new girlfriend... not even a current one. But I think I badly need one.'

I thought he would laugh at this, but he just smiled and nodded.

'So, you've got the old poetic guts-ache, have you, son?'

'What's that?'

'It's what all blokes get around your stage of life, some earlier, some later.'

I was very interested. Maybe there was a cure?

'Is it the same as growing pains?'

'Sort of. Growing pains are usually actual pains, in your joints, when you get the big growth spurt at fourteen or fifteen.'

'So, what is this poetic guts-ache then?'

Tommy thought for a moment. He looked rather serious.

As soon as he started to reply I knew what he was up to. It was the voice he used when he quoted, 'The Sentimental Bloke'. I had heard him before, and he could do almost all C.J. Dennis' poems perfectly…accents and all.

*'What is the matter with me? I dunno.'*

Tommy smiled at me… and now I realised I was about to get the answer.

*'I got this sort of yearning here inside*
*A dead-crook sort o'thing, that won't let go*
*or be denied.'*

Tommy paused in his recitation. I realised I was nodding furiously. This was a bit like Uncle Bill who said Shakespeare had words for every situation. But I didn't know that Tommy could also pull pieces out of the air, to help him make a point.

He went on.

*'The smiling girls walk up and down all dressed*
*In clobber white*
*And as their snowy forms go by*
*It seems I'm seeking something on the sly.*
*Something, or someone…I don't rightly know.*
*But, seems to me, I'm kinda looking for a*
*girl I knew a hundred years ago*
*or maybe more.*
*What is it… that I've heard them call this thing?'*

I waited, surely there was more of this wonderful stuff. But Tommy had finished.

'I could go on, mate, but you get the idea. Some of it wasn't in sequence but I was looking for the right words. What do you reckon about the part where the poor bastard realises he is totally rooted, because the solution to his emotional problems is a sheila beyond reach… his true love probably only existed a hundred years ago?'

'It's great stuff, Tommy… I was beginning to wonder whether I was the only bloke in the world who ever felt like that.'

'The French probably have a really good word for it.'

I was surprised to hear this from Tommy, so I also tried to sound knowledgeable.

'Maybe melancholy, or something like that?'

'Come off the grass, son. Anyone can get melancholy, even your grandmother. This is a blokes' thing. It's sort of about girls and sex, but more complicated as well. You go all dreamy and worry about the bloody meaning of life, and your emotions get all mixed up. The sex part is when you get sudden stiffies at the most inopportune times… even when you're not thinking about girls.'

I didn't know what to say. Quiet little Tommy, of all people, with the help of C.J. Dennis, had nailed my problem.

'Don't worry, Colt, it will pass, and I have seen worse cases than you. When I was young, one of my mates was so distracted he walked out in front of a car in Barolin Street and broke both his legs. No one blamed the driver… we all knew Ronnie had a bad case. Being a bloke, particularly a young bloke, is not easy, you know?'

Thank God for older, wiser men like Tommy. This was the profound discussion I should have been having with big brothers, uncles, even my Dad.

*A poetic guts-ache.* That was the perfect, most accurate diagnosis of my condition. Bugger the French. Who cared if they had a special word for it? Our own terminology was much better.

It was as if the two words, 'poetic' and 'guts-ache', had been created solely for this purpose. They had been sitting patiently, in separate sections of the English Dictionary for hundreds of years, in dusty old libraries, waiting to be united. And some unknown Aussie had done it before anyone else.

I really liked the idea that what I was suffering from was poetic. That covered the sweet, sad, and lonely bits. And, when I thought about it, the guts-ache description was also appropriate. Heartache didn't convey the right sort of feeling.

Sensitive European men like Romeo might get heartaches and pine over a girl's name but Australians, like The Sentimental Bloke, and me — we copped it in the guts.

How could I thank Tommy? He had always been my best source of information about our craft, now he was giving me emotional comfort and valuable information about this important period in my young life — best of all, there was nothing for me to feel embarrassed about.

# CHAPTER 10.

## 'Brisbane is fucked'

*Everyone knows it will be nuked by the Russians and the Government is holding public meetings to tell people how to shelter and avoid the black clouds of radiation when the bombs and missiles start falling.*

About the same time that I was being trusted to cover town events and meetings on the night shift, the Cold War between the Soviet Union and the 'Free World' started to heat up.

Only a few years earlier, as schoolkids, we would commando-crawl through the Old Gardens nature reserve along the river and sneak a peek at the Pitts' poultry farm near Millbank. Everyone knew they were commos from the old days before the war. I never did see anything subversive, just a lot of chooks.

Cliff Dullaway, my mate, had an Uncle at Biloela who was a commo, but he was also a Kokoda veteran and it didn't make sense. I'd met him when we went up there shooting wood ducks on his farm and he seemed normal to me. He could even call dingoes into range by howling just like them — I didn't think a real communist could do such an Australian bush thing as that.

But the Governments of the day were taking the threat of war with the Russians seriously. Civil Defence was the big thing and I had covered large public meetings where representatives from the police, city council, ambulance and fire brigade, would run through the National Civil Defence manifest.

To me, this seemed to mainly focus on getting under a desk or a table and shielding your eyes from the blast that would even rock Bundy after the Reds nuked Brisbane in the early stages of World War 3.

It was obvious that if you lived in Brissie, you were 'fucked.' Rod MacAlpine told me those were the words he should have used on the heading of my story from Civil Defence, but the *News Mail* was a family paper and he couldn't do that. Rod took the threat of a nuclear holocaust seriously and put a more acceptable bold heading on one of my stories — 'Nuclear Bomb Warning'.

Queensland Police Force Sergeant A.R.K Martens carried the news that places like Bundy, and other centres a similar distance to the south of Brisbane, would have to take care of thousands of homeless and horribly burned people once the Russian missiles hit the State capital.

He stressed it was imperative for people to, 'know what to fear and to learn how to deal with the effects of such an explosion'.

There was debate in the office about how bad the radiation would be. Rod said the poor bastards from Brisbane who survived the blast would probably have all their skin burned off and might even glow in the dark — he was pretty sure that some of those radio-active elements did that. He had been in the Navy and was doing an Arts Degree by correspondence.

I was tentatively taking girls out at that time, and I contemplated using this perilous situation to my own advantage, Maybe I should warn them that the world, and our young lives, could end soon — possibly tomorrow. None of them seemed worried about these doomsday predictions or saw a need to act imprudently.

However, I did think that World War 3 would probably break out before television reached Bundy. It was a rational thought and a view shared by many others who had also attended the terrifying Civil Defence meetings.

Later that same year, the *News Mail* ran a local story that confused me even more. The Government was preaching doom and gloom and stressing that the Russians were really our bitter enemies. So, how come they had allowed the Soviet Ambassador to Australia, Mr. Ivan Kurdivkov, to visit our little town?

Percy covered the story when this high-ranking communist official inspected a farm at Bingera. The Ambassador even took up a cane-knife and cut a few stools of cane.

Mr. Kurdivkov then asked to meet some workers and, as Percy duly reported: 'He was taken to the house of Mr. and Mrs Bill Streeter, where Mrs. Streeter was baking biscuits, which the party sampled.'

I was confused but encouraged. If the Russians were planning to nuke us, they were unlikely to do it while someone as important as Ivan was cutting cane at Bingera and sharing Anzac biscuits with old Bill Streeter and his missus.

But I also realised that war was no joke and that everyone in my family who was older than me had experienced its horrors, even if they weren't on active service. This was brought home to me every time we visited Pop and Grandma Sorrensen at Millbank.

I was only fourteen years old when my grandfather confessed he had planned to kill my mother and me, the unborn child in her womb.

It came as quite a shock and it didn't help much when Pop Sorrensen tried to explain that I probably wouldn't have felt any pain when he gave mum her dose of arsenic. Poisoning his only daughter, as well as his wife and then topping himself, apparently seemed like a good idea at the time.

Teenagers don't think much about their own mortality. Accidents and wars involve older people and you have to spend many years growing really, really, old before you die. So, when Pop's words finally sunk in, I realised that I would never again take my own existence for granted.

Pop was a sensitive old bloke, and unlike many others of his generation, my grandfather wasn't an adult male who'd had much to do with killing during his lifetime. He'd almost lost his arm in a mining accident as a young man so missed out on the horrors of World War One. He was an electrician not a farmer, so I suspected the only livestock he'd ever killed was the odd boiler from the family chook pen.

He was a small, quiet man and didn't look like he'd descended from a race of Vikings and Southern Ocean whaling ship captains, but I knew he'd had a tough life and provided for a large family during the depression

I loved visiting Pop and Grandma Sorrensen in their little housing commission home at Millbank. It was on the outskirts of Bundaberg and we would often continue out to The Springs for a picnic and some fishing.

They had a shelf in their lounge room that displayed wedding photos and memorabilia that included a French currency note that had a scorched bullet hole drilled neatly through it. It was recovered from the body of Grandma's younger brother, Geoffrey, who was killed in World War One and had been sent back to the grieving family by his commanding officer. I had been given the middle name, Geoffrey, in his memory. But what intrigued me the most was a mysterious, small, square wooden box with a red cross on it.

I asked about it a few times when I was younger, but the adults just ignored me. It was a few weeks after my fourteenth birthday when, out of the blue, Pop took me into the lounge-room, carefully lifted it down and showed me a little empty bottle inside with the word 'poison' printed on the label. He told me it was safe now, but he still didn't like other people touching it.

He said I was old enough to know about these things. It was a bottle of poison he got from a chemist friend in Childers where the family was living with mum, who was pregnant with me while my dad was away at the war.

It was early 1942 and that part of Australia, above the 'Brisbane Line', was preparing for imminent invasion. Families around Harvey Bay and Childers had been told to evacuate further inland and I ended up being born in Murgon.

It was feared the Japanese invasion fleet, which at that stage seemed unstoppable, would harbour in the lea of Fraser Island and disgorge many thousands of bloodthirsty battle-hardened soldiers to ravage through Northern Australia.

But, all through this, Pop had the poison with them, and by agreement, they would take their own lives rather than be subjected to the brutality of the Japanese who were committing terrible atrocities on their advance southwards.

Apparently, the Government's campaign to focus on this brutality to promote awareness and strengthen the national resolve, was also terrifying the residents of Northern Australia to the verge of panic.

Pop told me: 'I was responsible for them you see? My boys and your father were all way fighting in the war and it looked like we were about to be over-run in this part of Queensland. We made a terrible decision but believed it was the right one at that time. I would do everything I could to protect grandma and your mother, but we would not risk capture.'

I was told that the turning point had been the Battle of the

Coral Sea when Mum's family had moved further inland to Murgon where I was later born. The Jap advance was also later stopped at Milne Bay and Kokoda and Pop had tipped that bottle of arsenic into a deep hole and buried it early in 1943.

'We kept the box and the empty bottle just as a reminder. Whenever you think life is treating you badly, just thank your lucky stars and remember that life is precious. Things can never get as bad as they were back then.'

He looked like he was ready to answer questions, but I couldn't talk — I couldn't say anything. Until then I had seen no indication that he was the hugging kind of grandfather. I didn't let him see, but there were tears in my eyes.

Since then I have heard some people claim that desperate actions like Pop was planning are cowardly, but I came away thinking my grandfather was probably one of the most courageous Vikings of modern times.

Pop said it was the Yanks and the Battle of the Coral sea that saved us. Uncle Bill said it was the Aussies at Milne Bay and Kokoda. I didn't get involved in the debate — I was just eternally thankful that our side won.

In later life I took a keener interest than most in the US Alliance and Battle of the Coral Sea commemorations and made sure I visited the Bomana War cemetery at the start of the Kokoda Trail when I first went to Port Moresby.

I wasn't an ex-serviceman, but my interest was still deeply personal — I could have been collateral damage in World War Two at the hands of my gentle grandfather, if the tide of battle had swung the other way.

Through unusual circumstance I found myself standing beside the then Australian Minister for Defence Kim Beasley and Lamar

Alexander the personal envoy of the President of the United States of America, at the 50th anniversary of the Battle of the Coral Sea in Townsville in 1992.

My protocol role was to quietly keep both VIP informed about the order of service and to escort them and our Mayor Tony Mooney to lay wreaths on the newly dedicated memorial.

I had heard the Last Post played at many ANZAC Day services and had seen what emotion it could release from even hardened old war veterans, but I had always felt like an observer — I was just a civilian, albeit one with a couple of years of military training.

This time, as the crowd of 15,000 people paused for a minute's silence, even the raucous black cockatoos in the sea almond trees stopped squawking. Then, it happened — I cried openly for the first time in my adult life — not only openly but in front of a huge crowd. I managed to control the sobs inside me, but not the flood of tears.

No-one seemed worried by my tears — it was, after all, a very emotional service. However, I'm pleased I didn't have to explain that as those sixty seconds of silent contemplation ticked away, I'd heard the voice of my old grandfather from all those years ago and could almost feel that hug again.

# CHAPTER 11.

# Out of probation and into the pub

*Cows moo, dogs bark and journalists drink. End of story.*

I had finally been introduced to The Imperial through the personal sponsorship of Tommy and Mervyn. Tommy told me that the gradual introduction of a cadet to a public bar was an important part of my training, particularly in the early, formative years.

Universities were for engineers, lawyers, doctors and architects, but the local pub was for young journos to learn about life and their craft — simply by watching, listening and keeping a low profile. I realised it was problematic for someone of my age to be served at the bar, but it was also kind of an honour because they banned women — no matter how old they were.

Public bars were no place for a lady, and they were confined to dark little 'ladies' lounges' which all seemed to be furnished with old upholstered chairs that smelled of mould and cigarette ash.

I also learned quickly that even under-age drinkers still had responsibilities within the bar culture and that added to what was probably an emerging self-confidence. This was part of growing up on the job. Bevan and Percy warned me that 'we' had several blokes who needed watching in the pub, and they included Tommy and one of the linotype operators, Stumpy.

Stumpy was special because he had the protection of the printers' union and was managed by his brothers in The Chapel. By agreement they were handed his pay packet from the pay-master after Stumpy had signed for it. They then allocated a few shillings for one session at the bar and held the rest of the money for his wife.

Sometimes only a short session was too much for little Stumpy, but the printers always made sure he was okay to ride his bike. My status rose considerably when I was commandeered to load his bike into the back of my little Morris Z utility and drive him home to East Bundy. There was always one of his union mates with us, which made it a cramped journey. The printers had guaranteed to see him home safely on pay night, and they were always good to their word.

His wife always greeted us warmly. There was no embarrassment and no stigma. It just seemed to be the right thing to do, like he was sick or something.

A few years later he had to retire at sixty-five. There was no superannuation then and his special gift, after a lifetime of loyal work as a master tradesman, was a leather rocking chair with a footrest. Stumpy died in it within the year.

I asked Percy why journalists spent so much time in the pub. It seemed okay for journos to call into bars even when they were working. Percy's observation was simple, and I suspect, also well-rehearsed. 'Cows moo, dogs bark, journalists drink.' End of story.

Journos just seemed to cover for their alcoholic mates and turn a blind eye, while the boys out the back intercepted wages and transported their comrades safely home from the pub with money to spare for the wives and kids.

It was soon after my acceptance into the culture of The Imperial that the legendary Myles Carruthers burst through the hotel's bat-wing doors and ordered his 'double brandy on a double brandy' With Myles it wasn't a case of dogs barking or cows mooing, it was more in the volume of elephants trumpeting and lions roaring.

Looking back on his grand entry that night I had sensed that something momentous was happening, mainly because of the way the other hardened, and more worldly drinkers, had also reacted. At that stage, we didn't know he was a reporter looking for work on our newspaper.

It took a lot to silence the bar when it was in full swing. Thirty or forty thirsty canecutters, fisherman, accountants, real estate agents, printers and journos could create a din that sounded like a cross between a breeding colony of magpie geese and a meeting of agitated Italian tobacco growers in a tin shed at Alloway.

But Myles could do it — bring the place to a hushed silence while everyone focused on what he was doing or saying. The clever part was that Myles never gave the impression he was seeking attention — some unseen spotlight just followed him around.

There was a plummy accent, which was no surprise because he looked like a foreigner, but all his words were sharp, clear and rich which gave his opinions an added sense of authority.

Even at my young age, I sensed that statements or stories that were delivered with power and confidence might sometimes lack credibility, particularly as Myles had a habit of repeating stories when he was drunk and changing things around — as if he'd suffered a severe memory loss or was just making things up as he went along.

But what great stories they were. Even cynical Percy would often be silent as Myles recounted his wild times with the rich and famous in Europe and America before the war. There was always a humorous twist and some clever link to contemporary events. Some incident or comment at work, on in the pub, could spark Myles off and I, for one, wanted to believe it all.

I had always been interested in geography and history and could feel myself being transported to far-off places when Myles started to paint some of his marvellous word pictures. Maybe one day I would get to some of these big cities and fascinating countries — it seemed so easy if you travelled light like Myles and turned your hand to whatever writing jobs that were on offer.

He could recount things in amazing detail and seemed to have such a highly developed journalist's desire for accuracy that he would correct himself if he started to embellish a story.

'I was pissed as a parson and tearing along a narrow English lane at 90 miles per hour in the Duke of Manton's borrowed Bentley, when I drove slap-bang into two huge circus elephants towing a cage full of lions. No, let me retract that, it was one of those early Bentleys that had the radiator problem… so I was probably only doing 70 when we pranged.'

He seemed to know what the response from the boys would be.

'Who gives a shit, Myles? What happened to the fucking lions?'

I enjoyed the stories and the man's company so much that I found myself sneaking into The Imperial more often, because that's where Myles was at his best. He naturally entered the newsroom structure at much higher level than me, but from the outset he treated me very much as a fellow journalist, despite my youth and inexperience.

Looking back, I realise now that Myles also provided an emotional balance for the ribbing that cadet journalists and printing apprentices were burdened with in the early stages of their employment. I suspect he knew what it was like to be a victimised minority group.

Even in my second year Bevan and Mervyn still had a crack at me. They were trying to wind me up about the dangers of sex for a young man of my age, and I was playing along with their ploy. Mervyn was in full flight.

'Take care son, or you could end up being a sex wreck. One of those poor bastards who think about girls and sex all of the time. It keeps intruding into their thoughts, especially if they see girls with any exposed skin, like at the beach or swimming carnivals.'

'Give me a break, Mervyn… that's just normal.'

'Do you think about girls and sex a lot?'

'Of course I do and so do my mates. We talk about it.'

'Well, I'm not so sure about the company you're keeping.'

Bevan looked at Mervyn, 'He doesn't think we're serious about this, mate.'

Just then, Myles arrived at the lunch table and I shifted my seat to make room.

'These jokers have been winding me up again, Myles. Trying to con me into thinking I might be a sex-wreck. Just because I'm interested in girls.'

Myles drank his milky cup of tea with the characteristic little finger pointing up in the air. He looked at Mervyn and Bevan and shook his head.

'Gentlemen, you are dealing with a sensitive subject. The Colt here is on the cusp of life and, an only child to boot… he has no male or female siblings to help or inform him on this delicate matter. In regard to coitus, his mind is almost a blank page and you are writing the text in indelible ink. Let it be useful and informative, spiced even with some classic erotica, but please, no toilet graffiti on this young mind.'

Myles put a protective arm around me. 'We should all be cautious about any advice we give.'

Bevan took up the challenge.

'Well, Myles. You're supposed to be a man of the world… in a few words what sound advice can you offer the lad.'

Myles put his teacup down, wiped his lips and stared at the ceiling fan.

'Patience my boy, patience and consideration for your partner. If, at any stage, she seems uncomfortable with what you have initiated, back off immediately. You will find there are many and varied options as to sex and, as strange as it seems just now, the ones you end up preferring might sound uncomfortable, or even disturbing to some potential partner… depending on her sophistication, her life experiences, her religious or cultural constraints.'

I sensed there as more to come, so I waited while Myles picked up his tea and finished drinking.

'Yes, back off immediately, my boy. Wait for at least thirty seconds, but no longer than a minute, and then revisit the task at hand. The Greeks camped at the gates of Troy for years without success but achieved victory though persistence and stealth.'

It was too much for Mervyn and Bevan, who burst out laughing. Bevan slapped me on the back. 'The words of wisdom son, and you got it here from old Myles. In the smoko room.'

Mervyn couldn't stop chucking.

'Myles, mate you take the workplace send-up to new heights. He didn't fall for our line but now, thanks to you, he's really fucked in the head.'

# CHAPTER 12.

# Using adjectives can get your arse kicked

*Lessons in the journalist's craft at the News Mail could be emotionally draining, physically painful and sometimes bizarre… it depended who was in full voice at the time.*

I thought I was doing a fair job in avoiding adjectives, but sometimes the sentences didn't seem to make sense if you tried to exclude them altogether. The boss had threatened to kick my arse if I used them outside quotes, but he never told me what I should replace them with. Tommy was the sub who handled most of my copy, so I asked him.

'Mate, the other day you turned in copy saying that "good rain" had fallen at Wallaville. Can you tell me the difference between good and bad rain?' He put up his hand like a stop signal before I could answer. 'No, you bloody can't. For a reporter, there is no such thing. Tell the readers just how much rain fell and let them make up their own minds whether it was good or bad. Or quote some bastard and let him take ownership.'

I sort of knew that, but it wasn't what I wanted. 'But, are all adjectives bad… for reporters I mean… what about heavy rain?'

Tommy looked surprised, but not angry, that I had asked a question.

'Look, Colt, they are a bit like snakes. Not all of them are poisonous, but generally you should stay away from the mongrels. Heavy rain is okay if it's supported by facts in your copy that show ten bloody inches fell in a few hours, dams filled, and creeks flooded.'

I nodded.

'But be careful of adjectives that show you are intruding into the copy with your own views. Emotive words in particular. I don't want to see you writing that things were "horrible", "shocking", "sensational", "unacceptable" or even that a fire was "spectacular" or "fierce".

'We want a full bloody description of the fire instead. Was the smoke so thick the coppers closed the roads? Were the flames so high they melted the wires on the telegraph and power poles... the heat so intense that paint blistered on nearby houses and their glass windows cracked? I will throw the bloody copy in your face if you start a story like that by saying there was a "spectacular" fire in East Bundaberg.'

'Thanks, Tommy, I think I understand now.'

'Mind you, as a sub-editor I'm allowed to use adjectives, if the story warrants one. "Spectacular fire in East Bundaberg" might be a reasonable heading for the sort of fire I've been talking about... as long as all those supporting facts are in your copy to justify it. Good newspaper copy should be able to make people thump the table in anger, cry like a baby, or laugh their heads off... and you must learn to do that without colouring the copy with fucking adjectives.'

'Are there any other words I should avoid?' I wanted to know more. I was finally getting the good oil from a sub, but not just any ordinary sub — one the editor reckoned could even improve the published words of the Lord Himself.

'Colt, we'd be here all day while I ran through the list of words that should not appear in a quality newspaper story. Did you read the piece in the *Courier Mail* last week about two fishermen missing in Moreton Bay and they actually used the phrase, "shark-infested waters"?'

I hadn't seen it, but I still nodded.

'Can you believe it? Of course, there are sharks in Moreton Bay. But don't you think the average reader is also well-aware of the fact that sharks live in the bloody sea and that those poor blokes are in deep shit floating around out there in the night? They don't need some poorly trained reporter putting his own spin on it. And, where in the story is there anything to support the claim there's so many bloody sharks in the bay that it's now "infested"? No quote or warning from a scientist or even fishermen… just some journo trying to colour his story. If that is the standard, we should also be reporting about a child being lost in "bandicoot infested" long grass, for Christ's sake.'

I enjoyed Tommy's mentoring especially when he was off the drink. It was like his writing and his subbing — focused, factual and easy to understand. Myles, on the other hand only offered advice when he was on the grog and it was much harder to interpret.

Was it an outpouring of sage advice from a Fleet Street veteran, or the ramblings of an advanced alcoholic whose muddled mind functioned on the edges of fantasy? Tommy talked about craft, while Myles often wandered off into metaphorical discourse that was meant to enlighten, but more often added to my confusion about how I was supposed to think and act as a journalist.

'One day, Colt, the holy grail of journalism will be revealed to you. I've noticed glimpses in your copy coming across my desk… the attention to detail in daily shipping notes, the disciplined absence of adjectives in your coverage of the Methodist Ladies Annual Flower Show, and that tight piece about the child being stung by bees at Bargara. Little things call them portents if you like, that suggest you, my boy, could be one of the chosen few.'

We were drinking in The Imperial, me keeping my furtive low-profile and Myles with his fine tenor voice and perfect diction ringing confidently throughout the bar.

I knew Myles exaggerated, but it also sounded like praise to me and I was troubled by that. Come to think of it, I had never heard a sub at the *News Mail* praise anyone for their copy, not even the senior reporters.

'You, young man, will not only survive the four years of your cadetship, but progress through gradings to a lifetime in rewarding journalism… righting wrongs and all that. In your old age I hope you look back at this moment and remember that this wonderful establishment was much more than a watering point on your Road to Damascus.'

I knew full well that old Myles was about to have one of his regular raconteur moments and feared that it might involve several rounds of his double-brandy on a double-brandy order.

So, participating as the only drinking mate in a session with the brandy-quaffing Myles, I would be financially disadvantaged, even if my weekly salary had risen to the princely sum of five pounds, ten shillings and six pence in my second year. I wanted to walk out through the pub's old batwing doors there and then, while I still had a clear head and some change in my pocket, but I was fasci-nated by this holy grail thing.

'Okay Myles, I know there's no chance of stopping you anyway… and you blokes are always telling me I should ask ques-tions because that's what a good roundsman is paid to do. So, what is this holy grail of journalism?'

'Well, I cannot be definitive, surely you understand that this is something very esoteric… the sort of thing that drives pilgrims on long journeys with sharp stones deliberately placed in their shoes, or holy men who climb icy mountains with their genitals only party covered in the search for truth and the meaning of life.'

I didn't want to encourage him too much, so I just nodded.

'It is all about the coming of age, so to speak, the gaining of wisdom. That's why I am so pleased Tommy and Mervyn got you into this fine establishment at such an early age.'

Myles stood back and swept his hand across the bar in a wide and expressive gesture. 'Surely, my boy, you have felt the presence of Lawson and Patterson when listening to your countrymen reach full voice debating politics and life in this wonderful setting? Maybe you have noted the appropriate intrusion of Oscar Wilde and Brendan Behan when I skilfully introduce an international theme that resonates with reporters, printers, canecutters and honest coppers across culture and time itself? You never know where or when the spirits of great writers will emerge and share infinite knowledge with others.'

I decided to play it safe and nodded once again. I couldn't quite get a grip on what Myles was saying but I suspected those sorts of things could happen if you stayed in The Imperial long enough drinking double brandies like he did.

'Okay, Myles, but give me a better lead on this? Don't try to explain the holy grail, just tell me how it appeared to you?'

'Excellent. Yes, quite excellent, let us approach this mystical subject in practical, journalistic form. When I started sub-editing, I became fascinated with introductions. I was reading widely and researching during stints at all the famous national dailies in Britain and Europe while lecturing in Cambridge to make ends meet.

'Then, it came to me. The perfect introduction is exactly 17 words in length… no less, no more. This is a universal truth for broadsheets as well as tabloids and it also holds for BBC radio or television news broadcast. It's not 23 words as previously believed. Just delete six words on the next 23-word intro that crossed your desk… be it a story on last week's cane crushing figures, or the coverage of the annual meeting of the Federal Pipe Band… and you will see what I mean.'

Myles drained his brandy and looked at me expectantly. I didn't even know that people in our profession had been arguing for years about how many words should be used in an intro, but he wasn't drunk, and he sounded serious. The boss had told me to toughen up and be more assertive, so I knew I was expected to have a crack at this.

'So, that's it… you don't claim to have discovered the perfect introduction, but you know that if it's not exactly 17 worlds long, it can never be classed as being perfect?'

'Exactly so. I could not have put it better myself.'

'So, what ultimate goal is there left for me and other young journos entering this game. It sounds like you old blokes have it all sorted?'

I was still sipping my beer with the dash of sars and Myles had given up on me ordering a new round for him, so he caught the attention of Mother Moore, pointed at his empty glass and then to my pile of change on the bar and smiled pleasantly at the ceiling.

I took the hint and nodded to Mother Moore who hit his glass with two more brandies.

'Again, good question, Colt. One would assume the perfect heading is out there somewhere, but I'm not sure. These are serious questions, so I wouldn't like to speculate… we are both working journalists, not columnists, so we need to deal with the facts.'

I didn't want this to become one of those one-sided lectures from old Myles, so I decided to have my own two-bobs worth and throw something even more outlandish into the pub talk. 'What about a mysterious three-word heading, that might cover all news stories… that would be handy?'

'You mean all news stories ever written, as well as those yet to come?'

I was following his lead and warming to his quirky approach, even though Myles was ignoring the fact that my outlandish proposition was sadly lacking in facts.

'Why not, it's supposed to be a challenge, almost the impossible journalistic dream?'

'Yes… the perfect heading, now that's a thought. Three words only. One verb and two nouns… a total absence of adjectives. How clever would that be?'

I cut in. 'Maybe it was the heading on the tablet for the Ten Commandments and got lost in the desert somewhere, or some hidden Egyptian text, deep in one of the pyramids. Holy men, tomb robbers and scholars have been searching for it for centuries.' I was about to laugh at my own inventiveness, but Myles cut me short.

'That's it. That's exactly what probably happened. It's the heading of all headings, the mother of them all. What you have just witnessed is not the discovery of a journalistic holy grail, it's the creation of a new one. You do realise my boy that the blending of two minds have created something that may not be fantasy at all… such a perfect heading, could indeed exist out there, on the edge of mankind's rationale.'

I had seen it happen before. Our Myles would go off on some absurd tangent to keep everyone's attention, and what started off as pub banter bordering on gibberish would end up being a profound truth — for a while anyway.

He gripped me firmly by both shoulders and his eyes were glistening. Then he raised his glass high into the air, and I realised that Mother Moore and all the other drinkers in her bar were staring at us.

I excused myself very quickly and took off up the side stairs into the newsroom next door. Myles looked so elated that I feared he'd shout for the bar, and leave me with the tab. He was good at finding reasons for celebration, but often absent when it was time for him to shout.

I might have been only seventeen, but I was learning about life and the newspaper game very quickly — probably because I was mixing with the likes of Myles and the boys in The Imperial. I thought it smelled too much of stale beer and cigarette smoke, but maybe it was a fitting place for a young journo like me to start his career?

# CHAPTER 13.

# The Australian political system is rooted

*The press is rolling, dawn is approaching, I'm in the company of wise men and Myles is about to reveal a great truth.*

The late shift finished at 2 a.m. and there was hell to pay if the ancient flat-bed press wasn't churning out papers by then. The front page, and most of the set, apart from the local stories and editorial, were the responsibility of the late-stop sub and his main aim in life was to beat the State daily, the Brisbane *Courier Mail.*

We all shared the same tele-printer news service, so this could only happen if there was a very late breaking story, one that arrived when the last edition of the *Courier* was already being printed.

There was a price to pay for this, because the printers longed for an early cut. An early cut put the paper to bed before their shift was finished, so they could play cards, drink beer and eat prawns in the boss's time before they went home.

This power rested with the sub who usually ensured the printers got an early cut once or twice a month. Pissing the printers off was not a good idea.

In my second year, I would often stay on after my shift ended at 10.30 p.m. It was always exciting to see what went into the final run.

When Myles Carruthers was relief night sub, the editor would roster me on the late shift to 'keep an eye on things'. I knew enough by then to understand my real job was to see Myles stayed sober long enough to put the paper to bed.

It also meant I got even closer to the real power of the paper, the compositors, linotype operators, proof-readers and pressmen.

I didn't play cards… I didn't know the rules for most of the games and wasn't interested enough to learn them. I sat on a high bench, watched and listened.

Bevan had done night classes when he returned from the war and prided himself as being, 'fairly well read', so he loved to debate with Myles. He probed or questioned most thing Myles said or did, except the Oxford and Cambridge degrees. Bevan left those alone.

'Colt, if you're up against someone and there is a risk you could get done, like pub debates, rugby league, or war, you might as well take on the best there is. I've played A grade League, fought the Africa Corps, the Foreign Legion and the Jap Imperial Guards, and now I'm in an intellectual exchange with an English academic who has a swag of degrees.'

'So, you think that's important, Bevan?'

'I noted it from one of the self-improvement library books they used to send up from Brisbane. Plato, or one of those other ancient Greeks, said a man should be judged by the quality of his opponents… not the number of friends he's got.'

I watched later as the card game discussion enter the murky area of law, justice and the ordinary bloke and heard Myles defer to Bevan's view at the end of prolonged argument.

'Touché, Bevan, hoisted on my own petard, entangled in my own hawser, checked and mated. I would describe you as an Australian treasure. Yes, indeed an eighteen-carat bush lawyer, the equal of any silk at the Old Bailey, in your grasp of issues.'

Bevan looked over to me and gave a quick wink.

Myles continued. 'You have a wicked cut and thrust in intellectual debate my friend. You are a fountain of knowledge, in any cardroom in the world, with any level of company. As I have stated in my constant flood of correspondence back to the Old Country, judges, professors, gentry and the like, I am constantly amazed by the intellect which is deposited here in provincial Australia, deposited in the same fashion as this nation's famous alluvial gold... just under the surface.'

'Myles, you're so full of bullshit you should have been a politician. You duck and weave. You're silver-tongued and as crook as the best of them. And then you piss in my pocket to keep on side, just like they do.'

Mervyn shuffled cards and joined in. 'Don't get us started on bloody politics. I sometimes wonder if I wasted five years of my life defending the system that has produced the current mob of drongos running this fucking country.'

'And it's impossible for an ordinary bloke to get elected,' Bevan said 'You're either tied to the unions or need to be born with a silver spoon up your arse. What do you reckon, Myles?'

'Actually, I believe it would be fairly simple to get elected in Australia.'

'You must be bloody kidding.'

'I'm sure even someone like me could come up with positive policies that would be well received by your electorate and quickly adopted by the legislature. Things like twenty-four-hour drinking in the pubs, no excise on beer.'

'Go on, mate.'

'Double time on double time for night shift printers, lowering the age of consent and making it compulsory at seventeen. Good, solid, social policies will always win through.'

Myles suddenly stood up, stepped unsteadily onto a steel folding chair brushed his long hair off his face with a sweep of both hands and stood there with his shiny pink legs, short socks and plastic shoes.

Mervyn turned to me. 'Don't bloody move son, not even to take a leak. He's about to get on one of his rolls… just look, listen and bloody learn.'

Myles nodded, almost slipped off the chair, steadied himself and then addressed the card players.

'Ladies and gentlemen, good electors of the borough of Bundaberg.'

Someone clapped.

'Exercise your democratic right in the most effective manner and vote one… Myles Harrington Carruthers… for sane and sensitive government.'

'What are your promises?' interjected Bevan.

'Good question, my excellent fellow, what indeed are my promises, or those of the other candidates?'

His rich English accent rose, and he looked at us with his honest, pleading, blue eyes.

'I promise to give you all, each and every elector, a dozen bottles of the finest Australian ale.'

More applause.

'Each soldier, sailor and airman who fought for King and Empire will get a gold watch, a share in a known fast-finisher at Randwick, or a new set of lawn bowls. You have a choice, gentlemen.'

'What about the workers, Myles, what about jobs?'

'My dear comrades. Yes, of course, the workers. I will personally create rewarding and productive jobs for all. Ours will be a socialist utopia. Unlike Hitler who burned books I will burn all tools that have a handle… that curse of mankind which always leads to hard work and blisters.'

Myles was having trouble staying on the chair, especially when he tried to use his hands expressively. He stepped down carefully and re-joined the card players.

'I would win handsomely, engage in corruption of the sweetest kind and never have to deliver any promises.'

'Why not? Isn't your word any good?'

'Mervyn, dear chap. My word is as good as the next fellow's but, unlike our poor class subverted voters in Britain, the average egalitarian Australian is worldly-wise in terms of politics, and you have cynicism of the highest order.'

Mervyn looked unconvinced.

'Let me explain this way. You, Mervyn, are an observer of nature, a breeder of poultry and a racer of pigeons, are you not? Have you ever noticed that a duckling on breaking free of the eggshell, even before taking its first squirt, will look instinctively and fearfully towards the heavens? It will then flatten its fluffy yellow body to the ground should a shadow pass overhead, even the benign shadow of your friendly hand.'

Mervyn nodded, and Myles turned to the rest of us.

'As Mervyn can attest, the duckling, upon entering this harsh world of ours, somehow has remarkable prior knowledge of the sudden stoop of the fierce peregrine and the deadly grip of the great goshawk.'

'But what has fucking poultry got to do with Australian politics and political promises?' Bevan challenged.

'I am simply drawing comparisons. What the astute Mervyn and others have observed in nature can be applied to homo sapiens in social, cultural and political terms.'

'Get on with it then. Get to the bloody point.'

'As a candidate for this or any other seat, I can promise what I like. I don't have to consider budgets or whether the policies are good or bad. They only have to be popular. I simply have to offer more than my opponents. The bigger the lie, the better the political manifesto. You still haven't grasped the wonderful irony of it.'

We all looked at each other. Bevan was shaking his head.

'That's why I would sweep into power in this enlightened land.' He held up two fingers in the V for victory sign.

'Because, my worthy workmates, you Australians, unlike any other race which burdens itself with democratic government, know instinctively, most at birth and all by the age of nine, that politicians, whoever they are and wherever they are, never, ever keep their promises.'

Myles sat down and wiped his brow.

Bevan leaned back in his chair and spoke over his shoulder.

'You hear that, Colt? You should have been taking notes. Myles carries on like a pork chop at times, but he was spot on then, son. Spot on. The system is rooted.'

Mervyn nodded gravely, as if a great truth had been revealed, and they returned to their cards.

# CHAPTER 14.

# A Bible lesson on the comps' floor

*Jesus was in the building trades when He was a young bloke.*

I was working on the late shift more often and was quietly absorbed into the production area culture. This was a gradual process, but my acceptance on the comps' floor became obvious when printers would even move their chairs to make room for me around the canteen table out the back.

Amid all the rush and noise that seemed to be essential ingredients in actually putting the news into print, the compositors, lino-type operators and printers had their own form of decorum when drinking tea or eating pies and sandwiches.

Darryl, one of the younger comps, had recently become religious and was very keen to spread the 'good word' he'd received from Jesus via his pastor. He was a nice young bloke, and no one seemed to object to his preaching, even though several of his younger mates joined in with spirited debate at times. However, I was surprised when Bevan challenged him about his attitude to language.

Darryl insisted that we should not take the Lord's name in vain. So, the words 'Jesus' and 'Christ' should be replaced with some other more acceptable forms of exclamation. As swearing was also the 'work of the Devil', the word 'fuck' and all its derivatives had to go as well. Darryl's vocabulary had, almost overnight, changed to 'flogging hell' or 'flog me dead', with an occasional 'flip me' or just 'flip it'.

Bevan pulled him up one night and politely asked him not to swear while they were eating. Poor Darryl was shocked and embarrassed. He started to respond, but Bevan held up his hand and quietened him.

'Look, son, we all know what you actually mean with those silly new words, and you do as well. Just remember you can't get away with this in front of a woman, or the girls down in the front office. It's still swearing, dressed up as something else, but everyone can see through it.'

'I'm sorry, Bevan. I'm not actually using the bad words… but I never looked at it that way. What should I do then?'

'Stick to your religious beliefs, mate. If swearing is a problem, just stop bloody swearing. We won't think any less of you if you do.'

'You're right, I just need to stop swearing all-together, to be a better person.'

'Well, good luck… if you think that's what it takes. But have you ever thought about whether Jesus himself might have let fly with a swearword or two, particularly in his younger days?'

Darryl looked shocked. 'How can you say that?'

'I'm what could be described as a "questioning Christian". I've been through a bloody war and I did terrible things to some very nasty people. I'd be a mess if I didn't believe that God can forgive us for our sins… but I'm not sure I agree with you that retaining some old Anglo-Saxon swear-words in our vocabulary is a mortal sin.'

'My Pastor says they are words that Christians should not use.'

'Well, let me ask you a couple of questions. Jesus was an apprentice carpenter, wasn't he? His old man, I mean his dad here on earth, was a chippie?'

'Yes, the Bible tells us that.'

'It also tells us that he was like us, in that he felt pain and he suffered greatly on the Cross… for all us sinners.'

Darryl nodded. But then looked worried.

'Bevan, you're my boss... but I want to warn you not to suggest Our Lord used bad language while he was on the Cross.'

'Settle down, son, settle down. That's no place for him to start swearing... just not on the cards, is it? He had his mother there, along with his family... and there were women and little kids in the crowd as well.'

'Thanks, Bevan...I take your point.'

'But let's take the story back a few years. We have a normal bloke... well, a normal bloke in physical but not spiritual terms... working in a carpenter's shop.'

'Yes, that's what made him so special.'

'Well, wouldn't you expect a normal young bloke, at some stage of his apprenticeship, to take a mighty swipe at a six-inch nail with a four-pound hammer, miss, and smash his thumb?'

Darryl was left sitting, with a strange look on his face.

Bevan touched him gently on the shoulder. 'Mate, he was in the building trades for God's sake.' He then stood up and went to the sink to wash his teacup.

Darryl looked at me, as if I might be able to add something. I just shrugged my shoulders. This sort of stuff was way out of my league.

I didn't think Bevan had tried to subvert the young man's faith, but suspected Darryl would have some interesting questions to ask his pastor next Sunday.

Darryl kept his faith, and, for a while, he seemed keen to convert me to his particular beliefs. For my part I wasn't sure. Deep down I felt he answered to a different God to most of the people I knew.

I gave him a lift home one night and accepted his invitation to sneak into the kitchen of his parent's home for a cup of tea. As I had expected, the tea included a sermon. Darryl was convinced that my soul would suffer unless I joined him to receive God's message passed down through the local pastor.

I politely resisted his pressing invitation for a quick prayer and Darryl eventually let me return to my little Morris ute parked out in the dark suburban street. When I reached for the keys deep in my coat pocket, they were missing. I must have left them beside my cup of tea in the kitchen. The light was still on, so I hurried back and gently knocked on the door.

Darryl opened up, stared at me for a moment and before I could speak, he quickly stepped down and embraced me like a long-lost brother. 'Mate… you came back. You won't regret this.' He looked up towards heaven and the starry night sky and I could see tears of evangelical joy glistening in his eyes.

Asking him for my car keys was one of the most difficult things I ever did in my young life.

# CHAPTER 15.

## Even really old people like Myles are doing it

*Of course, Myles has a secret girlfriend. How else would a woman's lacy underwear get tangled up in his bedclothes?*

It was unusual for Myles to be late for the night shift. That's one reason why his heavy drinking and strange manners were tolerated in the newsroom. He was reliable.

So, when Myles was twenty minutes late and the boss hit the roof, I scuttled off to find him, not at The Imperial next door, but at *The Royal* two blocks away. Myles always told me that, 'a gentleman never lodges where he drinks'. It just wasn't the done thing. He said I should heed this advice when I left home and got a job down south.

I took the broad, winding, stairs two at a time and knocked loudly on Number 28. There was no reply, but I could hear snores. I tried the doorknob and it wasn't locked.

I pushed in and saw Myles, dead to the world, mouth wide open and dribbling. It was a hot evening and he was only partly covered by a sheet.

Then I saw them, on the bed, caught up in the sheets. Ladies underclothes. Black panties and a white lacy bra.

I pulled back the curtains and opened the window. The room reeked of brandy.

Myles sat up, startled. I could see he had no pyjamas on. He stared at me for a moment then pulled the sheets up to his neck, like a woman trying not to expose herself to an intruder.

'Better get a move on, mate. The boss sent me to find you. The wire service run has started, and the bloody tape is piling up on the subs' floor.'

I picked up the panties and gingerly dangled them on one finger in front of him. He tried to focus his bloodshot eyes, moved his head back and blinked.

'Oh Christ... no.' He took a deep breath and went pale.

'You look crook, Myles. You want to get to the bathroom?'

'Err, Colt, let me explain. This unfortunate scene here in my boudoir is not what it seems.'

'It's okay, I don't want to know about it. It's more important I get you to work before the boss loses it completely.'

'What you see before you is the debris of an encounter of coitus. But I need you to give me your word, dear boy, a gentleman's word, to keep this confidential because a woman's reputation is at risk here.'

'Sure, Myles, I won't say anything. I don't even know who she is, do I?'

'Suffice to say that a very charming woman has cast her carnal attention on me. I would not be surprised to find feet marks on the ceiling, such were the energetic and acrobatic efforts of the evening's dalliance.' Myles rolled his eyes towards the heavens.

I stared at the ceiling, my imagination running wild. Geeze, even old pink people his age are doing it.

'But now, duty and our esteemed editor calls us both. Report to the good Montgomery Nash and tell him that Myles Harrington Carruthers is on the way.'

I sprinted back to the office where Percy told me the boss had gone out somewhere and was still fuming about Myles.

Percy and Tommy were going through the race form, quoting odds and quietly arguing about a jockey called Sellwood.

When I charged in from waking Myles, the boys stopped talking and looked at me.

'Okay then, Colt, out with it, where is the old queen? Was he out cold or still missing from last night?' Percy asked.

'He's coming, Percy.' Then I added 'You know you shouldn't call him that.'

Percy folded the turf page and stared at me. Tommy looked uneasy.

I'd started it. I had to finish it. 'I know people say it, even to his face, like a joke. But it's not fair to him.'

They both stared at me waiting for more.

'Don't ask me how, because it's private, but I know he's got a girlfriend.'

'How do you know that?' Percy demanded. 'You don't strike me as a bloke who would perve through his keyhole, so this is probably Myles bragging about some conquest?'

I was in too deep to back out. I had the facts and for a change Percy didn't have a clue.

'Look, I've been asked to keep quiet about this, but in Myles' defence I saw plenty of evidence that he had a woman in his room last night.'

Still blank stares from both of them. I was getting a bit angry. Everyone was expected to believe everything Percy said or wrote. What about me?

'Okay, if you must know there was a woman's sexy underwear, a bra and panties, tangled up in the sheets. Myles was a bit embarrassed, as you would expect.'

'So, Myles and his entanglement with ladies' underwear means he has a girlfriend?'

'Yes of course, how else would it get into a bloke's bed?'

Tommy began to chuckle.

'Yes,' I said. 'It was funny catching old Myles out like that. Myles of all people, I mean at his age. He must be 50 at least.'

That really set Tommy off. He laughed so much he began to choke, and tears came to his eyes.

Percy just shook his head, but he didn't look angry. He was sort of grinning as well.

'You're all right, son. Everyone needs a mate to stick up for them… even our Myles.'

They both returned to their Underwoods and began bashing out copy. The noise these two blokes could make at work was like a thunderous duet from one of those German warrior queen operas. I loved it.

When I sat down at the phone desk, I started thinking about who the woman could be, what did she look like and how on earth had a scraggy old bloke like Myles got her into his bed.

Then it dawned on me. No wonder Percy and Mervyn were sharing some sort of joke at my expense. Myles, the old dog, must be paying for it. What a revelation. There was actually a prostitute working in my hometown. Who would have thought?

It became more obvious the more I considered the options. A man of the world like Myles, no matter how old he was or how crook he looked, would know about these things. With all his experiences in foreign places and the big cities he would be able to find a woman of the night, even in a little place like Bundy.

I would let things die down a bit and then in a few days talk to Percy and Mervyn about it. Let them know I wasn't as naive as I looked. I was starting to know, 'who's up who and who's paying the rent'.

When Myles limped to the top of the steps a few minutes later, Percy and Tommy ignored him. I'd expected Percy to react for sure. He loved taking the piss out of Myles. They didn't snub him, just acted as if nothing had happened between us.

Myles looked a bit worried, so I winked and gave him the thumbs up.

He tapped his nose with a finger, paused to give a short obscene thrust of the pelvis and whistled his way to the sub's room.

I knew something that the others didn't — even if it was a bit sordid. For once I was 'in the know'.

Then one evening the following week, I raised the matter in private with Myles.

'Myles, I just want to tell you that I know the truth behind you and the ladies' underwear. I don't believe you've got a real girlfriend. I might still be young, but I'm not wet behind the ears.'

It was the first time I saw him spill a drink. He looked nervously around the bar.

We had sort of become mates, so I patted him on the shoulder. 'But don't panic, mate. It's okay. I can keep a secret.'

'Colt, my dear boy.' I could see real tears glistening in his sad blue eyes. 'You are a good friend. I've been worried sick ever since. There are so many ignorant and intolerant people out there. It could have been very damaging.'

'I know, but your secret is safe.'

Mother Moore topped up his glass and he raised it for a toast. I clicked my beer against his double brandy.

'But, Myles, I'm still baffled.'

He drained his brandy and looked at me with a slight frown.

'How the hell did you find a prostitute in a place like this?'

His face suddenly changed colour and soon went from pink to bright red. He thumped his chest a couple of times as if the brandy had caught in his gullet.

Just then, more of our mob came in. Myles tapped the side of his nose with a pink finger, grinned at me, looked up at the ceiling and started to hum a little tune.

I just knew he wasn't going to tell me who she was. Even good mates can have their own secrets.

# CHAPTER 16.

## Rubbing shoulders with the communists

*Are you a comrade or a brother?*

Weekend work was the pits, but I loved night rounds. Besides the usual visits to the police, fire brigade and ambulance, there always seemed to be a meeting of some sort to cover.

Everything was open to the Press. Each suburb had a progress association or action group eager to promote their problems with potholes or garbage collection. Even at that early stage of my career I realised there was power in the columns of the 'local rag'.

The Harbour Board was a 'secret society' and produced hand-outs which our editor and senior reporters treated with the utmost disdain, but the Hospital Board let us sit in for all the reports except the medical ones.

There were a host of sporting clubs, a civic band, a drum corps and Scottish pipers, as well as several choirs and the amateur players, church groups, the CWA, RSL, card clubs, you name it. Even orchid growers and goldfish fanciers and their committees could expect a reporter to turn up at their monthly meetings.

In most places, we had a special table and chair set aside. Sometimes it would have a sign with the words Press in capital letters.

Then, out of the blue, the one group on the top of the small list of local 'secret societies' also opened its doors to us. The Bundaberg Branch of the Queensland Trades and Labour Council. Not quite the Heart of Darkness, but close to it when you consider the widespread fear of communism. Not just Russian missiles and the threat of a nuclear holocaust but subversion from within.

When the boss brought out the letter from the local branch and read it to the staff it caused quite a stir.

'At the April meeting of the Bundaberg branch of the Queensland Trades and Labour Council it was resolved that the Bundaberg *News Mail* Editor be asked to send a reporter to the Branch's monthly meetings (second Tuesday night of the month) at the Federal Band Hall. Facilities will be provided for your representative who will be offered unfettered coverage of our activities, deliberations and decisions.'

It was signed 'Artie McLean, president'.

The next meeting was in two weeks. I moved over to the roster and saw I would be on rounds that night. I was excited and uneasy. This job was obviously a big deal.

The editor was talking to the others when I brought them my news. 'Maybe you will want to change the roster?'

The boss looked at me. 'Don't you think you're up to it?'

'It's just that it seems to be such a big deal… for them as well as us.'

'Well, it's a surprise I can tell you, but it's just another job for a competent reporter. Listen carefully, take notes, ask questions if you have to and do a bit of research… you've got two weeks.'

I started my research the next day. I spoke to Bevan and Mervyn who were union men and Rod one of the subs who was doing political science subject by correspondence. He was soon to become the first journalist in the newsroom with a degree.

I was told that communists look like us, but they call you' comrade'. The other mob, who are trying to kick them out of the unions, are easy to pick. They call you 'brother' and most of them have Irish surnames. Quite a few of the comrades are skinny and have Scottish or English accents that are hard to follow.

Most of the brothers are fatter and laugh a lot more. They don't fight in the pubs or anything like that, but they get stuck into each other at the Trades and Labour Council meetings.

The 'good oil' seemed to be that the union movements were also having their own battles with communism. The commos had got themselves elected to key positions and were forcing the conservative officials out of the unions' top jobs.

This was being contested by the anti-communist unionists. According to Bevan it was pretty much the Catholic socialist brothers versus the communist comrades.

Rod said it was a bit more complex. Seems that some of the commo union leaders had worked hard for the workers and had become popular but there was also a violent element as well — on both sides.

'Don't be surprised at your first meeting, Colt, if they start belting the bejasus out of each other.'

He was also interested to see how Mr Nash would handle it all.

'There's a bloke called Santamaria who's leading the National Civic Council. The boss thinks they're one step removed from the Gestapo and that it's all one big witch hunt.'

'How do you know that, Rod?'

'Jeeze, didn't you read his editorial in today's paper?'

I'd been caught out.

'I've been flat out… only had time to see how my own copy ended up, but I'll get straight on to it. So, it's a good editorial?'

'Make your own judgement. Just remember this boss of ours thinks the South African Apartheid policy is a bad thing. Can you imagine the black Africans running the show over there?'

I was a bit tense in the build up to my first coverage of the TLC.
I didn't know what to expect from a group of veteran trade unionists. This wasn't a normal comfortable night rounds job. I was in
unchartered journalistic territory.

When I arrived at the Band Hall for the TLC meeting and
introduced myself to the president, I was relieved to see the father
of a good mate Ron Davis, who was a train driver. 'I know this
young fellow. He's a mate of my son's.'

A skinny, hard looking bloke with long hair and a Scottish accent
walked over. 'We are all comrades here, so welcome… Comrade
Hannay… a good Scots name as well.' He had a grip like a carpenter's
vice and looked around challenging as he said the word 'comrade'.

A much taller bloke, around my own height, came up and
shook my hand even harder. Had I stumbled upon a secret society
that required initiates to endure the pain of hands being crushed by
men specially trained for the task?

'As a representative of the Amalgamated Metal Works Union I'd
like to welcome our brother from the *News Mail*. He looked at the
Scot and also stressed the word 'brother'.

The president, Artie McLean, came to rescue. 'We will now
convene our meeting and as chairman I will ask you all to refer to
this young gentleman from the Press as Mr. Hannay. He's not one
of us, and to be professionally independent he can't be one of us.
This is an important occasion and I'm sure the paper has sent one
of their top men.'

'*Shit.*'

There was no punch up but plenty of local news copy — which
surprised me. I sensed Artie McLean was a shrewd operator. He
had several resolutions that were passed unanimously but had
nothing much to do with unions as far as I could see.

They supported the Bingera canegrowers in their requests for more lights on cane train crossings; backed the Norville Progress Association in their petition to have the town's sewerage scheme extended to that area; and opposed any plans to relocate the main street World War One monument which the council believed was now impeding modern traffic flows.

The big one was the controversial Kolan River Dam which would secure a large section of the sugar lands against drought and open new cane crop assignments for the next sugar industry expansion. Bundy would miss out if the dam didn't get the nod from the Feds. In this instance, the workers were backing the bosses.

It was also obvious that the Feds, Prime Minister Bob Menzies and particularly 'Black Jack' McEwen his deputy, were seen as the real enemies of the working class. That was the one thing that both the 'brothers' and the 'comrades' seemed to agree upon.

The *News Mail* night rounds-men covered the Trades and Labour Council meetings for almost a year until word somehow got to the Trades Hall bosses in Brisbane that the Tory Press had infiltrated their ranks.

Obviously, the national struggle between communist and anti-communists in the trade union movement was also being fought locally in Bundy and, with pressure from the Trades Hall bosses in Brisbane, the comrades outvoted the brothers to ban the paper from their meetings.

I knew we had never misquoted any of them, so I felt pissed off about the decision. Percy said that being angry was a good sign for a working journalist and that I'd probably have more doors closed in my face in the future if my generation kept up the fight for a 'free press'.

# CHAPTER 17.

## Major Carruthers of the Irish Guards, his wounded knee and General George Patton's role in his recovery

*No-one every questioned Mervyn's story about stopping a Jap bullet at Kokoda, but did Myles really bleed all over the back seat of a famous American General's staff car?*

I was copping it from Percy, the office cynic, who told me I was too gullible, particularly when I started repeating some of the fantastic stories Myles had shared with me. 'You're supposed to be a cadet journalist… don't believe everything this bloke tells you until you've checked it out. Ask some questions for God's sake.'

'Do you really think he makes all this up? Why would he bother to do that?' I didn't want to lose faith in Myles and his wonderful adventures, and I knew some of the things that I previously doubted were turning out to be true — or least partly true.

'Look, you know that limp of his? That so-called bloody war wound?'

'Yes, it's obvious, but I try not to look at it. I don't want to embarrass the man.'

'Embarrass him my arse. It's not a real limp.'

'What do you mean not real? His knee's as stiff as a board. A sniper or something on the Rhine. I heard him tell the boys it was one of the last shots fired in the war in Europe.' I'd begun to enjoy my new role as defender of the faith.

'That old con man probably never heard a shot fired in anger.'

'Why do you say that?'

'Because I watched him the other night after cards, from the front window over there. It was pouring down rain and he was so drunk he didn't notice. Suddenly, it dawned on him halfway across Targo Street that he was getting drenched and he scampered off, like a startled rabbit. Not a stiff knee or limp in sight.'

Percy picked up his coat and moved to the top of the stairs just as Myles reappeared at the comps' door.

Myles hesitated, and Percy pointed at him.

'I'm on to you, Myles. On to you in a big way... and you bloody know it.'

After Percy had left Myles pulled up a chair and sat next to my desk.

'Colt, my boy, don't think too harshly of Percy. He has the questioning mind of the police reporter. Always suspicious. It's a mindset from birth and it cannot be taught. It's why he's the senior staffer here.'

I couldn't help myself. I kept staring at his exposed knee at the bottom of his daggy corduroy shorts.

'Myles is your leg still giving you trouble, or is it improving?' He stiffened and licked his lips.

'I mean, you were seen sprinting across the street, when it was raining.'

'Ah, the ever-vigilant Percy, assuming the worst as usual.' Myles began to relax.

'My boy, I will confide in you, but none other, on this embarrassing subject.'

He became serious and spoke softly even though were we alone in the room.

'You see, I am sartorially and financially embarrassed just now, and my wardrobe is rather lacking. In fact, it comprises this excellent if somewhat worn pair of shorts from St Vincent de Paul, this sturdy nylon shirt and a spare pair of merino wool socks which I'm saving up for next winter.'

'But what has that got to do with running in the rain?'

'It has everything to do with it, my boy. When I started to get really wet, I had no option but to protect my clothes. As it was, I had a terrible time getting them dry for my next shift. Percy, and those less kindly disposed towards me, would have realised I am desperately short on clothing, a particularly sensitive dilemma for a man of my background.'

'Why is that?'

'I am a man who is normally accustomed to the fittings of Saville Row and the finest European tailors. Appearances you know. Very important.'

'But how did you manage it? Run across the street with your wounded knee?'

'With grit and determination, Colt. However, I must admit I did cry out at one stage when jagged pieces of Krupp steel grated against a tendon in this unfortunate joint.' Myles patted his left knee.

I winced. 'Bloody hell, mate.' But then I looked closer at his knee. It was skinny, pink and unblemished. 'They did a great job in patching you up, didn't they?'

'Ah, yes, my observant young friend.' Myles rubbed his chin and stared at the ceiling for a moment.

'Fortunately, I was attached to the Americans at the time. Seconded from the Irish Guards to General Patton's staff. Old Blood and Guts. He got his personal driver to rush me back to an airfield and I was whisked away to London and then on to the Royal College of Surgeons in Edinburgh.'

'Jeeze, Myles, you had better luck with your war wound than Mervyn did. He said it took him two days to get down from Shaggy Ridge to get his leg treated and another two weeks before they shipped him to a camp hospital in Townsville.'

'Yes, I'm afraid I jumped the queue somewhat, but the Americans are like that. I understand they did bill my old regiment for refurbishing the back seat of Patton's car... seems I bled all over the upholstery of his Mercedes Benz.'

Myles then proudly displayed the whole of his pale English leg.

'Remarkable. Two operations lasting five and seven hours. You would never think I'd suffered such a terrible wound, would you my boy?'

'No, mate, I would never have guessed.' Then I added 'Apart from the limp of course.'

'Ah, yes, the limp...I've never been able to disguise that.'

Myles stood up and walked back to the subs' desk, his left leg stiffer than ever.

A few days later I had an encounter in The Imperial that convinced me I should not dismiss every story that Myles told me. A respected member of my own family suggested that this strange Englishman might actually be worth listening to.

Being young, I was influenced by the more vocal of my elders who initially dismissed Myles out of hand. My mentors at work were cynics of the highest order and Percy openly scoffed that if Myles had been to Cambridge and Oxford as he claimed, then he'd probably achieved a 'double degree in embellishment and won the chancellor's medal for hyperbole'.

In retrospect I owe much to one of my tough old uncles, Gilbert, who'd worked in the Outback most of his life, as a scrub-feller, timberman, canecutter, tin-gouger and gold miner. He owned a cane-farm just outside town and drank occasionally in The Imperial. Somehow, I just knew he would never tell my Mum and Dad that their little boy was drinking illegally with the newspaper mob at the far end of the bar.

I was also chuffed about being in the same company as Gilbert — even the hardest men amongst the canecutters would nod and make way for him if the place was crowded. Dad had told me his older brother had managed to send home extra money during the depression, but no one was allowed to tell Grandma Hannay that Gilbert had earned it with his fists when touring with Jimmy Sharman and his boxing troupe.

He was the shortest but toughest looking of all the Hannays and the darkest, like our Spanish-Argentinian ancestors on that side of the clan. Gilbert was also well-read and could quote extensively from O Henry the famous American short-story writer, a champion of the under-dog and the marginalised. Sometimes the O Henry quotes upset my Dad. He thought Gilbert was a 'border-line Labourite' who was still resentful about how hard life had been for our family and others in the bush in the pre-war days.

Gilbert pulled me aside one day and asked me what I thought about Myles Carruthers — it was a bit hard to drink anywhere in The Imperial and not hear Myles deliver opinions or share encounters in his rich, theatrical voice.

I told my uncle what I thought he wanted to hear, that Myles was full of bullshit and no-one took him seriously. I wanted to prove I was growing up quickly and didn't want to sound naive.

'Well, Elliot, I hate to spoil our family image for you, but he reminds me very much of your own grandfather... an eccentric remittance man from the Old Country.'

I couldn't say I was shocked because I'd heard talk of this, but never from my Dad. I was named Elliot, after granddad, but he had died when I was very small, so I just nodded.

'He was thrown off the family estate in England and sent to the Argentine but came back with mix-raced kids like me and was packed off again to the wilds of Australia with some Hannay-crested bed linen and silver spoons from Sebrengham House.'

This was nothing new and I wasn't sure what my uncle was getting at.

'So, they are both Englishmen… what's so special about that?'

'He's not just English… he's an English misfit, like my old man and they're a different breed altogether…believe me.'

I must have look confused because Gilbert went on: 'I'd be tin-gouging out the back of Chillagoe and come across someone just like him living in bark humpies or under sheets of iron… convinced the land could talk to them if they sat long enough under a tree. More often with an upper-class accent… not a pretend one, like some of these ten-pound Poms. I met them right across the north and down into the Pilbara and Marble Bar where I mined during the war. You could never tell whether the desert life had made them crazy, or whether their stories were true. It was like they were somehow looking for sanctuary in the wildest places, and the gold was a secondary consideration.'

He bought us both another beer and then suddenly digressed from the subject of Myles Carruthers. 'Do you know I was living on a gold show with your Aunty Jess and little Marjorie with a family of desert blacks north of Marble Bar and your father used to fly right over our camp on his way to bomb the Japs up in Indonesia and Borneo? There was a top-secret base on Corunna Downs and Jess used to panic if the same number of Liberators didn't fly over on the way back from the raids. The old women, who seemed to be half deaf as well as half blind, could hear the planes a good thirty minutes before us.'

I waited, sensing there was more.

'How's that for a coincidence… two brothers living on the opposite sides of the continent brought together by war? One trying to hide in the desert and the other struggling to make his fortune from it. That's pretty much the history of this country isn't it?'

This was all very interesting, but I still couldn't understand what Gilbert was trying to tell me about Myles.

'These other eccentric men you met… they don't sound much like Myles to me at all. I don't think he'd last two days in the bush.'

'Come off it, you know what I'm trying to say. These types are a dying breed and a reporter like you should be absorbing all this and making up your own mind. Just remember: 'there's nowt so queer as folks', so don't be too hard on the man. I suspect that when you're my age, you'll look back on this Carruthers bloke as some sort of highlight.'

# CHAPTER 18.

# Enough to make a grown man cry

*Not one, but two tragic love stories that needed to be shared.*

It was ninety miles to Miriam Vale in the clapped-out green delivery van and Myles kept falling asleep on my shoulder. The Morris was flat out at 50 miles per hour, the brakes were spongy, and it possessed a fierce desire to wander off to the left. No wonder the printers had refused to drive it.

When the weight, the cramps and the brandy breath became unbearable I jabbed Myles with my elbow and propped him up again.

'Sorry, Colt, not enough sleep you know. Must have drowsed off.'

Myles squinted at the countryside. I was enjoying the drive. Rolling low hills covered in golden spear grass and swathes of stark black ironbark trees.

'Miles and miles of fuck all. Just like Rhodesia.'

'So, you've been there as well?'

He nodded gravely. 'Did you know that Cecil Rhodes used those actual words when describing that great slice of Africa that he personally carved up for his own empire?'

This was getting a bit much. I knew Myles probably wanted me to press him further, so he could drag out some long-winded story of dubious credibility peppered with the names of the rich and famous.

I said nothing, just gritted my teeth and struggled to keep the van on track.

He shut his eyes and rested his head against the side window. Good. The last thing I wanted was for him to fall asleep again and slump back over me. I also baffled about why Mr. Nash had insisted that I take Myles on this trip to Miriam Vale. The Bushman's Carnival was all camp-drafting, buckjumping and woodchops.

I acted as soon as I heard the first snore and bumped him hard with my shoulder.

'You bring a note-book, mate?' I asked loudly.

Myles opened his eyes but ignored my question.

'You got something to write on?'

'Alas no,' Myles patted the pockets of his shirt.

'I'll give you a few pages from my notebook. There are pencils in the glove box.'

I reached over but Myles gently took my hand and placed it back on the steering wheel.

'Excellent. The generous young Colt offering me the tools of our trade to ensure I don't become idle during what should be my rest period. But, my dear boy, I shall politely decline pencil and paper, quill and parchment, chalk and slate, and do you know why?'

'No, but I'm sure you'll tell me.'

'It's for your education young man. For no other reason than to give you the unique opportunity of seeing Myles Harrington Carruthers consign several one-thousand-word complex pieces of rural reporting to the greatest note-book of all.'

He paused, and I took the cue. 'And that would be?' Myles tapped his left temple. 'The human brain. The most complex and mysterious of all our organs. The brain which records all we see and hear through a lifetime in this worrisome world.'

'Isn't that a bit risky? Percy reckons that memories can't be trusted. Take notes, he says, and don't ever thrown a notebook away. File them all in the cabinet at work.'

'Fear not, my good Colt. Poor Percy has never encountered a mind such as mine. Part of my training in the War Office. Very handy for members of our profession. A cut above the old notebook you know. I will teach it to you some day. Master to apprentice. Maestro to child prodigy, bishop to page. Archangel to cherubim.'

I had to cut in. He was on a roll again.

'Well, I hate to tell you, but Percy also reckons your memory isn't so hot. How are you going to get the details? The facts and figures. If you don't use a notebook?'

'Ah, the perceptive Percy, not only highly observant, but also so generous in the broadcast of any information he gathers.' Myles sighed. 'Was Percy specific with these examples of what he assumed were my memory losses?'

'He says you wrote two totally different in-memoriam notices about the same woman… one last year and another this year, in August.'

Myles stiffened.' You mean the notice in memory of my poor sweet Vivian?'

'Well, there were two. The last one said she died in 1950 from consumption or something.'

'Ah Colt. The pain is still there, just below the surface, even after the passing of time... I shifted hemispheres, but she still haunts me, my dear, sweet Vivian.'

'But Percy checked back, and the first one, last year, had her dying in an air raid during the war.'

Myles shut his eyes and muttered softly. 'Vivian. Vivian.'

Something wasn't right. He was acting up again.

'Myles, I'm sorry, mate, but most of the blokes at work think you made it up. There never was a girl.'

'Why hasn't Percy challenged me on this? You know very well he's my most ardent critic in the newsroom. Not that there's a problem in having critics, my boy. One should not go through life without some worthy adversaries.'

'I hate to say this, Myles, but he reckons it's not worth taking it up with you. You'll just put up smoke.'

He sighed deeply again. I tried to watch the road and catch his eye at the same time.

'Colt, the answer to this is as simple as it is tragic. It's most painful for me to recount this, but I'll confide in you, and you alone. Because, my boy, your mind is more uplifted than some of our colleagues. Percy is understandably confused, because there are in fact, two Vivians.'

Two Vivians? This sounded a bit rich, but I didn't say anything, I just stared at the road ahead and waited to see how Myles would get out of this one.

'The first Vivian was a wartime romance, hot and intense. We had very little time and I was operating in a hush-hush section of His Majesty's Armed Forces. We lived as if there were no tomorrow. No hope at all for long term happiness.'

I let him run with it.

'Vivian and I were returning late to her billet when the Hun came over and we took shelter against the brick wall of a partly bombed out building. There wasn't time to take shelter in the underground, so I pushed her against the wall just as a stick of bombs fell in our area.'

Myles let out a soft sob.

'The shock from the explosions caused most of the wall to collapse. I didn't have a scratch, but Vivian was buried under tons of rubble.'

'I was left holding her hand my boy, do you understand? Her poor pink severed hand, with the engagement ring on her slim little finger picking up the light of the incendiary fires all around me.'

His eyes began to water.

'Jesus, Myles, that's the most tragic thing I've ever heard.' It was the spontaneous tears that had started to dilute my suspicions. Surely a man would not work himself into such an emotional state if he were just bullshitting? How could I have been so insensitive — chuckling with Percy and the rest of the crew behind this poor man's back?

Then I said it. The most supportive personal thing I could think of. Even though he was old, and I was only a young bloke.

'You poor bastard, Myles.'

'Yes, I knew you'd believe... I mean understand when I explained it.'

His eyes stopped watering and he seemed to get his second breath. 'It was several years later that I met my wonderful second Vivian. I was drawn to her like a month to a kerosene lantern at a Salvation Army footpath service on a Sunday night in Targo Street.'

I waited, knowing there was another very vivid word picture on the way.

'She knew about my tragedy and was quite happy to refer to herself as Vivian Number Two. I had this strange, haunting feeling that I was meant to find true love with another woman named Vivian. True love, my boy, you do understand true love?'

Before I could even think to answer, I saw his eyes watering up again.

'In life, Colt, one must prepare for more tragedy than joy, but for my part the cup of sorrow runneth over. We had been together for only two short months and were returning to her home late at night from Lord Charlesworth's Ball when it happened.'

'Jeeze, mate, not another tragedy?'

Myles nodded. 'The ultimate. A wound upon a wound. A burn upon a burn. Hard to believe it could happen to one man twice in his lifetime, isn't it?

'What happened?'

'It was a foggy London night, but Vivian was caught up with the romance and delight of the evening. She was in high spirits and we were drinking from a bottle of Chateau Laffite as we walked along. Actually, I was drinking from one of her handmade Italian shoes and Vivian did several beautiful pirouettes, spinning in her lovely blue ball gown.'

His voice quavered but he went on. 'She was trained in Russia before the war and was so fantastically light on her feet, but unfortunately slightly unbalanced because she only had one shoe on.'

Myles' eyes reddened again.

'I blame myself, Colt. You see she spun herself off the footpath onto the carriageway just as a London double-decker bus emerged from the fog. The driver didn't even stop. Vivian was such a slightly built beautiful creature that he didn't notice the bump as both sets of wheels went over her.'

I gripped the steering wheel tighter and sat in silence, trying to ignore the pity welling inside. Then I remembered this year's memorial notice. Despite all the displays of emotion this had to be bullshit.

'What about the notice, Myles? There was no mention of a bus accident. You said it was consumption.'

He was genuinely in tears now and I could hear him taking deep breaths after each sob escaped him.

'I couldn't do it, Colt. I could not tell the terrible truth in a public notice... it was just too painful to relive the accident. It sounded much better, much cleaner and produced a better memory to have her dying from consumption.'

Suddenly Myles put his face in his hands and rocked back and forth on the car seat. 'Oh, my God, it's coming back to haunt me. The old wound is open and bleeding. My poor, sweet Vivian.'

He gripped my arm as I struggled to keep the van on a steady course. 'Pull over, Colt. Pull over. I must urinate. It's all been a bit too much.'

I stopped the van on the edge of the road and we both walked through the tall spear grass to the nearby ironbarks.

I had seen grown men cry before. At funerals and racecourses but not one cramped beside me, shuddering and shaking, in a little Morris van bouncing along the potholed Bruce Highway — and it was all my fault.

I pictured the first Vivian. Her delicate hand with a bloody stump still held protectively by Myles. The rest of her squashed flatter than a cane toad on the road to Bargara. Vivian the Second dancing like a star from Swan Lake then wham! A red double-decker emerges from the gloom and she's cane toad number two.

I could hear soft whimpering noises coming from Myles as he leaked against his tree. I was so knotted up I could hardly piss. Full of guilt I swallowed hard and tried to share his pain, picturing the two horribly mutilated Vivians and raging against the tragic fate that had been dealt to my older colleague.

It was all a mate could do.

# CHAPTER 19.

## You can't arrest me... I'm a journalist

*Rum drinkers and Myles revive the spirit of Brendan Behan
at the Miriam Vale Bushman's Carnival.*

Myles went to sleep again on the final leg to Miriam Vale, but I felt so sorry for the man that I put up with his snores and the weight of his grey head on my shoulder.

As well as covering the Bushman's Carnival, I also needed to check with the local police, the legendary Sergeant Arthur Pitts and his sidekick Constable Thompson.

As Percy Grey said, many coppers were only really legends in their own lunchtimes, but Pittsy was the real deal. He was often featured in the Brisbane papers and had apprehended more dangerous criminals on the Bruce Highway than any other cop in Queensland.

The Highway went right through the town and any stolen cars, wanted criminals and even the occasional escaped prisoner, found themselves passing right in from of the police station and the sergeant's residence. The Pitts family was a big one and their father ensured they all had copies of wanted number plates. A family of copper kids sitting on the stairs of their high-set house waiting the highway traffic go past — all acting as little eagle-eyed bounty hunters.

Percy reckoned that Sergeant Pitts as an honest copper who'd obviously upset some of his crooked copper bosses in Brisbane — that's why he was stuck way out in Miriam Vale.

The Bushman's Carnival was in full swing when we arrived. And Myles woke as our little van rattled over the cattle grid at the main gate.

'What's that horseman doing, Colt? The one twisting and weaving. Chasing a cow all over the place?' I sighed. 'Myles, this will all be new to you. I'll explain when I can, but I've work to do. It's called a camp draft and it tests the skill of the man, and the horse, in cutting out cattle.

'Don't worry my boy, I am actually familiar with the rural scenes. Cowboys in Calgary, Gauchos on the Pampas, Hungarian horseman descended from Attila the Hun.'

Then I saw it. The bush bar was open. A corrugated iron roof of sorts, bloodwood posts and timber slabs for the bar top. A wooden keg covered with two wet sugar bags and a crowd of drinkers. Cattlemen, timber cutters, railway fettlers, road workers and locals.

How Myles might fit in with such a gathering was a question only God could answer, but I had no alternative. I had to get rid of him until I sorted out how I would get access to all the results and the judges.

'Mate, you might get a bit of colour over there, at the bar. Just while I sort out the admin with the organisers. Okay?'

Myles had obviously not seen the bar or in any event had not recognised it as an outlet for alcohol which surprised me. 'Excellent, quite rustic isn't it? Fear not my boy. You handle the nuts and bolts and I will slip silently into the local scene. By the way we are on expenses today, aren't we?

'You've got to be joking. It's a wonder they didn't expect us to pay for the fuel to get us here.'

'I'm sorry old boy, but our early start caught me financially embarrassed. Could you spare a few shillings?'

As soon as he referred to me as 'old boy' I knew he was on the bite. It was his way. I also knew that 'spare me a few shillings' meant he was unlikely or unable to repay the debt. If he wanted a loan, he would ask for one, and you were sure of being repaid.

Desperate to get rid of him and get on with the job, I handed him a ten-shilling note.

'I need to speak to Sergeant Pitts, so come and find me if you see any coppers. I'm assuming they're in uniform but with these blokes you never know. They might be in Stock Squad gear... big hats and riding boots.'

'Fear not, my boy. I can identify a member of the constabulary anywhere in the world and I don't even have to see their faces. It's in their carriage, you know?'

I hurried off to the sports ground office to sort out copies of all the day's results. We needed first, second and thirds in every event and I would need to interview all the judges and stewards for comment. If they didn't take copies of the results, I would have to get the Underwood out of the van and set up with Myles reading them to me while I spent a large part of the day bloody typing.

What luck, two birds with one stone! As I entered the office, there they were. Sergeant Pitts and Constable Thompson in uniform talking to two carnival officials.

'Morning gents. My name's Hannay, from the *News Mail*, here to cover your carnival.'

Constable Thompson put his hand out and I reached forward to shake it, but Pittsy suddenly stepped between us.

'Just steady on there for a minute, young fella.'

He turned to the constable and the two carnival officials, a big bushie wearing a battered hat and a small man with glasses. 'Don't believe a word this bastard says. We've been warned about him. Poses as a reporter, but he's a conman. All sorts of convictions with money and girls. Underage girls.'

The emphasis on 'underage' was obvious and the bemused stares of the two officials rapidly changed into threatening frowns.

'Come on, Sarge, you know me. I call you or the constable every day on rounds.'

'See what I mean?' Pittsy turned to the others 'Talk his way out of a rabbit trap. Escaped from police custody twice I hear, but that's not going to happen this time, is it son?'

In one quick motion, he gripped me by the shoulder, grabbed my other arm and twisted it behind my back. When he applied only the slightest pressure, I could do nothing but walk in the direction he wanted, straight out the bloody office door.

I turned my head even though it hurt and looked back hoping everyone would see the desperate innocence in my eyes. 'Come on, Sarge. A joke's a joke. I've got work to do.'

The coppers ignored me but took great delight in walking me past gaping groups of spectators towards the police car which was parked behind the office.

I thought it would end there, but I was bundled into the back seat and driven back towards town. We passed through the sports ground entrance before they both burst out laughing.

'Welcome to Miriam Vale, son. You went as white as a ghost when I frog marched you out of the office.'

'Jeeze, Sarge. What are the officials going to think now? Half the carnival crowd saw me being arrested and thrown in the police car.'

'Correction, please. You were not thrown into the police car. Throwing people into police cars is not permitted.'

'Well, not in front of a crowd anyway,' Constable Thompson offered. They were both laughing almost uncontrollably now, and Pittsy was digging me with one of his massive elbows.

'Okay… I can take a joke. What happens now?'

'What happens now, son, is that we escort you to the back private room of the local hotel where you repay us for our co-operation with the *News Mail* by shouting us several cleansing ales.'

'I don't have an expense account, Sarge, but I'd be happy to shout. Why didn't we just do it back at the sports ground bar?'

He shook his head. 'Son, we're in uniform and it's a mortal sin for a copper to be seen drinking in public while in uniform. It's also risky for us to be seen allowing a young bloke to consume alcohol in a public place when I hold a reasonable suspicion that he's not yet reached twenty-one. That's why we are here in private. You, my boy, are going to compensate us for being woken up with your bloody police rounds calls after we've been out all-night catching crooks and keeping the public safe.'

I nodded, but also regretted handing over the ten shillings note to Myles. I felt I might have need of every penny in my pocket to pay the paper's moral debt to these two blokes.

I had bought them a second round when I decided that these buggers also owed me something to make up for the grief, they'd just put me through at the sports ground. So, I decided to get something out of Pittsy in return.

I'd seen what looked like a twenty-two rifle in leather gun case in the police car beside Constable Thompson and I remembered talk at the office about how the Sergeant had arrested two wanted Melbourne criminals by driving up beside them on the highway while Thompson pointed a rifle through the window at the driver.

Queensland policemen didn't normally carry guns and it was a complicated process to get one issued. At the court case in Gladstone the allegation of the Melbourne crims about misuse of a firearm in their arrest was dismissed. I thought it would be great to go back to the newsroom with the good oil on this incident. As the editor said, he expected all his reporters to be 'in the know'.

'So, Sarge, the rifle in the back seat. What's that for?'

They looked at each other and I realised they weren't smiling any more.

'It's for the snakes,' the constable said. 'A bloke got bitten at Colosseum Creek and died very quickly. They know now it was a taipan. No one thought they were in the district until now. That snake bloke, Ram Chandra, looked into it.'

Pittsy visibly relaxed and took up the story.

'Never know with snakes when they're bad. A wheel can throw them up under the bonnet and whack. Some poor sod opens up to check the engine and cops it. You can also have a terrified woman with little kids being confronted by a snake in the house while hubby is at work. So, it's handy for us to have a rifle if we get a call.'

We all nodded.

'So how many dangerous snakes have you used the rifle on so far? Not counting those two crooks from Melbourne?'

Thompson laughed so much he spilt some of his beer. I copped a huge slap on the back from the Sergeant.

I took advantage of their current good humour. I checked my watch. 'So, can you get me back to work now?'

'Sorry, mate you're on your own now.'

'What do you mean... on my bloody own?'

'That's the stuff. It's not a real joke unless someone gets really pissed off, is it?

I didn't reply. I was really getting pissed off, but I had to be careful. We all knew I was still under-age.

'It's not a long walk back to the sports ground, just over a mile, and we can't wait to hear how you talked your way out of this one without our help. Looks like his third daring escape from custody doesn't it, Thommo?'

Constable Thompson grinned. 'There are tough blokes down there who just might make a violent citizen's arrest if they thought an escaped crim had shown up again.'

I downed the last of my beer and I walked out of the door in rising panic. How much more time would I waste and what sort of condition would Myles be in now?

I got a lift before I'd walked a hundred yards. Everyone was heading to the Bushman's Carnival and the family from Gladstone in the old Dodge sedan who squeezed me in the back with the kids obviously didn't know I was a conman, notorious seducer of young women and escaped prisoner.

I fronted straight up to the office. A year or so ago I would have been shaking with fright, but I was now third year trained, on an assignment out of town and had deadlines to meet. I was angry rather than afraid.

The big bloke still had his hat on and the little one peered at me through his glasses. Before I could say a word, they both smiled, and the big fellow held out his hand.

'I'm Jacko Ryan the president. Hope you'll give us a good write-up in the paper Mr. Hannay.'

I was so stunned my handshake probably felt like handling a dead fish.

'I can explain. About Sergeant Pitts, I mean.'

'You don't have to. We all know about Arthur and his jokes.'

The little man mumbled 'financial secretary' but didn't offer a name when we shook hands.

Jacko Ryan probably saw I was still confused. 'Your boss, Mr. Carruthers, set us straight when he came looking for you.'

'My boss?'

'Yes, the editor or something. Asked whether we had seen you and when we explained what happened he vouched for you. He's an interesting bloke. If you're a mate of his you must be okay.'

It was too much. Myles bloody Carruthers, the lost sheep, having to rescue me and my reputation at the Miriam Vale Bushman's Carnival. Now on a first name basis with the event officials. One minute I'm a conman and potential child rapist and now it's all okay because I'm a mate of Myles.

'So, what did he say exactly?'

'Quite a lot, actually,' the little man took time to polish his glasses and squint back at me before continuing. 'I don't believe he said he was the editor. Sounded like Editor at Large to me. Explained that he's been head-hunted from Fleet Street to manage expansion for the *News Mail*. I'm sure he has shared his vision for your newspaper with the staff, but it sounds achievable to me. I have a background in rural banks you see.'

Jacko joined in. 'Ronald here picked him for a man of finance, and I know cattle and horses, don't I?'

I could do little else but nod in agreement.

'Myles told us how impressed he is with the quality of our livestock and the calibre of our riders. Said our camp draft was the finest example he had ever seen of the relationship between rider and horse when cattle were being worked. Spoke with some authority on the subject. Normally you wouldn't expect a pom like him to know so much about camp drafting.'

Mr. Financial Secretary nodded and joined in. 'He dresses and acts a bit strange, but that's the English for you, particularly the landed gentry like Carruthers. I'm not surprised he has misplaced his wallet and was actually looking for you to borrow money.'

Jesus wept. I had to act quickly, somehow isolate Myles and get him on the job with me. He was already broke and trying to bum money off tough bush characters could be a disaster. 'I suppose he's back at the bar? Sorry, I've got to find him, or I'll run out of time before we have to head back to Bundy.'

'It's okay, Mr. Hannay, he's told us what your paper needs from us. All the results will be copied for you and we've arranged for the judges and stewards to supply notes on anything outstanding. Most of the woodchops are all in and the bull rides are about to start.'

'That great. Thanks a lot. But I still have to get going.'

'Just one thing before you go,' Mr. Financial Secretary asked in a polite voice. 'The ten shillings?'

I stiffened. 'What ten shilling is that?'

'The ten shillings we advanced Myles. He said you had authority to reimburse on behalf of the *News Mail*. Much less messy than us sending your employers an invoice?'

He smiled sweetly and reached out as I fumbled in my pocket and handed over ten bob in assorted and rapidly depleting coins. They might be boys from the bush, but they weren't mugs.

As I walked through the door, I heard Jacko remark. 'I knew from the start that it was a joke.'

I tried to slow down to hear some more. 'He's too tall to be a conman. They're always little blokes.'

I had hoped for absolution of my other supposed crimes of ravaging young women, but there was just silence.

I left Myles at the bar after checking that he hadn't been involved in a painful clash of cultures. I shouldn't have worried. As usual, he was the centre of rapt attention.

Fortunately, the organisers were true to their word about providing copies of all the results and some basic notes from judges for me to follow up. After the delay caused by my kidnapping, I had been worried, but I now knew that the job was manageable, even with a distraction like Myles, and we'd get back to the office in time for the sports' page deadlines.

When I did collect Myles several hours later, the man behind the bar was fussing over him. Myles had a huge capacity, so it must have been a massive session because he was only just able to stand up. Two other brawny drinkers offered their considerable support to walk him to the van.

They were singling Myles' favourite dirty ditty about a boy called Perkin 'who kept on jerkin' his gherkin'. He sang with a sweet, high pitched voice which made the crude bits somehow seem okay, even in public.

'Take care of him, won't you, son. He's been a drawcard. I've seen some drinkers in my time, but this bloke has probably spilt more alcohol in his lifetime than I've served in my thirty-five years as a barman.'

He pulled ten shillings from the till and handed it to me. 'Give this back to him. You can't really take money from a bloke who is as entertaining as Myles... can you?'

I was stunned and kept staring at the ten shilling note this tough old bush publican was refunding.

'Like, I mean, it's not every day I serve someone who was a close friend of Brendan Behan. Do you know that the last time Myles saw him, Behan... *The* bloody Brendan Behan... they were both throwing up on a green velvet carpet in the dress circle of a Dublin theatre? How good is that?'

All I could do was stare.

'You're a reporter, so you must know about Brendan Behan, the Irish playwright… only the greatest since fucking Shakespeare?'

I nodded.

'Well I'm a Behan too. My mob are from Mundubbera… and Myles is a second cousin of Brendan's, so that makes us sort of relatives, doesn't it? As Myles kept saying after he saw my name on the bar licensee notice… *the world's a small place and we Behans stick together.*'

I just nodded politely to the barman, walked away, put the ten bob note straight into my wallet and zipped it up tight. As Percy said, at my age I needed to learn something every day and I'd learned a lot today on this trip to Miriam Vale.

# CHAPTER 20.

## Boris bungs on a blue

No-one told me that journalists might have to defend their profession and the freedom of the press with bare knuckles in smoke-filled noisy bars.

I wasn't really surprised when there were rumblings from the rougher drinkers on the far side of the bar during a night session about a week later. Myles had been in full voice telling one of his fantastic stories and he'd also started acting out some of the scenes — even the female parts.

Mother Moore ran a tight establishment, but her favourites were all on the south side of the big horseshoe bar. That was us, the *News Mail* mob plus a few of the local businesspeople from nearby Targo Street shops.

This left the northern side for any casual drinkers who wandered in, plus a small group who included the night watchmen, some of the itinerant canecutters and a couple of so-called hard men who had been featured in some of Percy's court stories — assault, resist arrest.

One of them, a squat round-shouldered bloke called Boris had been a year behind me at school, but a decade ahead in terms of fist fights, arrests and general thuggery. Boris and I did however share one thing in common… we both had very short careers as boy boxers at the Austral Hall further down Targo Street.

Word was out that the legendary Jack Lowe from the Burnett Star Boxing Club had expelled Boris once he started to make regular appearances in the Magistrate's Court, branding him as a thug and not someone fit to practice the 'gentle art'.

I had also been rejected by Jack, but much earlier and for a different reason. I joined the club when I was at school and, because of my height and long reach for a thirteen-year-old, Jack concentrated on my straight left. What he called the 'gentleman's punch'.

I got pretty good at it during training but came a cropper when matched up against another scrawny kid from Mount Perry.

There was not much chance of either of us being hurt under Jack's watchful eye, but I copped a hiding, I was just too lanky and slow. Jack knew I had also joined the archery club and told me straight after the fight that shooting arrows was a much better choice for me than the ring.

On this particular night in The Imperial, Boris and his mates were being noisier than usual with Mother Moore occasionally calling out, 'Language gentlemen... language please.'

So, I was surprised when Boris stood up and loudly proclaimed that the fucking *News Mail* was a rag you wouldn't wipe your arse on. That silenced the bar and most of the other drinkers turned to stare at us, the *News Mail* mob.

We knew it was because Boris had been charged in court the previous day for taking under-size mud crabs and had copped a stiff fine. Percy's story had been the lead on page three that morning, so I knew immediately why Boris had his dander up. He'd been offered the ultimate insult on our local news page — Percy had printed his full name.

The dreaded Boris had been christened Lancelot by his doting and apparently classically influenced parents. Now, this deep, dark and very personal secret was out. The truth of his birth certificate was known to all and it took the shine off his nick name which he also carried in tattoo form on one of his muscular biceps.

I expected Percy to respond to Boris' insult, but it was our paper's recently arrived new manager, Roy Theodore, who took up the challenge. He was the boss, so I suppose it was his job to defend our paper. Roy was a Kiwi, a former journo and features editor from the Brisbane *Telegraph*, who had gone into management. He looked fit enough but wore thick black-rimmed glasses and was too old to be taking on a street fighter like Boris.

'You're a dickhead, Lancelot.' It was a beautiful insult in its own right — fit for a newspaperman responding to a crude insult to his journal and his profession. Short and expressive without reverting to his opponent's bad language in front of Mother Moore and her girls. Roy had pitched his response perfectly to show the difference between the 'dickheads' and the *News Mail* boys. Percy nodded approvingly.

'Why don't you go and drink somewhere else?' This was brilliant stuff from our new boss. A veiled threatening insult, *piss off and never come back here you prick*, pitched in the guise of a friendly suggestion.

The reaction was instantaneous. Boris started to barge his way through the packed drinkers, heading straight for us. Roy took off his glasses, put them on the bar, scooped up a pile of coins and gripped them in his right fist, squared his shoulders and widened his stance. Percy stepped up beside him and suddenly I found myself standing beside them.

Mother Moore yelled at Boris, telling him he was barred, but he kept coming. He only stopped when Percy called out: 'You're in enough trouble already. Do you want to make page one as well?'

At the same time, several of the printers, including Bevan and Mervyn, appeared at the side door.

Our attacker stood for a few seconds and I could see his eyes shaking in his head. He was taking deep breaths as if he'd run a four-forty flat out. Both his arms were by his sides, but he kept flexing his fingers in and out. He looked as if God had asked him the meaning of life and he was desperately trying to find the right answer.

Then it came to him. 'You can all stick this bloody pub up your arse.' He turned as if to walk out the main front doors, then swung around and pointed straight at Myles. 'You drink with a poofter like him, a bloody tan-tracker, but think this place is too good for me.' He gave us all the two fingers then crashed through the batwing doors.

It was all over as quickly as it had started. Everyone had been preparing for a blue, but things changed as soon as Boris stormed off. A couple of his drinking mates soon followed in a show of solidarity and the bar quickly returned to normal, the loud buzzing noise of dozens of drinkers talking, and the steady clink of glasses.

Roy put his specs back on and emptied the heavy coins from his fist. Myles went back to his brandy. Everything looked like it was back to normal, but I knew it would never be the same now one of our workmates had been singled out like that in the public bar. It would be all around town the next day.

I was so upset that I was shaking when I tried to drink my beer. I was also embarrassed because I didn't know whether I was shaking with fear or anger.

Bevan saw it and came over. 'You did the right thing, Colt, standing up with Roy and Percy.'

'I didn't realise I was doing it, Bevan. I don't know what I would have done if he'd bloody kept coming.'

'Oh, he was mad all right and looking for a scrap. But he started to lose traction when he found himself alone out there just when we all turned up.'

'I'm told I've only got one punch and it's not a big one... the straight left. Don't think I'd have been much use. But Roy looked like he knew what he was doing.'

'Fighting in pubs is a mug's game anyway, son. But if anyone ever comes at you like that again, just make sure you kick over a bar stool in front of him, if you can. It's surprising how something like that will distract them. Your hat, if you've got one, is also good. Throw something in their line of sight near their feet, don't throw it at their face or anything.

'How does that help when some bloke is coming straight at you, determined to knock your block off?'

'Not really sure… don't know the science behind it… but believe me it does work. I've had them stop and stare like they've never seen a bar stool or a bloody hat before. You see that 'what the fuck' look in their eyes and you've got only a second or two to move. Either whack him hard in the nose with your straight left, or bolt for the back door and get as far away from the bastard as you can.'

'Right. Thanks, Bevan.'

'In your case, mate, I recommend the second option.'

We both laughed, and I found I could finish my beer without shaking.

I looked around for Myles, but he'd disappeared. 'You heard what Myles copped, didn't you?'

'Yes, Colt… and so did everyone else.'

'What do you think will happen now?'

'Don't know… but I can tell you one thing.'

'What's that?'

'Our old mate Myles has been through shit like this before.'

## CHAPTER 21.

# Tommy tries to end it all

*God created broadsheet newspapers, but tabloids are the Devil's work.*

No-one spoke about the verbal abuse Myles had received in our confrontation with the town thug. But he was less vocal in the pub and stopped drinking alone in the bar even under the protective eye of Mother Moore. He also eased off, or at least reduced his brandy intake from heavy drinking, to steady drinking. I was far more worried about Tommy, who was obviously in a dark place.

I felt close to the man, both as the mentor who'd shown me the ropes at work, and as an elder who had eased me through my 'poetic guts aches', but I was now covering for him on a regular basis. I assumed he would eventually get on top of the grog — but I was wrong.

Drinking on the late shift was tolerated, but only if it didn't result in a late run on the presses. Late runs left the paper delivery contractors with less time to spread copies throughout the district. It was the ultimate newspaperman's sin. The *News Mail* was a morning paper and it was supposed to be delivered at 'sparrow fart', so its contents could be consumed along with the bacon and eggs at breakfast.

Tommy was the acknowledged night sub on Sundays. He not only put the front page together but subbed all the state, national and overseas copy as well. On a good night, he could do the Sunday night set alone and produce a quality Monday paper. On a bad night, when he'd had a terrible Saturday at the races, or even worse, a good Saturday at the races, Tommy was in trouble.

If he seemed to be under the weather on a Sunday night, I would stay after my reporter's shift finished and give him a hand, but on this occasion, he simply didn't turn up. I didn't dare sub any of my own stories, but I started to feed the boys out the back with the Country Press copy, hoping that Tommy was just running late for some legitimate reason.

I was about to call the boss when Tommy finally turned up, full to the gills. He wasn't just drunk, he was confused and depressed, could hardly stand up and kept repeating the one phrase over and over.

'It's not on, Colt… It's not on I tell ya.'

He wouldn't answer when I asked him if there was anything I could do. He staggered around, tore off several yards of copy from the tele-printer, threw it into the air and started out the door into the production area with some of it still tangled around one leg.

I realised I would have to call the boss. Tommy was out of it and someone would have to sub the paper. Before I could dial the editor, Mervyn burst through the door.

'Colt…call Roy for Christ sake. Tommy's been on a bloody bender and he's threatening to jump off the gantry.'

This didn't make sense. Surely Tommy wouldn't want the manager to see him in such a state. 'Why does he want the manager? I'm about to call the editor because I can't take over on my own.'

'How the fuck do I know…he wants Roy. If he does bloody jump, he'll go straight through the newsprint. The press hands have spent ages setting it up for tonight's run and Wendell is threatening to strangle Tommy if the fall doesn't kill him outright.'

I called Roy and he didn't sound happy. He was still in his pyjamas, dressing gown and slippers when he stormed into the production area ten minutes later.

Tommy was sitting on the gantry, a steel-framed platform with guard rails about three metres above the floor of the press room. He had positioned himself at the top of the stairs, which looked more like a rickety steel ladder than an actual stairway.

Mervyn told me that our gentle mate had kicked out viciously at anyone who tried to get him down. His message was garbled, but simple. He would jump off the gantry unless the manager came to talk to him. He kept muttering something about 'It's not on... it's not bloody on.'

At that height, the fall would not be fatal. Tommy might break a bone or two, but the real risk was to the big stretched section of newsprint between two of the rollers on the press.

To all the linotype operators, compositors and pressmen involved in getting the next day's paper out on time, this stretch of printing paper was far more precious than the safety of their old mate Tommy.

If Tommy did jump, he would end up in a large tray of black ink, about the same area as a bathtub, but much shallower. Wendell, the leading press hand for the night, was far more agitated than poor Tommy.

While Roy was talking to Mervyn and assessing the situation, Tommy suddenly realised that the man he wanted to see to had arrived.

'Roy, Roy... it's snot on mate... It's snot on. Call it off, or I'm gonna jump.'

Roy seemed calm, but his voice was shaky when he replied.

'Tommy, you've gone too bloody far this time. We're heading for a late paper and it's your fault. Now get down here, or I'll fire you on the spot.'

Something must have registered with Tommy. Maybe he hadn't realised that the paper would be late.

'Roy… Jeeze mate, wait. I'm coming down.'

Tommy rose unsteadily to his feet reached out for the stair railing, missed by miles and fell forwards, legs stiff, arms spread wide like Jesus on the Cross, straight through the stretched news-print and into the big tray of ink.

There was a strange splashing sound and I looked down to see a wide black stripe of printer's ink extending from my left shoulder, across the front of my good white shirt, to the right shoulder.

Roy had a similar mark and Mervyn looked like one of the South American Indians with a jet back band right across his eyes.

There was a dark stripe, looking very much like a high tide mark, around the walls of the press room. It was only interrupted where some unfortunate printer, press hand, reporter or manager had been standing at the time.

The black tide was almost geometric, as if a draftsman had used a spirit level to get it at the exact same height and depth. Tommy's drunken plunge had created a work of industrial art.

He struggled up and slipped again in the ink bath. He looked like someone from an Abbott and Costello movie or a minstrel show.

Roy and Mervyn had to restrain Wendell who was threatening to strangle Tommy in what remained in the ink bath. Wendell, who was normally a very quiet bloke, was graphically describing how he wouldn't stop holding Tommy face down in the ink until the last of his gasps for air stopped bubbling to the surface.

Tommy was rushed outside and hosed down. One of the apprentices took him home in the little company van.

Roy told me not to bother the boss and he sat down at the subs desk and showed me how it was done. After all he'd been the features editor at the Brisbane *Telegraph*, he wasn't your normal newspaper manager. He was one of us.

We got the paper out. Not quite on time but some sparrows were probably still farting when the last deliveries were made.

The issued looked good to me — it was different. Even though we were rushed, Roy did more than run all the body text in single columns. There were double column sets and blocked items, so the news was presented horizontally instead of vertically, at least on some pages.

Roy said there were big changes ahead. Offset printing, cold type. A few weeks later he asked me to write about skindiving along the coast and out at Musgrave Island on the Great Barrier Reef. He even included some of my underwater photos. Roy controlled the Saturday feature section and things were certainly changing. I was permitted to use a few adjectives and scored one of the *News Mail*'s first by-lines... By Staff Reporter Elliot Hannay.

Tommy took sick leave and also took out a personal prohibition order. It was stuck on the walls in all the local pubs, complete with his photo so he could be easily identified by the publicans and the bar staff. That seemed odd because they all knew Tommy anyway. Still, it was courageous on his part, for an alcoholic to admit publicly that he needed help.

I thought things were getting back to normal at work, but I was wrong. A month later, my world at the *News Mail* was turned upside down. We were converting from a broadsheet to a tabloid newspaper. For some of us, this news was more threatening than the Russians.

The ancient flat-bed press was being scrapped, printers were being trained to take on new technology and a rotary press was being installed. Jobs would probably go, and Tommy admitted that his big alcoholic lapse had been at least partly due to a fear that the new management would see him as a liability in the new age of newspaper production.

Mr. Nash, who told me in my first year that broadsheets were God's favoured method of producing newspapers, became even grumpier than usual. No-one, not even the old hands like Percy, was game to ask the boss what he thought about all this change.

The printers said it was being driven by advertising and the desire to print ads in colour, or at least in a couple of choices of colour, that might make products stand out better.

Rod reckoned it was all about television and trying to stop big advertising accounts changing to the new media.

I asked Tommy. He said tabloids often had the best turf coverage in the country, but broadsheets had more status, as well as more room to run stories.

'Everyone will have to sharpen up now, Colt, you mark my words. Your writing will have to be as tight as a fish's rectum and the subs will be carpeted if they let anything run for more than a column and a half. You young blokes will be crying tears of blood when you come running in with the in-depth coverage of a yarn you think is worth a thousand words and I have to slash it down to a few hundred that still makes sense.'

He shook his head and lit another cigarette.

'No more sending out subbed copy with single, double and three column headings and letting the printers and comps fill up the inside pages with bulk. We'll have to design marked-up layouts for the whole book, not just the front, local and back pages as we do now. More time and effort, the same production deadlines, but nothing to cheer about with extra pay... not for the journos anyway.'

'What about the printers, Tommy?'

'Colt, they are streets ahead of us and always will be. Say what you like about The Emperor and his bloody Chapel, but they have hammered out a deal nationally and it's got more packages than Buss and Turner's store on a big sales day. Packages for retraining, re-skilling, new classifications, job security and better pay. Our mob just jumped up and down a bit. Older hands like me will probably be the first to go and the AJA will do nothing.'

'But we aren't allowed to go on strike like the printers, are we? Isn't the news too important and we're not supposed to take sides anyway — isn't that a problem for journalists?'

'Out of the mouths of babies, Colt… you've nailed the problem of the Fourth Estate. We're sometimes so far up ourselves it's painful. The printers go on strike and that's it… no bloody papers until they get what they want or at least agree to return. We strike, and management will still find a way to get some sort of rag out onto the streets to carry their precious ads, because they'll still be able to roll the presses. Forget about solidarity of the workers, the boys out the back would be happy to print it just to show everyone who has the real power in this game.'

# CHAPTER 22.

# It's like kicking a puppy tied up on a chain

*There's got to be a better word than poofter.*

Tommy was on the mend, but Myles was a changed man after the abuse he'd received from Boris a few weeks earlier. His sessions next at The Imperial were almost furtive, his voice quieter and even his stories seemed to have lost some of their colour. All because some thug had called him a poofter in public.

I might have been naive when I defended Myles about the women's underwear more than a year earlier, but I'd always known the man was different. Okay, so he wasn't attracted to women, but he didn't chase after blokes either.

The longer I worked at the paper the more I had heard the whispers that he was a homo, a poofter, a tan tracker, a queer. But none of those words sounded right and they never came from the older blokes, those who didn't only put up with his eccentric company but enjoyed it as well.

There was a barber in town who was rumoured to be one. Even he was given a more refined tag. He was just 'a closet poof', but he still made a decent living and gave good haircuts. There was the brother of one of our distinguished civic leaders as well. He had also been a prisoner of war in Japan, so he had special status and was just described as being, 'queer'.

Even my mother's youngest brother, Uncle Arthur, never married and lived with another man. But he was a 'bachelor' — a bachelor who was into weights and speedo togs and who giggled when he wrestled with his friend on the wet lawn at the back of my grandmother's place in Brisbane.

Mum told me that when I was very young, she used to make me little cloth boxing gloves before my Dad showed up at the end of the war. The poor woman encouraged me to punch at her hands, like a sparring partner, because she was worried that I might grow up into a 'sissy boy' if I was only exposed to her soft and gentle nature in those formative years.

Maybe she'd realised that my father would have had problems with a son who was like her younger brother — sensitive and lacking any interest in girls.

Why hadn't the English language, or someone responsible for inventing new words, come up with a much better name or category for blokes who were different, or who preferred men — particularly blokes like uncle Arthur and my mate Myles?

I knew that the Yanks, who were supposed to be a progressive race of people, had a special name for them, 'faggots' but that sounded even worse than the English and Australian insults.

What Myles did on his days off was a mystery. The boys out the back, who were keen lawn bowlers, had given up inviting him to their social games or the Saturday night bowls club dances.

Being a sub, he could always rely on having Saturday off, and he'd sometimes show up at a morning session in The Imperial. That's where the local stringers, Tommy and Bill McCarthy, would file turf stories for the Brisbane Sunday papers. That's why none of us actually saw what happened to Myles on that fateful weekend, but I was the one who found him, covered in blood.

It was about two on a Monday afternoon when the publican from the Queen's Hotel rang the boss. They were mates. The hotel people knew Myles had gone into his room late on the Saturday night, they had heard him, but he refused to let the cleaner in when she had knocked about an hour ago.

When the publican beat on the door, Myles refused to open up, but asked that the hotel tell the *News Mail* he was too sick to come to work.

I was about to start my shift, so once again I was sent off to check on Myles. I had grown up a bit since the last time when there was confusion about the ladies' underwear, so I was clued up enough to realise my assignment was to see if Myles was really sick, or just hung over. If he was hung over, I should do my best to get him to work or the boss would step in.

'See what the fuck is going on, Colt. For a big drinker he's usually reliable, work wise. If he is crook, see if he wants a doctor.'

I spoke to the publican when I arrived. He was pissed off.

'Tell the old bastard that if he won't let Merle in to clean the room he'll be changing his own bloody sheets. What does he think he's bloody got? The plague or smallpox?'

When I knocked, I called out loudly. 'It's me, Myles… the boss wants to check if you're okay… If you need anything, I mean.'

I heard shuffling and then he opened the door. He was covered in dried black blood. That's the first and only thing I saw. There was so much of it that for a moment I couldn't focus on anything else.

It was all over his favourite nylon Hawaiian shirt. Blood was soaked in a wide dark red sash like a soldier in dress uniform, only his uniform was minus trousers. His snowy white undies and skinny pink legs looked pristine in comparison with his gore stained shirt and face. Blood was even matted in his yellow grey hair.

Moving stiffy to the bed, Myles sat down while I closed the door. I hadn't said a thing. I didn't know what to say. Even at my age I'd seen some black eyes and a busted lip or two, mainly from sport or accidents, but this was something different.

One eye was closed, puffed up like a ripe plum, and that side of his face was also swollen out of shape. The black and red bruise looked like a huge birthmark. He could talk but seemed to have trouble with his tongue. He spoke with a bubbling noise, as if he needed to keep his busted lips closed. He peered through his one good eye, but it was also reduced to a thin slit.

'Thank God it's you, Colt and not one of the others.'

He moved his head backwards and winced in pain, then leaned towards me and I realised he was trying to put me in focus.

'Double vision, I'm afraid... Not fit to appear at work tonight... might even take a day or two. Can you cover for me, old boy?'

I had been shocked at the first sight of Myles, now I was just plain bloody angry. Myles was a mate and you didn't let things like this happen to one of your mates.

'Christ, Myles who did this to you?' It didn't make sense to me. 'Who the fuck would want to belt up a bloke like you?'

'A bloke like me, Colt?'

Myles was doubled up, had his hands over his eyes, and was shaking his head.

'Seems not everyone wants a bloke like me walking the streets of your cosy little town on a Saturday night.'

He put on a strange emphasis every time he said the words 'a bloke like me'.

I patted him on the shoulder. I had to say more. 'What I mean is mate... what sort of sick bastard would do over a nice bloke like you?'

That's when he started to sob.

I tried to make him feel better by saying something more.

'Everyone back at the office will be pissed off by this. You're one of us … you're a mate.'

That really set him off.

I couldn't just sit there patting him. The bleeding had obviously stopped, but he looked like an accident victim and would need an ambulance to get to hospital.

I sprinted the two blocks back to the office, hoping that anyone seeing the final dash into the *News Mail* would assume I had a very urgent story to spike.

I blurted it out to Mr. Nash and his eyes seemed to go cold. At first, I thought he was angry with Myles, but he wasn't. 'Talk about flogging a puppy on a chain… What sort of mongrel would do that?'

'I don't know. Myles looked too crook to ask him about it.'

'Okay, I'll get Doc McKeon and we'll both go around a see Myles right. You get on with your rounds, and not a word to anyone outside this office, you understand?'

Doc McKeon was my family doctor. I knew he was also president of The Rats of Tobruk. By the look of Myles, I thought a war doctor was probably the right choice.

# CHAPTER 23.

# Why don't they arrest the mongrel?

*Everyone knew why poor Myles had been bashed,*
*and who had done him over so savagely.*

**M**yles didn't come came back to work until a month later. He took all his sick leave and some of his holidays as well. He was still a bit scarred, but the swelling had gone down, and he looked almost normal, apart from the cotton wool plugs in his nose.

He'd moved out of the *Queen's Hotel* for a week to recover after Dr. McKeon had patched him up in his surgery. Tommy said they had put Myles in a fishing shack at Burnett Heads, because he didn't want to go to hospital. The boss had given the Burnett Heads publican a good description of Myles plus strict orders not to serve him a drop of drink.

Apparently, Mr. Nash had a part share in the shack, and I was surprised that such a tough old boss would go to so much trouble for one of his staff. Somehow Tommy heard about it, so he made the occasional visit to cheer Myles up. The cheer also involved several bottles of Tommy's preferred Chateau Tatanunda brandy, but the boss wasn't to know about that.

In the coming days, I got angrier. Why hadn't someone been arrested?

I knew Myles had gone silent for some reason. Everyone else seemed to know why he wasn't talking, but I couldn't work it out. I even pressed him a couple of times, but he just averted his eyes from mine and muttered something about being very drunk and not seeing who attacked him.

I was occasionally filling in for Percy and covering the minor cases in the magistrate's Court and had seen people being punished for crimes much less severe than belting an old defenceless man until he was almost unrecognisable.

Even drunks who swore in public or abused the coppers would end up being fined for using obscene language. It was rather comical in the courtroom to hear the evidence being given... verbatim... foul language echoing around the chambers. Old ladies who said they could read your fortune in tea leaves or Tarot Cards would end up in court if they charged for their mystical services. Gullible people needed protecting and that's what witchcraft laws were for.

I had innocent faith in the judicial system but was learning quickly that our society wasn't as just as I thought.

I was stunned when an Aboriginal man stood up before Mr. J.S. Wills S.M, and appealed for the right to manage his own wages. I hadn't known that many Aboriginal people in Queensland were 'Under the Act' and were considered by the Crown to be so ignorant that they could not be trusted with their own hard-earned wages. Their pays went into a so-called Trust Fund which was administered by the local policeman or some regional government bureaucrat. These white fellows decided how much these Aboriginal workers could access from their own accounts.

It just didn't sound Australian to me. It was worse than sacking girls when they got married. What were the unions doing about it?

At least there had been some justice under Magistrate Wills. After some brief questions about the man's employment record, the presentation of two references and what seemed to be a half-hearted protest by a Police sergeant on behalf of the Crown, the

Magistrate hit the bench with his gavel and declared the man 'exempt from the Act'.

The black man shook hands with everyone, the coppers, the deposition clerk and even came over to the press box and reached out to me. It was one of the warmest handshakes I ever had.

I knew this was a bit unusual in the dignified courtroom, but Mr. Wills sat back and let it happen. Before he left, the man faced the magistrate, looked him in the eye and then gave a bow of his head, turned, and with shoulders squared, seemed to glide, not walk out of the courtroom.

I wanted to ask so many questions, interview everyone and write a special story about this, but I knew better. We only covered what was actually said in the courtroom, introducing 'extraneous matter' to a court story was too dangerous.

Still, the short single-column story about an Aboriginal man winning exemption from the Act managed to make page three, so our readers could see what had happened and make their own minds up about whether it was a good thing or not.

I spoke to Percy about it and he said he wasn't surprised I didn't know how bad things really were.

'Of course, it's all about race. Look at the White Australia Policy for a start, it's designed to keep out all the Asians and blacks. And, not being content with that, we go and make life miserable for the blackfellas who are already here and treat them like unwanted foreigners in their own bloody country as well.'

'But I thought that was just economic or something. There wouldn't be enough jobs for everyone if we opened up the doors.'

'Wake up, son. We act like a mob of racists, but we don't want to face up to it… which for my money is just as bad as the bloody

South Africans and those Southern States that oppose integration in America… at least they are being up front about it.'

I knew there was little I could do about racial injustice, but I was still worried about Myles. Someone had to answer for what had happened to him, but no-one seemed to be doing anything.

The boss put Myles on night shift, probably to give him time to improve before having to be seen by everyone in the main office downstairs on the on day shifts.

He still looked crook. There was a large healing cut, which had obviously been stitched just above his left cheek bone and he was very dark under both eyes. He seemed cheerful enough but was more withdrawn than usual. After a few days back at work he started drinking again in The Imperial, but never alone.

One night, when there was just me and Tommy with him for a couple of quick drinks at smoko, the legendary Detective Sergeant Neil Harvey walked straight over to us. He didn't say anything, just gave us the nod as he approached. For the first time in my life he seemed to include me in the nod. I realised it was a big moment in my career. I relaxed a bit.

I had never seen him speak to Myles, not once, not even when he came over to get race tips from Tommy. But now he was speaking directly to Myles and, what's more, he was calling him, 'Mr. Carruthers.'

'Well, Mr. Carruthers, I see you're recovering from your injuries?'

Myles, as ever, took it all in his stride. 'Yes, thanks… very unpleasant indeed but I'm mending.'

'Unpleasant is the word all right, Mr. Carruthers. Such a pity you weren't able to recognise your assailant, but I wanted to let you know that I now have a personal interest in this.'

Myles looked surprised.

'What's more, I'd be very concerned if it ever happened again…
to you or any other person like you.'

I realised then that this copper wasn't really speaking to Myles,
he was addressing the whole bar. All eyes were on our little group.

Detective Harvey then turned to Mother Moore and in an even
louder voice ordered a drink. 'Mother, a double brandy on a double
brandy for my friend, if you please.'

Mother Moore was sharp.

'On your special slate is it, Neil?' Meaning that the coppers never
paid for their drinks.

That was the first and only time I ever saw the man smile.

'No, Lucy… take it out of this.' He then dipped into his coat
pocket flattened out a ten-shilling note on the bar, adjusted his tie
and walked out.

I thought Myles would have smiled or something, but he
couldn't seem to speak.

As soon as Mother Moore served Myles his brandy, and pock-
eted the ten shillings, Myles regained his composure. 'We have all
learnt something tonight, something very unexpected.'

Tommy cut in. 'You can say that again.'

'Yes… who would have thought that our esteemed Mother
Moore's Christian name was Lucy?'

We all laughed. It was typical Myles.

He was still swilling the brandies around in his glass and looked
deep in thought. 'You may recall, Colt that I have great regard for
the works of Brendan Behan.'

I nodded, remembering the Miriam Vale saga.

'Brendan said that he had never seen a bad situation that could
not be made even worse by the appearance of a policeman. Very
clever, very astute don't you think?'

I nodded. Tommy was still chuckling.

'Well, tonight Detective Sergeant Neil Harvey put the torch to that and made one of the world's great writers sound like a smart-arse.'

Myles raised his brandy glass high, gave it the stare, but before downing it in his usual one gulp he turned to us. 'Gentlemen, to Neil Harvey... and his ilk.'

We drank the toast seriously. I was old enough now to realise it was probably the first time anyone had ever drank to the health of a policeman in the Imperial Hotel — and really meant it.

Myles looked particularly pleased about the outcome — Bundy's top detective had publicly identified my old mate as someone who was now under his personal protection.

I felt elated as well, because I was almost certain I had also received the ultimate nod from Neil Harvey. In recent years, I had worked it all out. A basic nod was usually a greeting, often in the street. A special nod was a sign of approval — there was longer eye contact, but the ultimate nod represented deep social and personal endorsement of the recipient. The ultimate nod was hard to explain. but when you saw one, you knew exactly what is was.

I was sure I had just seen one, but was I included? Tommy was an expert, so I asked him straight out. 'Tommy, that nod from Neil Harvey....' I was having trouble framing the question and my mate sensed it.

'You want me to rate it, don't you, son?' He was grinning.

'I mainly want to know if I was included... what do you reckon?'

Tommy dragged it out by picking up a saltshaker from the servery at the end of our bar and shaking some into his beer glass. The beer started to froth again — it was one of Tommy's tricks.

'Relax, Colt. It might have looked like a group nod, but it was meant for the three of us… as individuals. It was more focused and could more accurately be descried as a *collective* nod. It should have been bottled in spirit alcohol and preserved as a fine example of its species.'

So that was it — confirmation from the highest authority. This was one of the turning points in my career. I was still underage, only nineteen going twenty, so I was very lucky to receive acceptance with an ultimate nod in a public bar from a feared and respected copper.

But there was still a problem. The mongrel who we all knew had done Myles over so savagely, was still out there — free as a bird.

# CHAPTER 24.

## Who dinged my ute?

*Revenge is best taken as a cold meal.*

My new car was a beauty and I was pleased that people were noticing I had upgraded from my little rag hood Morris Z utility. I was so proud of it that I didn't park it out the back of the *News Mail*, but left it in Targo Street, right in front of The Imperial.

On that Friday night, or more accurately, early Saturday morning, I found someone had smashed a dint into the bonnet. Holden utes were built from rolled steel, they were tough as tanks.

The dint was on the driver's side, closest to the gutter. It was about the size of a plate, pushed in a few inches and was splattered with what looked like blood. The pub was closed and in darkness.

On the Monday at work, when I was on the early shift, I asked around but no-one in the office had any idea what had happened. Maybe some drunk had tried to climb up the front of the pub and had fallen back onto my car?

I was about halfway through my shift when Bevan walked in. 'Colt, I've had a look at that damage to your ute.'

He opened his wallet and pulled out a ten-pound note. 'Just between you and me ... this should cover the panel beating.'

I tried to ask him what was going on, but he walked away, turned at the door leading to the production floor, looked at me and put a finger to his lips. I knew I shouldn't ask any questions.

It was all revealed later that night. Tommy was full of it when he arrived for the late shift.

'You know that prick Boris? That dodgy young bloke who tried to bung on a blue in the pub… the one who called poor Myles out in front of everyone?'

I nodded.

'Well, it's all caught up with the bastard. Someone gave him a proper towelling on Friday night. Neil Harvey, the copper, told me at the races on Saturday.'

'What happened to him?'

'He copped a bloody hiding, didn't he? You know everyone thinks he's the bloke who bashed Myles?'

I nodded again. Myles had never named anyone, but I was surprised that the coppers hadn't homed in on Boris — because everyone seemed to know about the earlier incident in The Imperial.

Tommy hated not being 'in the know' and I could see him pondering. 'They must be linked don't you think? Even if it is justice being delivered six weeks after the event.'

I shrugged. 'How bad is he?'

'Neil reckons he looks like he was hit by a six-tonne beer truck. Whoever it was should get a medal but they're keeping mum about it. Everyone says that young prick can fight like a thrashing-machine, so it must have been a hard man who did him. You got any idea who it might have been?'

I shook my head and kept subbing copy. 'Not a clue, Tommy… not a bloody clue.'

But, in my mind, I kept seeing an image of Boris having his ugly face smashed into the bonnet of my ute and I was surprised about how happy I felt. Justice hadn't come through the courts, it had been delivered by a middle-aged war veteran with a cheerful smile who knew several ways to kill a man with his bare hands.

After all my mulling over the lack of justice in our society, I now knew that someone had finally paid for the crime committed against my old mate and that retribution had been in a most fitting physical form.

Had there been Bevan's trademark thrown hat or a toppled bar stool to distract the advancing Boris on that Friday night? Probably not. If it had happened in a bar, the whole town would be talking.

I suspected the justice had been administered silently and unexpectedly. One of Rommel's Africa Corps sentries on a desert outpost at dawn or a Japanese marine kneeling into a jungle stream to quench his thirst in fading light — all of them had been 'grist for the mill' for Bevan and his mates.

Just the same, it didn't seem right that no-one might ever know how it really happened. I'd been the one who found poor Myles in his pulped state and it troubled me so much that I felt a need to recreate the vengeful event.

Boris had been banned from The Imperial, but he'd most likely walked past late that night on his way up from the Tattersalls Hotel, into the main part of town. I envisaged Bevan seeing the unpunished thug swagger past. A challenge, a wild punch thrown with youthful confidence, an arm and shoulder suddenly caught in a commando lock with the assailant swung, face down, with his full body weigh smashing onto the bonnet of my Holden.

A broken nose, three top teeth knocked out, a cracked bottom jaw, two black eyes with possible retina damage, contusions and abrasions. Those were the sort of injuries I assumed one might receive if hit by Detective Neil Harvey's metaphorical 'six-tonne beer truck' and that just might balance the 'butchers bill' that was owed to Myles — a tooth for a tooth.

## CHAPTER 25.

# Myles pulls the plug

*Myles, off on another worldly adventure, warns about getting stuck 'in the dark corridors of provincial journalism.'*

So, Myles was leaving. It was really happening, and it wasn't a bit like his arrival when a crowded bar of noisy drinkers had all been silenced and left wondering what the fuck this strange bloke was doing holding four shots of brandy high in the air before downing it in one gulp.

This time, Myles was virtually slipping away, disappearing before our eyes. Roy, the manager, had agreed, for some unknown reason, to a shortened period for Myles to work out his notice and still retain his holiday benefits. I realised one day that he only had about a week to go before he headed south on the train.

Myles also wasn't working every day and the boss didn't seem to worry, so he must have been involved in whatever arrangement had been made about Myles' last weeks with us. I did catch him a couple of times at the telegram counter at the Post Office. He was polite but a bit short with me and just said he had some overseas business — family business, to attend to.

I was on day shift and in the pub with Bevan on my lunch break when Myles peered through the side door. We both knew that he didn't drink alone anymore, but he must have felt comfortable enough with Bevan and me, to come over and shout us both a drink.

Bevan didn't muck around. 'Myles, where are you off to mate? You've been so secretive about it that poor bloody Mervyn is taking bets out the back.'

'No mystery gentlemen, all organised and above board. I will send a forwarding address to Roy. It will be in Canada, Toronto most probably. Family stuff you know?'

I raised my glass. 'Well, good luck then, I envy you a bit, but I thought you might be heading to somewhere more exotic… like Tahiti or Timbuctoo.'

'Please, Colt, promise me you won't just sit back in this delightful town for the rest of your life and expend your journalistic energies in the dark corridors of provincial journalism.'

He looked at both of us and then quickly added, 'Not that there is anything wrong with this fine regional daily… It's just that a whole world awaits you my boy.'

'How do you think I'd go in England, Myles, job wise, I mean?'

'Colt, I'm sure Fleet Street will snap you up. You've had an excellent grounding here.'

'If I do go, would you be able to pass on any contacts or tips?'

Myles stared at the ceiling for a few seconds, deep in thought. 'Of course, my boy, I have many contacts, *The Times*, *The Guardian*, *The Observer*, you'd adapt quite quickly and be an asset to any one of them but…'

He leaned over and gave me a fatherly pat on the shoulder. 'But, on consideration, it is probably better that you find your own way… I know you'd feel much better about that, professionally I mean, rather than me opening doors in high places.'

I could see Bevan give me a quick wink.

The boys all seemed to have different versions of where Myles had gone, and what would happen to him. Where there is mystery, legend starts to flourish.

Our manager, Roy, tried to settle it soon after Myles left. I believe I was the first to learn the truth… or at least the truth as it was presented to Roy when Myles gave notice.

'Like everyone else, I thought Myles wanted to leave because he'd had enough of Bundy,' Roy said. 'And you couldn't blame him after what happened. But it was family business and Myles asked me not to talk about it until he left.'

I nodded. I was intrigued.

'It was all about a family inheritance. An aunt died in Canada and the lawyers in Toronto tracked Myles down here. There was money in the bank and property… lots of money and property.'

'How do you know it's true, Roy… we're talking about our Myles, remember?'

Roy grinned broadly. 'I've been dying to show this to someone… take a look for yourself. It's a photocopy Myles left it on my desk with his letter of resignation.'

There it was, on formal letterhead from a Canadian legal firm, addressed to Myles. It was brief and to the point. It would be advantageous for Myles Harrington Carruthers to contact them as soon as possible as the estate was an expansive and complex one and he was the sole beneficiary.

I must have looked stunned.

'I know mate… I know. Un-bloody-believable. Old Myles being left money.' Roy tapped the copy in my hand. 'It's all in there… like something out of Dickens… It's even got the maiden aunt… it doesn't mention an amount but read between the lawyer lines and its screaming wealth, affluence, good fortune… take your pick.'

I handed it back and started to think about Myles turning up in a bar in Toronto, possibly still in his St Vincent de Paul shorts with the soiled pockets, ordering a double brandy on a double brandy and inspecting his raised glass.

What would he tell his new-found drinking mates? Would he return to his Saville Row suits and handmade Italian shoes? Would he talk about his adventures in Australia? What would he do with all the money?

I later asked Bevan what he thought. Was it all too fantastic to be true?

He shrugged and smiled at me. 'That's the beauty of a bloke like him. He's leaving us with another mystery to ponder over. But, one thing I do know, the old bastard was in the Middle East at some stage during the war, I'm sure of that. He could describe exactly what a German 88 round sounds like going over your head… you'd have to be there to know that.'

I was intrigued. 'What does it sound like mate?'

'Like the gods… no the Devil and his armies from Hell ripping into heaven itself… a massive tearing sound like the sky just above you is being fractured, then a whip crack as loud as thunder that will usually blow your eardrums. But if you hear all of that, you know you're probably still alive.'

I was impressed.

'Mind you, those are my words. Myles just pulled some choicer ones out of the air, as usual, but he was spot on son, spot on.'

I was still impressed but should have known that a printer who could hold his own against Myles Carruthers in a pub debate could also string a decent descriptive sentence together.

# CHAPTER 26.

# Getting too involved in front page news

*Journos can write about tragedies and move on, but the families can't.*

About this time, I had the interesting experience of seeing my own name on the front pages of metropolitan dailies.

I was holidaying on my cousin's dairy farm outside Brisbane, when a distraught young man about our own ages skidded his car to a halt outside the farmhouse. We had to call the police — two of his mates had disappeared in a nearby flooded creek.

My cousin, Peter, like me, was a keen skindiver and I also had my gear with me. We raced down to the weir, put on face masks, snorkels, and flippers, and started searching where the two young men had disappeared.

It was like swimming in a giant washing machine. The water was turbid, and we had no visibility. We were free-diving, and in the darkness and turmoil I found it difficult to stay underwater for more than half a minute. We had to feel our way over rocks, broken concrete and pieces of reinforcing steel and sometimes found ourselves half stuck under a rocky ledge.

Hope diminished with every minute we spent searching, but we were desperate to find the boys as their families and friends gathered on the opposite bank. The floodwaters had cut the crossing and the Police were now holding people back.

When we first arrived and hoped to rescue someone, we hadn't wasted time putting on wet suits. But after a few minutes we both realised that diving in roaring floodwaters was pretty dodgy and we quickly suited up. We felt we had a bit more safety as we could dump the lead belt in an emergency and the buoyant neoprene suits would help float us to the surface.

On my next dive, I found one of them I touched, then grabbed a cold ankle and was surprised how easily he floated up with me as I kicked hard for the surface.

What to do? Get his head above water so he might miraculously start breathing? I didn't dare change my grip in the swirling waters, so I dragged him ashore to the waiting ambulance man and his little bottle of oxygen.

I tried to be gentle, but he was stiff and cold. I knew I hadn't been involved in a dramatic rescue, but the recovery of the body of some mother's son.

I left him to the ambulance man and a priest, or some kind of clergyman who had suddenly appeared. I walked back to where my ute was parked and got a tarp from amongst my camping gear. I felt he needed to be covered, he looked too exposed to me on that grassy bank, with his family crying out from the other side of the floodwaters.

But if we covered him, they would surely know he was dead, so I put the folded canvas tarp beside the ambulance man who was still pumping oxygen He just looked at me and nodded his head. Pete found the second body soon after.

The young fellow who had raised the alarm was a mess. Between sobs he told the police sergeant that they hadn't planned to go swimming, they just wanted to look at the floodwaters pouring over the weir.

Then, one boy jumped in close to the bank, for a bit of a lark, and was quickly swept under. The second fellow hadn't hesitated — he dived in to rescue his mate, but also disappeared.

The priest had anointed the forehead of one of the drowned boys and seemed to be praying. The other body was still covered up with my tarp, so I pulled the flap aside, so the man of God could do the same for him. My bloke had been identified as the one who had dived in to save his mate.

The priest just shook his head. 'Sorry, I can't do that.' I realised what was happening — he wasn't a Catholic and the priest couldn't help my bloke get to heaven.

I had followed my older cousin Pete's lead and kept cool and rational through all this drama, but now I felt a terrible sadness welling up in me, sadness tinged with anger. Not anger towards the Catholic priest, but towards whatever god had allowed this to happen. If there was a god who was prepared to accept the soul of the anointed boy, surely he would also accommodate the mate who had died with him?

Not all my anger was directed at the heavens, I was also troubled by the realisation that this was front-page news and felt ashamed that some poor young journo from *The Ipswich Times* or the Brisbane *Courier Mail* might be being briefed on intrusions to extract heart-rending copy from the grieving families of the two lifeless boys on the muddy bank in front of me.

I was so mad at the world that I began to shake and had to sit down with my face in my hands. I looked up when I realised that someone had draped an old grey army blanket over my shoulders. It was the old police sergeant. He didn't say anything, just gave me a look like he understood — like he'd done this blanket thing in the mud before.

I would have been okay, but he gave me a fatherly pat on my shoulder as well. That's when I lost it.

Naturally it made the papers the next day. Pete and I got a mention. But for the first time I realised how inadequate our journalists' craft was. What about the terrible sense of loss for the boys' families? What must it have been like to sit helplessly on the other side of a flooded stream and feel the minutes go by, hoping that two strangers, who appeared to be quite safe in the waters that had swallowed their boys, would also be able to perform some sort of miracle for them?

I realised then that behind every newspaper heading about a tragedy there was personal suffering, emotional pain and loss that would be felt for years to come. Journos could write stories and move on — but families and friends could not.

It happened again, about six months later.

Peter and I were at the wedding of friends in Brisbane, Trevor and Joc, and joined up with a fellow guest, Neil, for a spearfishing trip to an inshore reef just off Kingscliff.

I hadn't met Neil before, but he was a happy, fit looking man, a very experienced diver, with a lovely wife who was expecting their first child. He disappeared while were we were diving, and she was waiting on the beach.

There was a rather disjointed police search with local fishermen, and the groom, my mate Trevor, instead of being on his honeymoon, ended up searching for his best friend from the air in a privately chartered Cessna.

The body was sighted two weeks later by fishermen but was never recovered.

It was another front page in the *Courier Mail* and another example of how printed words are never enough.

# CHAPTER 27.

# Lessons from *My Brother Jack*

*Poncy English professors and mean-spirited book reviewers aren't the only ones engaged in the pursuit of literary merit.*

Our profession was also in the news in Australia, or at least one of our famous colleagues turned author was making headlines.

George Johnston had just published *My Brother Jack*. I didn't know what to expect when I started reading it and was excited to discover the story was about a young journalist growing up on the job and being influenced by older men who had fought in the war.

It was also a great story about family, and the generation gap. Best of all, here was a famous working journalist and war correspondent breaking all the newspaper rules by using repetition and loads of descriptive adjectives.

It was set 20 or 30 years earlier, but it seemed to be reflecting many of my own experiences.

Percy saw me with my copy at work one day and came straight over. I thought I might cop it, because Percy was more into newspapers than novels.

'Take a good note of how that's put together, Colt. You know he's one of us?'

I nodded.

'The academics and literary toffs often scoff at journalists and forget that words are our bloody craft as well. Reviewers, poets, essayists and poncy English professors aren't the only ones who understand the pursuit of literary merit.'

I knew what he was talking about but was surprised — I never thought I'd hear our old court reporter promote 'the pursuit of literary merit' as being part of the newspaperman's craft.

'Yes, Percy I know… Hemingway was also a journo.'

'Yes, but not a very good one with hard news, by all accounts. You should try to find some of the reports George Johnston wrote about the War in the Pacific… brilliant stuff. After you finish *My Brother Jack* go and re-read something Hemingway wrote.'

'I've read *The Snows of Kilimanjaro.*'

Percy thought for a moment. 'No, get something more akin to what Johnston was writing about… something with not so much stench from rotting animals or the recoil of an elephant gun.'

'What will I be looking for?'

'Style, of course, style in the economic use of words… they're both great wordsmiths, but Hemingway uses too many for my money and Johnston gets me there quicker, but with the same level of emotional involvement and a strong sense of time and place.'

Shit. This was Percy Grey, not our learned Myles Harrington Carruthers, and he was sounding forth on a subject far removed from courts, horse racing, lawn bowls, the bottling capacity of the Bundy Rum Distillery or the current district crop estimates. Then again, he was a proud 'hack journalist' and hacks could turn their hand to any job, and almost any subject.

About that time, was also exposed to the emergence in America of a reporting style that would have been branded as heresy by most of the *News Mail* subs. Tom Wolf's New Journalism and Hunter S. Thompson's Gonzo approach to hard news in a style that almost mirrored the style of the novelist, was filtering through to us in the pages of American newspapers and quality feature magazines.

I had the feeling I was stuck in a rut and being exposed to such fine writing was another incentive to strike out on my own, even if I had to cross hemispheres.

Rod, one of our sub-editors furtively passed on copies of *Esquire* and *The Post*, with warnings to keep them out of sight.

It was exciting and as far as our boss was concerned potentially dangerous to read the works of Gay Talese, Truman Capote and my favourite, Jimmy Breslin.

As a court reporter I was fascinated by the way Breslin could write a gripping piece about a big mobster with a diamond ring on one finger finally being convicted in court through the efforts of a shabby little attorney who wore glasses instead of jewellery. It was all about the setting, the characters and the tension — the case details didn't seem to matter.

Some years later, after the assassination of President Kennedy, I talked to Percy in The Imperial about Breslin's masterful piece in which he left the headlines to others and sought out the man who was digging the President's grave at Arlington Cemetery.

'I don't know what all the fuss is about, Colt. Isn't it an obvious peg for a working journalist?'

*Obvious? Come of the bloody grass Percy, it was the holy grail of journalism, unearthed in Arlington Cemetery by one of the world's truly great reporters.*

I just shrugged and bought my old mentor another beer. Years later I found another piece, also by an American, which I should have sent to Percy in defence of the 'new journalism' which Percy had so often dismissed as old journalism rediscovered by a younger generation.

When I was first sent out on the rounds without a clue, a young Hunter S. Thompson was writing his now famous cover letter seeking a start on the *Vancouver Sun*. In it he proudly stated that he had a healthy contempt for journalism which he believed was overrun with dullards, bums and hacks, and generally stuck in a bog of stagnant mediocrity.

Hunter said he preferred sports reporting but could happily write about everything from 'warmongering propaganda to learned book reviews'. In that regard, he would have been welcomed by Percy and my other workmates in country towns where journos were expected to be able to turn their hands to all the forms of newspaper writing.

# CHAPTER 28.

## The Colt's choice... Fleet Street or the Arctic Circle?

*Marching to the beat of a different drum.*

I sensed it was time for me to take off. One of my mates, Graeme, who was high up in the rum distillery, was keen to go overseas and we were considering teaming up.

I had parted with my latest and most serious girlfriend. The split had been her idea and had been awkward rather than sad. She was a mate's sister, which always made things difficult.

She also seemed to make heavy going about our differences, while I thought differences should have added to the attraction — that's what I found interesting about her.

I gave up opening the passenger car door when I picked her up because that was 'treating her like a cripple'. Walking on the gutter side of the footpath just got her sounding off about how she didn't need protection 'from horse-shit flung up by carriage wheels or assaults from low-class ruffians'.

It was supposed to be funny, but I knew a put-down when I met one. It had been a convenient relationship for a while, but I think both of us had silently agreed that it lacked any prospects for the future.

I had also started to feel that my hometown could be suffocating, and even good friends could grate on occasions. I was getting pissed off about something — but couldn't get a grip on what it actually was.

Then it happened. I threw the first punch at one of my best mates, Ashley.

I regretted starting the fight and I also regretted that it was with a tough, round shouldered, red-haired bloke who knew how to counter punch.

We both ended with black eyes and a renewed, much deeper friendship. But Bevan had warned me that 'fighting is a mug's game' and, the next day, I realised how bloody stupid I had been.

What if it had been on the concrete footpath outside a pub, instead of a wet grassy lawn in a backyard at Bargara? We both talked about it afterwards and thanked our mates who had pulled us apart. Ash agreed that, left alone, we probably would have tried to beat each other senseless.

Both of us had been surprised at how quickly a hidden capacity for violence had been released — after all, weren't we pretty peaceful types who never went around looking for trouble?

More than that we were spearfishing mates, who relied on each other in an activity that could sometimes turn dangerous. We were as close as brothers but had still wanted to knock each other's block off. It was a painful but sobering experience.

Some of my younger colleagues at work were also getting the jump on me by moving off to what seemed to be much more exciting jobs.

Rob Strathdee, who I had been mentoring on the council rounds only a year before, was now a war correspondent in Vietnam. The legendary Ken Blanch from Brisbane, who had covered the Kalkie murders in my first year, was visiting town after a stint with the Army PR team in Vietnam. We were sharing a beer in The Imperial and he was talking about the Battle of Long Tan — on equal terms as journos this time.

I had worked patiently for promotions through journalism's professional gradings and reached the B Grade ceiling. This signified that I was more than just qualified, I was equipped to handle any task an editor might throw at me — even on a metropolitan paper. To become an A Grader, I would have to wait for my older mate Percy to die. So, I obtained a good reference from the boss before taking up Roy's offer of leave of absence.

The idea was to get part-time jobs on English newspapers and have a good look at offset printing and the new system of cold type. It didn't quite work out that way.

My sense of adventure and fascination with fabulous people in far-away places had been sharpened by my friendship with Myles and my experiences with older workmates.

I arrived in London in a heatwave in 1967 with a contact in Fleet Street and almost certainly work on one of the regionals. But there was also the chance to trek up the coast of Norway, cross the Arctic Circle, and camp in the land of the midnight sun. The ice bears and snowy gyrfalcons called to me much more loudly than clattering typewriters in crowded English newsrooms.

Later, I got work picking hops in Kent rather than covering council meetings and then I crewed across the Atlantic to Barbados in a yacht with a 'knock down' in huge seas west of Madeira. I voyaged through the Caribbean on a tramp steamer, caught coral fish for export to aquariums in Europe, had a machine gun cocked and the barrel pressed into my navel during an unfortunate misunderstanding with a policeman in Venezuela, and dodged bullets in Quinn's Bar in Tahiti, the roughest drinking hole in the South Pacific.

Many ex-pat Australians of my generation decided to stay in England, but the call of the Sunburnt Country was too strong for me. I had stayed away almost two years and circled the globe by modes of transport that ranged from luxurious to life threatening.

I returned just when the prophetic words of Simon and Garfunkel were topping the charts. '*Home — where my love lies waiting — silently for me.*'

There was more than my love, my wife and the future mother of our four children waiting silently for me. My future would hold three years of hectic deadline television and radio journalism with ABC news before becoming one of the new generation of younger editors who were not actually appointed by God. I would be free to support a weekly and two daily newspapers with editorials full of opinionated adjectives, encounter an active chapter of the Ku Klux Klan during the years of the Mabo land rights campaign in Townsville, and be selected as one of six Australian journalists for China's first exchange with a Western nation. I would also have a crack at righting wrongs and exposing injustice, and cop million-dollar writs backed by death threats from underworld gangsters, crooked coppers and corrupt politicians who resented being exposed by the power of the written word.

In his own small way Myles, and my older workmates, had prepared me for all of this — during my transition from boy to man. The Colt has no regrets about the time spent with Myles and his ilk, in the days of hard copy and hot metal.

# CHAPTER 29.

## The Colt falls for a sea nymph at midnight on Kelly's Beach

*Was this the girl from the C.J. Dennis poem,*
*a lost love from 100 years ago?*

It was my twenty-seventh birthday and, in typical Bundy fashion, I was being celebrated around a keg of beer to which a sheep-dip dispensing gun with a very long tube had been connected. It was being passed around to allow the seated drinkers to refill their own glasses without crowding around the keg.

We were seated in a big circle on a backyard lawn, with the keg floating in a tub of ice and salt brine to super cool the beer. Taking the beer to the drinkers rather than letting the men gravitate to the keg was a local invention. It was much more civilised and sociable and also a very efficient way to empty an eighteen-gallon keg — you just needed a very long hose if there was a big crowd.

There was catering, of course. Ashley and Bob had brought a big esky full of sweet estuary prawns down from Baffle Creek and there was probably a loaf of bread somewhere.

I was back home, and as they say in the West Indies — I was a man full of sand. That roughly translates to a bloke who has sailed off into the sunset and returned much more confident and worldlier. A man full of sand is also bursting with stories, but they can only be recalled by polite prompting from old friends and recounted almost reluctantly.

When I came home, Bundy felt like a comforting blanket, and at first, I was happy to pull it over my head and forget about the rest of the world. There was a warm bed every night, a regular wage to keep hunger at bay and the risk of being robbed at knifepoint or accosted by little men in strange uniforms carrying machine guns, had greatly diminished.

But now, as the party moved into full swing, I realised that something was still missing — that sense of adventure and excitement which accompanies all travellers moving through far-off places — the heady mix of wonder, expectation and the occasional euphoric encounter with paralysing fear.

I was starting to worry that the familiarity of my hometown might change the Bundy blanket feeling into something that was smothering me — robbing me of the special kind of oxygen that 'a man full of sand' can become addicted to.

The last guests to arrive were a solicitor mate turned journo, and his girlfriend. No one was expected to bring presents, but John and Sandra pulled one out of the hat. They pushed Barbara forward and introduced her. She was a new flatmate, a Brisbane girl who had just started her career as a high school teacher.

I'm sure I couldn't speak and stood there like one of Tommy's moon-struck poddy calves. She was sensational, I had never seen another young woman like her in all my travels — the dancing girls in Tahiti, those English beauties riding in Hyde Park, or barefoot Swedish backpackers frolicking on the edges of an icy lake in Norway.

She was wearing some sort of white linen frock that was both elegant and sexy. It was short enough to show off lovely legs but had two big circular cut-outs on both sides from just above her hips up to her tanned ribcage. The snowy white fabric contrasted with the tanned skin, dark short hair, and sparkling eyes. I instantly recognised the whole package as a work of art — I had seen nothing like it before, not even in the Tate Gallery in London.

When she walked you could see her body moving through the cut-outs, the actual curve of her hips. I was sure I had visited countries where shoulders like hers would need to be covered in public, with an extra shawl on Saints' Days.

I changed suddenly from a man of sand to the Colt when he was a mumbling, fumbling sixteen-year-old, frightened of girls. Sandra gently pushed Barbara forward: 'What do you think of your birthday present, Elliot?'

Before I could get a word out, Ashley cut in. 'Mate... are you going to unwrap her now, or wait until later?' I saw the sudden flash in Barbara's eyes and panicked that she might spin on her heels and walk away from all these uncouth people. I got some of my sand back, extended my hand and gently led her to a chair.

I offered her the best prawn I could dredge from the esky — that's when I first saw her beautiful smile.

'Thanks, I love prawn cocktails, but I've never needed to peel one before... can you show me how it's done?'

The smile was all it took. I was full of sand again and also brimming with worldly prawn peeling knowledge. I deftly removed the head and black vein, tail and shell in two quick movements.

I dangled the morsel in front of her, but in that instance realised this was too soon and too intimate to drop food into the mouth of this lovely young woman. She reached out for it and took a delicate bite.

Watching her savour the flavour and seeing the tip of her pink tongue move against her lips I knew that God had created this particular prawn for this purpose alone.

The party went well, and I sensed that Barbara realised my mates weren't a gormless mob of yobbos, they all just had a strong larrikin streak. It also helped that most of them had nice wives or girlfriends. I made sure she wasn't too engaged by the couple of other single blokes who were also there.

Ashley's fiancée Beverly had kicked him so hard in the shins that he was still limping when he came over to us. 'Hi Barb… I'm Ash. Sorry about before, I was just trying to embarrass my old mate here, but I got you in the crossfire as well. I've mixed you a Bundy rum and Coke to make up for it.'

Later that night, a small party of us ended up at Kelly's Beach for a moonlight swim and the chance to see the turtles nesting. There were suitable stops on the way for people to get their togs and we found a big mother turtle laying eggs only a few yards away from where we parked the cars.

The water was a bit rough and floating strands of green and gold seaweed sometimes got in our way. There was also phosphorescence in the water. When you swept your hand through the waves it would leave a tail of golden sparkles from many thousands of minute sea creatures and plankton.

We body-surfed the small shore break in the moonlight. I realised that Barbara hadn't just been spending time at the beach to get her great tan, she also loved the water and was confident and graceful as she slid under the waves or turned and effortlessly caught one into the shore.

I stuck close to her and on two occasions we swept along together and were deposited in a tangled laughing heap on the sand at the water's edge. The next time, I held her by the hand, and we lay there for a while, being washed and gently rocked by remnants of the following waves.

When it was time to leave, I walked ahead to get her towel, but couldn't keep my eyes off this girl. I had this strange and urgent feeling that I needed to know exactly where she was at all times and if I lost sight of her, for even an instant, I would wake up, or she might suddenly disappear like the mystical girl in Tommy's poem.

I had walked only a few paces up the beach and turned to see Barbara come out of the waves in her white bikini. She was framed by the moonlight and laughed as she untangled a shiny crown of tangled seaweed from her hair.

When this vision walked closer, I realised she was glowing — like a sea nymph who had been dusted with fairy gold flakes. She was covered with phosphorescence from the Coral Sea. I must have been staring. She followed my gaze down, smiled cheekily and started to brush the gold specks off her bikini top.

That's when I did it. I had more sand in me at that moment than the whole of Kelly's Beach. I walked straight up to her, took her gently by those wonderful bare shoulders and, when she looked up into my eyes — I kissed her.

# PART 2
# THE
# EDITOR

# CHAPTER 30.

# A $3 million writ from a gangster — with my name on it

*Townsville, 1980. Newspaper editors, even those in the bush, must sometimes act like they're fearless — but was I just being reckless in confronting crooks, corrupt politicians and bent coppers who were running unchecked in Queensland in the years before the Fitzgerald Inquiry?*

I'd just got off the phone to Barbara to warn her I might be late. Dinners with our family had been important, almost sacred, over the past nine years, even with broken ABC shifts and my return to newspapers as the editor in Bundaberg and now Townsville.

Climbing the professional ladder while learning new craft skills, such as film scripting and editing also included new responsibilities such and hiring and firing. The downside was a more disrupted family life and a young husband on call until 2 am most days of the week.

But the board was having a special meeting and my desire to once again share a meal with my beautiful pregnant wife and help tuck our three littles ones into their beds would have to be suppressed.

I was expecting big news from the management meeting and feared it could end my short career as the youngest editor in the 100-year history of the *Townsville Daily Bulletin* — word was out that I'd upset a dangerous Sydney gangster from my cramped little editor's office way up in North Queensland.

Shorty McLean, our managing director, was a tough little ex-rugby league player who had the habit of head-butting a steel filing cabinet in my editor's office. It didn't happen all the time, but he used it as stress relief whenever he came through the door to share his feelings about the latest concerns of the board of directors of the North Queensland Newspaper Company.

I could usually sense just how serious the problem might be by the force of each head butt and I knew we were in trouble this time. Shorty was flat on his back on my office floor, his eyes were flickering and there was a dent in the filing cabinet. Even the big forwards from Mount Isa in the Foley Shield grand finals hadn't been able to flatten him like that.

I sat him in a chair while he refocused. I knew what this was probably all about. We had cracked a national story about Abe Saffron and Eddie Kornhauser, whose involvement in bids for North Queensland first casino licence had been hidden away in a maze of tender documents and holding companies.

When Shorty looked like he could focus again, I tried to lighten things up.

'Any imputation concerning any person by which the reputation of that person is likely to be injured…' It goes on for ages but was memorised by all editors and most young journalists of my era — we had to know about the Laws of Libel to avoid defaming someone with our printed words.

Shorty cut me off with a nod. 'Yes, it's happened. And I couldn't wait to rush in here and break the good news that you've also been named, personally, in the writ.'

I had hoped he might not have seemed so pleased about that part. 'How much?'

'They rounded off the damages at a neat three million dollars. I supposed fucking gangsters from King's Cross and dodgy Gold Coast developers don't bother with the small change?'

'You mean alleged fucking dodgy developers and gangsters? We didn't actually call them that in our story….so, what will the board do?'

'Contest it, of course. No retraction, no apology. I told them they should be proud that an exclusive front-page story here in Townsville can expose the dark side of the casino backers and obviously scare the shit out of some of the biggest crooks in the country.'

'What did they say?'

'Our chairman reminded me, quite politely, that the shit we scared out of them was being valued in the millions. The reason I'm so bloody angry is they want to review anything like this in future. They don't trust management and the editor to make the call like we did this time.'

'But I thought we had an agreement after what happened last time?'

What happened last time was that one of our directors had leaked. I was managing a red-hot story about allegations of financial fraud and faked invoices that involved the Commonwealth Superannuation Trust Fund. We were targeting one of Townsville biggest companies, Kern Corporation which was expanding nationally.

Our informant was a computer consultant who was converting their hard copy files and accounts. It was great lead and fine work by one of my most junior reporters, Jon Woodworth. Shorty and I briefed the board and our company lawyer because of the risk of action over libel.

We had obtained computer printouts that intrigued our company secretary, Jim Manion, who was also an accountant. My intention was to break a story after giving the company the opportunity to respond, check the legals and let the Federal Police decide whether they should investigate further because Commonwealth super funds were in the mix.

But we didn't get that far. Someone threated to break our informant's legs with an iron bar. Our contact, fearing for his life, lost all faith in journalistic confidentiality and jumped on a plane out of town.

Later, one of our board members admitted he had spoken to Kern Corporation, as an 'act of courtesy' and had let them know we would be seeking comment on a potentially negative story. Too much Rotary fellowship, not enough confidentiality?

Today, Jon Woodsworth rates the story as the best piece he ever wrote that was never published. Jon and I however, did have a private meeting with the then leader of the State Opposition who raised questions under Parliamentary privilege and suggested that the Federal Police should have a look at the company's books... bearing in mind that our informant claimed there was more than one set of books.

Looking back now, it's also interesting that Kern Corporation was involved a few years later in a Sydney Casino licence bid with none-other than a young Donald Trump. It's equally interesting that their bid failed because the New South Wales Police were concerned about the group's links, through Trump, to the American mafia. And, oh, yes, money from the Commonwealth Superannuation Trust fund was also in the mix again.

So, when we copped the writ about the Townsville Casino story, I knew that Shorty would have been under great pressure for not having informed the board about my plans to publish the offending story. I was quietly confident. We had good people on the story, and we'd checked the facts.

One of my senior reporters, Blair Roots, a boy from the bush, had uncovered a lead that had been missed by the big metropolitan papers and national TV news outlets. Blair went on to become a highly regarded presenter on the ABC *Big Country* series.

He'd been covering the local angle on bids for Queensland's second casino licence. Judging by the frenzy in business, political and financial circles over the awarding of the first licence on the Gold Coast, whoever got the nod for the next one in North Queensland would have a government permit to print money.

Blair had also worked with old hands, so he knew exactly what I was talking about when I asked him to find out 'who's up who and who's paying the rent' in the world of casino licences.

Blair had been trying to sort out what the company structures were and some of the listings were very difficult to track down.

I never asked him to reveal his source, but he discovered something no other media outlet had. That one of the bidders involved two businessmen who had close links to Russ Hinze, a senior Cabinet Minister in the Bjelke-Petersen Government. The names Eddie Kornhauser and Abe Saffron, sent Blair's alarm ringing. He now knew who was paying the metaphorical rent.

Kornhauser a multi-millionaire Gold Coast developer had been accused in State Parliament of money laundering but had only ever been convicted of tax evasion. Abe Saffron was also known as 'Mr. Sin' and the 'Boss of King's Cross'.

These were serious people. Kornhauser was reputed by the Business Review Weekly to be worth $340 million and Saffron, the Sydney underworld figure, had a highly successful track record in suing for defamation. Police were also looking closely at Saffron's associates over the disappearance of a high-profile Sydney socialite who had tried to block one of their big inner-city developments.

I learned later that Russ Hinze, also known as 'the Minister for Everything' in the Bjelke-Petersen Government, was backing them. He was a colourful character and I'd interviewed him several times, both as a newspaper journalist and while working for ABC News. He could never understand why people accused him of having conflicts of interest when he was Minister for Racing. Surely, he said, having stables of racehorses and trotters and a huge personal income from the racing industry was a, 'convergence of interest, not a conflict of interest'.

While doing his background checks, Blair was able to quote a magistrate from an earlier court case in New South Wales who had ruled that Saffron wasn't a fit person to hold a liquor licence in a country pub. As this bloke was in the front running for a multi-million-dollar casino licence in Townsville, we thought our readers might be interested.

I was emboldened by the fact that the most damaging statement we had published, in terms of injuring someone's reputation, had been made in an open court. There was, however, a question about whether it was contemporaneous, but I still thought it was relevant material that would serve our 'public interest' argument.

At that stage I though our only problem was the writ — I didn't realise we'd upset some very nasty people who had friends in high places. Back then, the Fitzgerald Royal Commission into police misconduct and corruption in Queensland was still six years away.

Most of the big names who were eventually jailed or charged on Tony Fitzgerald's recommendations were still running the show, including Police Minister Russ Hinze and the Queensland Police Commissioner Terry Lewis.

Soon after Shorty broke the news about the writ, I received a call from an old *News Mail* colleague, Rob Strathdee, the Queensland bureau chief of AAP news services. Word was spreading rapidly through the national media who had a fixation about the mysterious Abe Saffron.

Rob had good contacts in Brisbane, Sydney and Melbourne, and as journo who had sent dispatches from a war zone in Vietnam with the sound of gunfire in the background, I knew he wasn't the type to spread unnecessary panic. But his opening remark was now ringing loudly in my ears.

'Mate, I suggest you get a pistol licence and a very large pig dog... you do realise just how rough these bastards can be?'

I hadn't been dismissive, but I'd done my best to downplay the risks involved and reminded my colleague that even in North Queensland there was still the rule of law and crooks from Kings Cross would be operating far from home where they might have bought some protection from the authorities. He wasn't convinced.

'Just remember there could be more than $3 million at stake as far as Saffron is concerned and don't be surprised if things get rough, particularly with some of his associates. You do realise that the media in Sydney as well as the judiciary are all tyring to link him with the disappearance of Juanita Neilson? The list of his underworld associates is a mile long, believe me, he's the vicious end of this dodgy deal. Some of his mates have killed more people than you can roster on a day shift in Townsville.'

I was still absorbing Rob's warning when I took an even more disturbing call from another colleague who was also a key player in the casino bidding.

Word travels fast in a place like Townsville, so I'd expected an experienced journalist who was now the North's leading lobbyist and PR operative to hear about our massive writ. John Gagliardi and his wife Kay were friends. We babysat each other's children and I'd known him from earlier years when he worked on the Queensland Nickle project.

But John wasn't interested in quizzing me for details, he wanted to share something deeply personal and upsetting that he was sure was linked to the casino bidding and my writ from Saffron.

John's wife had received a note threatening to send his blood-stained severed ears to the family home in a matchbox. The warning was simple. Someone who had a lot to lose was trying to stymie John's effective advocacy in the bidding process.

Coming on top of Rob Strathdee's warning about the Saffron mob's track record in actually delivering death threats put recent events in sharper perspective. We agreed to meet privately the next day to share our concerns.

It now seemed obvious that the legal action against me and my employers and the threats against John Gagliardi and his family were designed to protect the licence bid in which Saffron and Kornhauser were hidden partners.

In my case they were trying to block the local newspaper from publishing adverse material and in threatening John they were trying to neutralise the most effective consultant in Queensland who was working against their interests by promoting one of the other bidders.

I was still feeling somewhat righteous about not involving Barbara in the darker side of my work as a newspaper editor.

We were now in the 'Age of Aquarius' and expectations were high for my generation to experience a new era of enlightenment.

*Jupiter aligns with Mars; peace will guide the planets; and love will steer the stars.* To accommodate this change that would last for another 2700 years, new-age blokes were now wearing their hair long and sporting purple flared slacks to work.

Barbara had also suggested it would be okay for me to spend more time with the kids and help with some of the family duties as well. It was all part of the modern social scene — sharing and caring.

But, copping a writ that had the potential to financially ruin one of Australia's biggest regional daily newspapers and send me into the ranks of the unemployed wasn't something I'd wanted to share with my pregnant wife. So, I felt justified, maybe even a bit noble, for not taking that one home with me.

But I was stunned when John revealed the death threat sent to his wife about severed ears in a matchbox.

Looking back after all these years, I can honestly say that what really frightened me wasn't the possibility of my own severed ears, it was the even more disturbing vision of our little curly-haired elder daughter Emma, running excitedly up the stairs of our high-set Queenslander in Townsville with a package from the postman for her mother.

Until then I didn't know there was a tipping point when protective anger can strip fear from a husband and father and prepare him to deliver equally unthinkable acts of violence to his fellow man.

However, for a husband whose wife was close to giving birth, I didn't handle things well at that time. I was thinking pistol licence, guard dog and more probing editorial comment when I should have been taking time off to support Barb in the last stages of her pregnancy, cooking meals, cuddling our three little kids and regularly telling the whole family how much I loved them.

I suppose staying silent and not bringing work home with me was my way of insulating my wonderful wife and kids from the harsh realities of life as a newspaper editor.

At least the Russians helped me refocus when they invaded Afghanistan. How outrageous, a major world power invading a small nation to stop Islamic revolutionaries from taking over?

The Western nations were furious, and it was appropriate that the *Townsville Bulletin* editor should add North Queensland's voice to the international chorus of condemnation. Could anyone imagine countries like America and Australia invading a place like Afghanistan simply because we thought the bad guys were about to take over?

This time, I was pretty sure there wouldn't be a defamation claim from the aggrieved Russians or death threats to local journalists. I had decided that the nuclear-armed Soviet Union seemed to be a much softer and safer editorial target than the Saffron mob.

I also needed to take professional care because the matter was now before the courts and further comment in our paper would be sub-judicial and create even more legal problems. However, there was no way we would back down to threats, direct or indirect. Our strategy was to let our lawyers earn their retainers and, hopefully arm-wrestle Saffron's people out of Court in the coming weeks or months.

I would now get my senior staffers who had worked on the casino stories to focus on regional issues including the controversial crown-of-thorns starfish plague. I had once spoken to a marine researcher who was adamant that if unchecked, the starfish would ruin the Great Barrier Reef in four years. Now seventeen years later the reef was still there, but so too, were the starfish.

I told my journalists that no newspaper in the country was better placed than us to inform the public about what was happening on the reef and what needed to be done.

A day later I pulled Blair Roots off the story and put him back on the casino and police watches because I had underestimated the influence of Abe Saffron and the extent of corruption in the Queensland political system and the Police Force.

Virtually overnight, the local coppers had declared war on the *Bulletin* and our staff. It was no use complaining to the region's most senior officer because he was calling the shots against us and had a fearsome reputation — not just with criminals but anyone who crossed him.

Almost 40 years later I was to co-write a book with Bob Katter junior, who had the misfortune to cross Inspector Mervyn Henry Stevenson around the same time I clashed with him as editor of the *Bulletin*. As a young Country Party Member of Parliament, Katter took up the case of two Charters Towers' policemen who were convinced Stevenson was a corrupt copper in league with cattle thieves and drug gangs and was probably involved in several mysterious deaths across North Queensland.

Back then I didn't know that a young policeman had been threatened by Stevenson who waved a pistol in his face, only to receive a truly courageous reply: 'Well Merv, you had better get me with your first shot…because I won't miss with mine.'

There was an inquiry of sorts, but corrupt senior elements of the police force managed to turn the spotlight on informants rather than Stevenson. Katter and the 'honest cops' admitted they were living in fear.

As Katter recalled:' Of the eighteen people who had evidence, or gave evidence about the Stock Squad's corrupt activities, within two and a half years, six were dead and the other 12 were on trumped-up charges or being investigated with a view to being charged. If you stood up to the head of the Stock Squad, you were quickly dragged into very dangerous quicksand and people genuinely feared for their lives.'

I wish I had spoken to him when all this was going on. I might have handled Stevenson differently when he tried something similar on me.

# CHAPTER 31.

## Outback hero or killer cop?

*Everyone laughed when the Acting Regional Superintendent*
*of Police showed me the concealed pistol in his ankle holster*
*before pointing a cocked finger to my forehead and popping off*
*an imaginary shot. But I didn't think it was funny.*

At first, I thought the police attention we were suddenly receiving at the *Bulletin* was payback for stories they didn't like. Journo-copper relationships were sometimes like that.

But it only took a few minutes in the back bar of The Great Northern Hotel with John Gagliardi, the colleague who'd also been intimidated and threatened over the casino bidding, to convince me that even though our ears had not yet been posted to our families in matchboxes, we were still being targeted by Saffron and his supporters. According to him, what we were experiencing was the whole Sunshine State package — corrupt politicians, bent coppers, and underworld figures with murderous reputations.

John confided that he was also being harassed by police and he believed it was all linked to the casino issue. Russ Hinze, the Minister for Police was also a friend of Eddie Kornhauser and both had been named in corruption allegations on the Gold Coast.

John had been pulled over at all times of the day and night. As he said, you know you're being given special treatment when you've been stopped, interrogated and inspected on three occasions on a short drive home from work.

What especially worried John was that the police didn't seem to be local and were mainly in plain clothes. At that time, the Bjelke Petersen Government had a 'Special Branch' that reported direct to Minister Hinze and kept a close eye on communists, trade unionists, deviates, hippies (generally anyone wearing sandals or beards) and political troublemakers.

His Brisbane contacts warned that elements of the Special Branch were also at the call of corrupt senior police to do 'private tasks' for certain politicians and their dodgy business mates.

I told John that our harassment had started with *Bulletin* logo cars being pulled over for roadside checks and drink driving tests by the local police so often that it was obviously meant to send us a message.

Soon after there had been a complete breakdown, with an unofficial but highly effective black ban being placed on all the police dealings with the *Bulletin*. Even 'Scoop' Hooper, our trusted former police rounds-man who was also their cheerful drinking partner, got the cold shoulder. The police prosecutors refused us access to the usual hand-up material in the courts.

The fellowship between police and journalists could sometimes become fractious when we ran stories about heavy-handed arrests or coppers being reprimanded by magistrates and judges, but this was different. I checked with senior staff and none of us could pinpoint a negative police story that might have upset them — which was why I believed John was right in connecting all our troubles to the casino bidding.

I wanted to write something in response, but all my old-school training warned me that I didn't have a very strong peg on which to hang a story. We had some facts, but not much substance, apart from speculation bordering on a conspiracy theory. However, something did happen soon after that gave us a chance to hit back.

Among the young journalists working for me at that time was Chris Mitchell, who later became Editor in Chief of *The Australian*, as well as Rory Gibson who edited the *Fiji Times*, returned to Townsville as Editor of the *Bulletin* some years after I retired, and now writes one of the most entertaining syndicated columns in Australia.

Rory and his mates, who rented a flat at the bayside suburb of Rowes Bay, had a late-night visit by the police who virtually trashed the place. I made inquiries, only to be told that it had been in response to an anonymous drug tip-off, and unfortunately the detectives went to the wrong address. We took it to the Police Commissioner's office in Brisbane and were told that mistakes like that happened all the time — nothing personal.

We ran the story on the front page, played it straight with no comment, but the facts themselves painted the police in a bad light. Some sections of the police force had been sending us warnings and now it was our turn to kick back.

However, the timing was also bad for us because the District Superintendent was on extended leave and I'd had a good working relationship with him. He'd been replaced by an officer who had genuine legendary status in North Queensland and the Gulf Country, Inspector Merv Stevenson.

Merv obviously preferred the legend of the respected bush copper and horseman who could track better than the Aborigines and who was relentless in his pursuit of armed cattle duffers. His detractors, however, were convinced he was dangerously corrupt and suspected him of several unsolved murders and unexpected suicides linked to the sale of stolen cattle and the expanding drug trade in North Queensland.

I had met Stevenson when I was working for ABC News the 1970s. Back then, he was happy to talk to journalists, particularly bush journos, but by the time I was editing the *Townsville Bulletin* he had developed an intense dislike for the media or anyone else foolish enough to ask too many questions,

He also had a habit of black-banning journalists who upset him, which made life hard for the editors of our newspaper in Charters Towers, where Stevenson was based. My colleague Max Tomlinson, editor of *The Northern Miner,* ran a court story that didn't surprise many of his readers but incensed Merv Stevenson. A witness alleged that the head of the Stock Squad was also involved in stealing cattle. He was named in open court.

Max quite rightly splashed this across the front page. It was the first time that these allegations had been exposed publicly. Stevenson complained to our management and board members and it was suggested that the *Northern Miner* should run some sort of 'balanced story' about the decorated policeman and his pending retirement, with a focus on all the positive aspects of his career. Max politely told management to piss off.

I assumed that Stevenson, an officer well known for leaning on friends in high places, was continuing a personal vendetta with the North Queensland Newspaper Company. Now he was acting as the region's most senior police officer, I could expect an official cold shoulder and even some stupid payback harassment.

Then, something happened that really jolted me and showed just how fragile media and police relationship could be in the Sunshine State. The Special Branch coppers threatened my police roundsman, Jon Woodworth, with trumped-up charges of resisting arrest and urinating in a police vehicle.

Jon had been at a public event in Anzac Park when two detectives apprehended a young man with what appeared to be unnecessary physical force. He was grabbed while sitting with friends, punched, headlocked and handcuffed in front of astonished families and children. Jon assumed he had witnessed the arrest of a wanted criminal, presumably a violent offender and approached the detectives in his role as the *Bulletin*'s police roundsman.

As soon as Jon questioned one of the arresting officers, he too was grabbed and thrown into the back of the unmarked police sedan and taken to the watchhouse. He was told he would be charged with resisting arrest and urinating the back of a police vehicle.

It was pure fabrication bordering on the ridiculous, but the coppers were serious and obviously very upset that their rough justice delivered at a public event was witnessed by a journalist who was likely to put the incident into print the next day.

I was stunned. Would the police in Brisbane arrest a *Courier Mail* or *Telegraph* reporter on false charges to stop them printing a story?

Even though Jon hadn't been rostered on that day, I convinced management that we should give him legal support and hopefully expose the much broader police harassment during the court hearing.

Of course, we ran the story about the arrest in the park and the fact that observers had been stunned by the heavy-handed actions of the police officers. We stayed silent about the unfounded threats to our reporter, keeping that in reserve as our 'dry powder' for any further battles.

Soon after, Shorty McLean, without any reference to me as editor, organised a 'cease fire meeting' at a local Chinese restaurant with Stevenson and two of his associates. He told me later that the Chairman of our Board, Frank Haly had organised it through his Rotary contacts.

I refused to attend until two conditions were met. Stevenson agreed to drop the ridiculous charges against my young reporter and I also insisted that out manager, Jim Manion, be included to make up the numbers for our side. But I was not happy.

The involvement of the two union reps was a smart move by Stevenson. It gave the impression that the dispute was an industrial issue — that the black ban was just a reaction from honest, hard-working coppers who were being 'victimised by a hostile Press'.

I just didn't buy that... I suspected they were Special Branch stooges from Brisbane, I had never seen them before. I told my managers before we entered the restaurant that there should be no apology for anything we had written. As soon as the niceties were over, I asked Stevenson how he felt about the possibility of a Kings Cross gangster cashing in on our city's new casino. Jim Manion followed my lead and raised the question of political influence in the highest levels of the Queensland Police Force — how did the police union representatives feel about that?

Both our questions were ignored. Stevenson just kept sucking out the claws of his chilli mud crab and black bean sauce while he treated us like suspects who should be quaking with fear in the presence of a master investigator.

'*I will ask the questions, not you bastards.*'

At first, I thought the sense of theatre was almost laughable, but there was more to come. He jokingly offered one of his colleagues a discarded crab shell that he'd sucked dry in front of us, sipped his beer and then used a large white serviette to carefully wipe all the chilli sauce off his face. Now he was the centre of attention. He was not only controlling the discussion, but more importantly setting the scene to his advantage.

Fuck this — we were being played. The only reason Stevenson and his boys were at this so-called peace gathering was to score a free meal and drinks and put the pissant local newspaper people in their place.

I recalled my early days of training under tough old journos and editors who probably would have done or said something to put a bloke like Stevenson off his game before he got the upper hand. But I was too slow to respond, and Shorty and Jim seemed more focussed on compromise and less interesting in challenging this bloke.

We copped a tirade about sensational reporting in the *Bulletin* which damaged reputations, compromised bids for important developments in the city and broke the bonds of trust between journos and coppers that had been developed over many years.

'You blokes have no idea. The bloody casino and all that money will probably go to Cairns, thanks to you lot.'

So much for him being worried about the image of his police force. What did our casino exposure have to do with this dispute?

I was waiting for him to finish so I could hit him with cutting observations of my own, when he did something that singled me out personally. It also cleverly ensured that any right of reply we might have expected was suddenly cut short.

He stuck his right leg out where I could see and pulled up the trouser cuff to expose a snub-nosed pistol in a leather holster.

Was it a jocular grin or a warning grimace that I saw when he kept his right hand on the butt of the pistol, leaned over the restaurant table, pointed a cocked left-hand index finger at me and popped off a pretend shot into my forehead?

'Bang! That's how I feel some days when I head of to work and know I'll be dealing with you and your mob… so don't bloody ask us to share the bill today.'

The two other coppers thought it was a great joke and Shorty managed a nervous chuckle to help ease the tension, but I didn't laugh. I certainly didn't like the strange look in Stevenson's eyes.

I assumed I could now have my turn as editor and defend the *Bulletin*'s right to publish without fear or favour. But Merv was too smart for that. He stood up, ignored me, but apologised politely to Shorty and Jim that he had to get back to an important investigation.

He left quickly, through the back kitchen, but chatted to the owners and staff just out of sight. It was probably for my benefit — still being in control, making sure it didn't look like he was retreating.

The two cheerful police union representatives were obviously settling in for a long afternoon. I left them to Shorty and Jim and tried to make sense of what had happened as I walked back to the office.

While the look across the table had been full of menace, it was the pistol put on public display for my benefit that really shook me. I had grown up with sporting and hunting firearms and I knew that a snub nosed 38 calibre revolver was designed specifically to kill people at short range, and Merv Stevenson was wearing one to a meeting with newspaper executives in a restaurant. He wasn't an undercover cop facing vicious criminals in a dark alley. Townsville wasn't such a dangerous place that senior police officers had to go armed in public.

Maybe some of the stories about Merv Stevenson were true — but how could someone like that also have police medals and be so high in the ranks as Acting District Superintendent?

Turning a blind eye to cattle duffing or drug production for some form of kickback might be described as one of the temptations of the job, but people going missing or dying under mysterious circumstances?

The man was a legend in a vast region of North Queensland, up into The Cape and west to The Gulf. Law and order were thinly spread in that part of the Outback, but Stevenson knew every isolated campsite, disused wartime airstrip and safe harbour in the mangroves that might be used by drug runners or cattle duffers.

The Tableland towns of Mareeba and Julatten were on my paper's northern circulation limits, but our country masthead, *The North Queensland Register,* known as 'The Bushman's Bible' across much of Northern Australia, was also running hard-copy crime stories as well as seasonal outlooks and beef prices.

In earlier times the *Register* journos travelled these remote areas with a swag, a tucker box and a water bag — now they included a rife.

The latest sensation was when cashed-up hobby farmers on a run-down property, William Clarke and his wife, were killed by shotgun blasts while asleep in their house at Julatten. Their drug operations in the North, which extended to remote properties on The Cape, were described as 'industrial in scale'. The investigating police officer from Mareeba closed the case without result and took all the police files with him when he was later transferred.

Mareeba, which was also a regular area of operation for Merv Stevenson, had made headlines only two years before when Senior Constable John Connor had bragged about a pending drug arrest that would 'shake Australia'. A few days earlier he'd been seen with a notorious drug dealer from Griffiths, where anti-drugs campaigner Donald Mackay had been murdered. The Mareeba arrest was never made, and Connor was found dead in his car, shot through the head with his service revolver.

Stevenson was part of the investigation, but no-one was ever charged. At the time of my confrontation with him I didn't know he was being watched by one of Queensland's top detectives, Inspector John Huey, who later headed the special task force created to assist the Fitzgerald Royal Commission Inquiry into Police corruption.

While I was fuming about police harassment, Huey was being pulled off his inquiry into cattle stealing and drug related criminal activity in North Queensland. A young Labour politician, Wayne Goss, had named Stevenson as a suspect under Parliamentary privilege, but probably did realise that Merv had friends in high places. Not only did Assistant Commissioner Bill McArthur stop the investigation, he also publicly praised his old mate from the Stock Squad days. 'I wish there were more young Stevensons in the police force today.'

Several years later Huey would finally give evidence about Stevenson when the Royal Commission was convened. He suggested that his earlier investigation should be re-opened because there was evidence that Stevenson had stopped a fellow police officer from making a confession about the death of the Mareeba policeman, Senior Constable Connor, the young officer who bragged that he was about to make a drug bust that would 'shake Australia'.

A year into the Royal Commission, when it was obvious that Tony Fitzgerald's team was doing a thorough search of police files across the State, the Charters Towers Police station was gutted by fire.

I shared a beer at a barbecue with Paul Burt, the owner of Burdekin Downs and a young policeman who was boarding at the homestead because the police barracks had also been destroyed. He and another officer had narrowly escaped on the night of the fire.

My friend Paul joked to the policeman: 'So, why didn't Merv Stevenson warn you there was going to be a fire that night?'

Those revelations were yet to come. I was still trying to come to terms with my strange encounter in the Chinese restaurant and realised it was a timely jolt of reality for me. There was no resolution of the dispute, just a display of force and a threat to the local newspaper editor cloaked in black humour.

If things got any worse with Saffron and his associates, there was no use turning to the local police for action or protection. In a subsequent call from Rob Strathdee he had also warned me about the most senior policeman in Queensland, Terry Lewis. Word was out that Commissioner Lewis was corrupt and few of the senior detectives in Brisbane could be trusted.

At 38, I was proud to be the youngest editor in the 100-year history of the paper but that also meant there was a young family and a pregnant wife involved. This darker side of journalism with its associated risk of severed ears, seemed more suited to powerful and influential old men with no young wives and little kids to consider.

Then, within a few months, most of the personal burdens relating to gangsters and crooked coppers became much lighter. The writ failed, mainly because the *Bulletin* refused to discuss an out of court settlement and we had always been on solid legal ground by quoting a Judge in an open court where bad things had been said about Mr Saffron.

Even though the writ failed, it probably served a purposed in limiting our negative coverage of the Saffron-Kornhauser links. They consortium didn't make the State Government final list for the casino, licence and I no longer had to worry about bankrupting the North Queensland Newspaper Company with a $3 million legal bill.

Stevenson was no longer the regional police chief and was desk-sitting the final months of his retirement in Charters Towers.

The local coppers, particularly the detectives, missed seeing their names in print and began co-operating again. Everyone had selective memory loss and I was happy to go along with it.

The gods of journalism seemed to be smiling on *The Townsville Bulletin* masthead and I was about to encounter two of the biggest news stories of a lifetime.

# CHAPTER 32.

# The six most excellent journalists in Australia

*Cold beer and mud crab diplomacy on the shores*
*of the South China Sea.*

Back in early 1980s the Fraser Government was cautiously following Gough Whitlam's lead in developing closer ties with 'Mainland China'. This was slow going because of the underlying Cold War concerns in Australia about communism, particularly in the aftermath of the Vietnam War and the Russian invasion of Afghanistan.

Behind the scenes, the Department of Foreign Affairs and the Australia China Council were working on an exchange of journalists. I was elated but also stunned when I was selected as one of the six journalists to represent Australia on the delegation. It was hard to believe that an editor from a community in North Queensland had been given a green and gold jersey by agencies based in Canberra. The assignment seemed to be too politically sensitive and of such international importance that only the cream of our profession would be considered.

People living in the so-called 'less progressive' parts of our country, including North Queensland, the Northern Territory and regional Western Australia, know too well what it's like to be silently tagged as rednecks by the cultural and political elite of the urban east coast, no matter what our backgrounds might be.

I suspect all the members of our delegation brought the baggage and the benefits of our own cultural geography to the exchange and it certainly influenced the coverage we gave the Chinese. There would be no common voice from the first Western journalists they had hosted.

We were a hardened group from the cynical days of journalism. Four men and two women from Sydney, Newcastle, Hobart, Ballarat, Perth and Townsville. No high-profile political columnists, no-one from the Canberra Press Gallery and no television or radio presenters. I'm not sure whether a similar delegation from the celebrity focused Australian media today would include anyone like us.

It was only after we met with the Beijing foreign correspondents that I realised Australia had stolen a diplomatic march on the rest of the western world. *The New York Times, Washington Post, London Times, The Paris Match, Reuters* and others were stunned when they heard about our itinerary and the rare access we were being given to locations and high-ranking officials.

We were also aware that our hosts, fellow journalists from *The People's Daily,* included high ranking Chinese Communist Party officials dedicated to expanding their party's political philosophy across China and throughout the world. Fortunately, we had also been briefed in Hong Kong by one of Australia's most famous foreign correspondents, the late Richard Hughes.

Even the most pedantic sub-editor would concede that the term 'legend' was appropriate for this famous journalist, whose real-life experiences had been used by Ian Fleming and John le Carre to create supporting characters for the James Bond novel *You Only Die Twice* and the spy thriller *The Honourable Schoolboy*. Like his mates, Fleming and Le Carre, Hughes was also reputed to be a spy.

I knew about the Cold War scoops and his fine reputation as a war correspondent, but I regretted not having read his 1972 autobiography *Foreign Devil… thirty years of reporting from the Far East*, which would have prepared me even more for encounters with the Chinese Communist Party and their political cadres in the coming weeks. Hughes told us he was frustrated by his tag of 'China Watcher', but he had been barred from entering the country after publishing *Foreign Devil*.

He warned us to keep our journalistic senses sharp and look for the issues behind the statements that would be made by our hosts, particularly the political cadres. He also gave tips on what a cadre might look like or how he or she might act.

As a fellow Australian, Hughes magnanimously asked us to allow him to absorb some of the pride we must be feeling as the first Western journalists to tour China in 30 years. I had been trained in an era of newsroom reprimand rather than praise from older and wiser journalists and felt strangely euphoric about being treated as an equal by this remarkable writer.

Once in China we were joined by the ABC Beijing correspondent and a senior journalist from *The Age* who was assisting *The People's Daily* to format a new English language edition.

At one of the earliest banquet welcomes, we were introduced by an interpreter as the 'six most excellent journalists in Australia'. We decided it would be undiplomatic and possibly embarrassing for our hosts if we corrected such an unfortunate misrepresentation. The fame only lasted one night, but I cherish the memory and find myself recounting the ego-boosting experience more often in old age.

Three things struck me about China. The first was the lack of colour and the uniformity. Everyone seemed to wear the traditional communist party Mao jackets and paint options were obviously limited to grey, white and brown.

Visiting the regional and rural centres was akin to stepping back in time. Crowded and modest brick and timber houses and farming that gave the impression of subsistence rather than prosperity.

It seemed that the Chinese had also abandoned road or traffic rules because vehicles were driven down the left, right and centre of unsealed roads while bicycles flowed like swollen streams in all directions.

Our delegation travelled at breakneck speed with red-flagged police escorts and blaring sirens warning the masses to clear a path or risk being run down. In the rural areas, farmers laid out hand-harvested wheat and barley on the roadways so the gain could be separated by the wheels of passing cars and trucks.

The third observation was our encounter with monumental drinking sessions at official welcomes. Polite and reserved Chinese hosts would insist we down shots of Mao's favourite drink, the fiery Mao Tai rice spirit, which kept the revolutionaries going on the Long March. Ten to twelve shots during an evening reception was not uncommon.

This was in contrast to the usual reserved and decorous conduct of our hosts but was never taken to the extreme.

There needed to be excuses for the toasts because alcohol consumption for the enjoyment of it would have been decadent. The Chinese were very inventive during their toasting sessions — peace, goodwill, friendship, happiness, good luck, safe travel. I even had one host insist that I drink a toast with him to our eyebrows. Apparently, Mao Tai is very good for eyebrows and bushy eyebrows are the sign of inner health.

Fortunately, the nights were not long, because it was also considered decadent to stay up much later than 8.30 or 9 o'clock.

The tour lasted over a month and we were welcomed into big cities and emerging industrial centres as well as 'forbidden territory' in sensitive regions such as Qinghai on the Tibetan plateau and Hainan Island in the South China Sea.

Hainan made the most lasting impression on me. The whole island was almost on a war footing, over tension with Vietnam and Russia and yet we saw our hosts visibly relax for the first time when we happily accepted their traditional cuisine of mud crabs washed down with ice cold lager ale.

I doubt that any delegation before or since our visit was able to show battle scars from World War Two as a spontaneous act of international fellowship.

There had been some panic when John Hall, the veteran editor of *The Ballarat Courier* declined to drink any more toasts because of a Kokoda war wound that had limited his kidney function. That quickly changed to celebration when the Hainan Governor stood up and lifted his shirt to show the blue scar bullet wounds from his own personal encounter with the Japanese Army. Brothers-in-arms, all formalities out the window.

For me there were echoes of Henry the Fifth and Shakespeare's rousing Band of Brothers piece. *'Then he will strip his sleeves and show his scars, and say, these wounds I had on Crispin's day.'*

Sadly, I'm not sure if Australian journalists would get such a warm welcome on Hainan Island today.

Things have changed dramatically since I stood on the coral shores of the South China Sea and listened to senior Chinese Communist Party officials speak with great passion about their country's ancient rights to not only harvest the sea's resources, but also to occupy and defend its remote reefs and islands.

Their fears centred not on America, or the Western Alliance, but on fellow communist states, Vietnam and the Soviet Union. Back then, they believed the United States was a non-threatening capitalist nation whose powerful military establishment accepted that the out-crops and islands as far south as the Paracels were 'owned' by China.

Some of my reporting is still on file in the form of yellowing newspaper clippings and one story in particularly doesn't seem finished with me. It's the Communist Party's blueprint for China's relationship with Australia which was full of hope nearly 40 years ago.

Vice Premier Gu Mu, the second most powerful man in China stunned the diplomatic corps and foreign correspondents in Beijing by offering a 'no questions barred' interview to our delegation.

Gu was second only to the Communist Party's supreme leader, Chairman Deng Xiaoping, but he was the man destined to set China on its course of modernisation, as head of international rela-tions and economic development.

The Australian Embassy sent one of their leading diplomats to our meeting and Gu immediately sought common ground by greeting us as fellow writers. He proudly told us that during the revolution he'd been the leader of the League of Left-Wing Writers and like us, he knew all about the power of words and the responsibility of using the correct ones when communicating vital information to the masses.

It didn't sound like a propaganda lecture to me — more like a bridge building excise across an obvious cultural and political divide. At that time Australia was, quite rightly, expressing con-cern about China's support for the murderous regime of Pol Pot in Kampuchea. Our government was irate about two off-course Aussie yachtsmen who had been tortured for months as 'American imperialist spies', before being publicly burnt alive in a town square.

I still have a copy of the story I wrote, which was grabbed back home by AAP as the first official comment to the western media on how China planned to develop its relationship with Australia in the years ahead.

Gu Mu spoke about a tolerant and productive partnership with Australia particularly as China worked to integrate free enterprise as an important supplement to the socialist state.

There would be no problem with Australia expressing the views of its people and its government, now or in the future, even if they were views not shared by China.

'It is not so serious for friendly countries if they have different practices in foreign policy. We can have different opinions, but they will not affect friendly relations between our two countries,' he said.

'We should also remember that our two countries do have views that are very close on many major international political questions.'

A partnership with a western nation as part of China's economic plan for the future underpinned with respect and understanding of each other's views that could be freely expressed on the international stage without recrimination? Such a statement would have been unthinkable only a few years before and, unfortunately, seems unlikely to be repeated given the 'current state of affairs'.

Gu Mu died in 2009 aged 95. A loss to both our countries.

I suspect that our escorts from the Australian Embassy were on tender hooks for most of our tour, fearing unintended but possibly damaging diplomatic *faux pas* from a group of amateurs. However, in terms of grassroots contact and personal exchanges we journalists probably left more long-lasting impressions with our Chinese hosts — particularly on Hainan Island.

It was a very big night when John Hall and the Chinese Governor shared their war stories and battle scars at the banquet table.

One of our hosts recited an ancient Chinese verse about the man who ate the first crab — they look so fierce and inedible

— and we all needed to honour and thank him for bringing such culinary joy to the world.

When it came to my turn to say something profound, I was a bit the worse for wear, having been nominated as proxy for John's share of the toasts to ensure his kidneys didn't fail.

I was surprised to receive a standing ovation, slaps on the back and requests to pose for photos. I had simply recited the piece about 'Charlie Mopps, *The Bloke Who Invented Beer*' — which my old sub-editor mate and mentor, Tommy Aitkenhead, had taught me years ago in The Imperial. It seemed appropriate because they were serving a very fine lager which was brewed on Hainan Island and eating mud crabs.

The cultural attaché from our embassy, Ross, happily did the translation for me.

*He oughta been an admiral, a sultan or a king*
*And to his praises we will always sing.*
*Look what he has done for us... he's filled us up with cheer*
*Lord bless Charlie Mopps... the bloke who invented beer.*

While our hosts knew they definitely had a valid claim on the first man to eat a crab, they weren't too sure about the history of beer — and graciously accepted that it was indeed a bloke called Charlie Mopps, from Australia, birthplace of such cultured and refined foreign friends.

I would not be surprised if that fact of history is still being taught to primary school children on Hainan to this day. As Tommy had argued at the time — stuff learned in a country pub listening to journos and printers could come in handy years down the track.

## CHAPTER 33.

# Confusion in the South China Sea

*Why are we no longer China's preferred foreign friends?*

Our relationship with China has gone horribly wrong in recent years. It's as if the budding friendship I experienced almost 40 years ago that was so full of promise, was actually the high point, and our political and cultural relationship has not grown at the same pace as China's remarkable development.

Sure, the trade opportunities have been realised, but tensions over foreign policy have risen, almost in lockstep with the growth of China's infrastructure and economic power.

I've been back privately on several occasions, and each time marvelled at the pace of development, while acknowledging the fact that we are no longer their 'preferred foreign friends'.

What went wrong? I will leave comment to those far more experienced in Australia-China relationships but feel comfortable about sharing my experience as one of the first Western journalists to question Communist Party officials about their hopes for the future.

Maybe there was more of an acceptance in the early years of our engagement that China, under communism, would be reluctant to adopt Western politic, legal and social values in its pursuit of a freer economic market for its masses. As China opened up in the ensuing years, we assumed they would eventually 'become more like us'.

Very early on our exchange I realised there was a vast cultural gap between me and my Chinese hosts. I was a father of three who travelled freely around the world as a young man and decided where I would live and work without regard to the national interests of my country, but one of our young interpreters saw nothing unusual in being separated from his new wife who had been sent by the State to teach children in a western province. They would be allowed to meet for a short holiday together after a year's separation.

When the State decided the time was right, they would live together and be allowed to have one child. A small personal price to pay to help China march towards its destiny as a respected world power.

Things have changed in the South China Sea since I was there almost 40 years ago standing with our group on the beach of a beautiful bay that reminded me of Magnetic Island off Townsville, complete with massive weather-worn granite boulders.

I quickly realised that, to our hosts, the bay had historic significance that bordered on being sacred ground. It was part of China's outpost on Hainan, overlooking the South China Sea and a famous poet and philosopher from one of the ancient dynasties had carved a warning text on one of the boulders. It was impressive calligraphy, deeply etched into the rock of ages.

Two of our older hosts from Beijing, a 'gunfire journalist' who served with Mao on the Long March and a female historian and archaeologist whose job was to repair the ancient cultural sites that had been damaged by the Red Guards during the Cultural Revolution, acted like pilgrims visiting a holy shrine.

The gist of the translation was: 'Beware of the thief who comes from the south in the dead of night'. The face of the boulder, that the patriotic poet had selected centuries ago to carry this warning, looked out over the South China Sea.

At that time, China's concern about Vietnam was still very current because the two countries had recently fought a short but quite bloody war over their nearby mainland border. The Vietnamese, fresh from resisting the most powerful military force in the world, had dared to claim some of China's ancient territory.

The Spratly and Paracel Islands weren't making news in the West, but they certainly featured in most of my discussions about border issues while on Hainan Island. Our old gunfire journalist was always happy to talk He also went out of his way to exclude America as a threat, because he viewed them as not being an 'expansionist nation'.

I recall that Roger Simms, editorial writer for *The West Australian*, was seated nearby at the banquet and joined in some of the exchange.

Our host said: 'You only have to look at the history of the United States to see the truth of my words. America was the most powerful nation in the world, and we were all lucky they weren't interested in expanding the boundaries of their country. They could have occupied half of Europe, all of Japan and a much bigger slice of the Pacific after World War Two, but they didn't.'

He had fought against the Americans during the Korean War but didn't rate them anywhere near as dangerous or untrustworthy as the Soviet Union or Vietnam.

'The Russians threatened us with nuclear bombs when we defended our borders in the north and reclaimed our stolen lands. Look what they did to Hungary and now the invasion of Afghanistan.

'Your Prime Minister, Mr Fraser, is quite right to be supporting America and speaking out so strongly against the Russians. China has no territorial ambitions, but we will always defend our own lands and seas.

'The Western world supported China's claims in the South China Sea before our people rose up and threw the nationalists out. Even the Americans acknowledge it is still our territory. The South Vietnamese invaded the Paracels and we had to expel them by force of arms... there was a naval battle. The Vietnamese wanted the American Navy to take the Islands back for them, but they refused.'

I am painfully aware my South China Sea experience was almost four decades ago and that Australia's once excellent relationship with our largest trading partner is now in a state of deep freeze.

Even Cabinet Ministers seeking audiences with their Chinese counterparts are put on hold, a far cry from the time when an Australian delegation of journalists could be welcomed as VIP's and given state banquets with Vice-Premiers, provincial governors and city mayors.

Vice-Premier Gu Mu's vision of a strong and enduring China-Australia relationship while accepting each other's differing views on foreign policy issues now survives only in old archived copies of a newspaper I once edited.

Since the Permanent Court of Arbitration in The Hague ruled in 2014 that China's claims are unlawful, tension in the South China Sea has been part of our 24-hour news cycle.

Will these rulings pass the 'pub test' in China? Or have we, in the West, underestimated the Chinese sense of national territorial pride and assumed that only Communist Party expansionist policies and decades of successful propaganda are at play here?

The Paracel Islands, which the Americans appeared to have accepted as being Chinese territory 40 years ago, became a flashpoint when a Chinese destroyer tried to block the passage of a US warship.

Paul Monk, formerly with the Australian Defence Intelligence Organisation, recently included China's claims in the South China Sea in his list of the 'Seven Great Myths About China', while Paul Dibb, from the Strategic Defence Studies Centre, has written about China's 'reckless aggression'.

Paul Kelly, editor-at-large of *The Australian*, has warned that if the dynamic with China continues: 'Australia faces a fusion of economic and security challenges for which it seems sublimely unprepared given its public complacency and domestic obsession.' Former prime minister Kevin Rudd, who now heads the Asia Society in New York, believes that the United States and China could be shifting from peaceful co-existence to a new era of confrontation — a new Cold War and then possibly a hot one.

Former prime minister Paul Keating believes our nation's security agencies are too 'hawkish' about China's emergence as a world power and should be 'cleaned out of office'. When he and veteran politicians and commentators such as Bob Carr and Graham Richardson join the fray, journalists start tagging participants in the debate as either 'panda huggers' or 'panda haters'.

My first editor sixty years ago stressed there were always two sides to a story and a journalist sometimes needed to walk a mile in the other bloke's shoes to make sense of it. Sure, it's a cliché, but that's what they're for, to deliver a universal and timeless message.

We are a nation that usually encourages informed debate on vital issues, but from my perspective, there is still a question that seems to be unanswered — or unasked. If we are to resolve this complex issue in our own national interests, what diplomatic strategies are in place to convince China, and its people, that their territorial claims are invalid?

Now, with diplomatic tensions rising, I wonder why our Australian Embassy escorts back then never challenged these claims or our hosts' perception that the Americans accepted Chinese ownership as far south as the Paracel Islands.

I am no China scholar, but as an old-school journalist I have many more questions than answers. Maybe I am promoting one of the 'Great myths of China' in writing about my experiences but, I do regret that Australia doesn't seem to have any diplomatic or journalistic shoes on the ground to view the ancient territorial carvings on that big granite rock, or to drink beer and eat mud crabs with the locals and ask how they feel about the South China Sea.

Panda hugger or panda hater... is there still a chance for Australia to act as an honest broker while maintaining strong ties with our American friends and allies and our Chinese trading partners? Or have our leaders lost the political courage and independent foresight that was displayed by Whitlam and Fraser when they first took us down this path all those years ago?

How different was leadership in the national interest back then, when foreign policy wasn't made up on the run to support candidates in by-elections, or to improve a former prime minister's poor rating on Newspoll?

# CHAPTER 34.

# A visit from the Ku Klux Klan

*Racists and bigots hiding under the banner of patriotism.*

I was not long back from the trip to China and was probably showing signs of youthful hubris. In terms of journalism it couldn't get much better than that — exclusive access to the inner sanctum of the Chinese Communist Party that had been off-limits to western journalists for almost 30 years and breaking international news back in Australia through my own newspaper and AAP.

But when three well-presented men from the big end of town walked into my office to complain about one of my editorials, their shocking opening remarks convinced me I was onto the biggest story of my career — bigger even, than anything out of China.

I believed I had a strong peg for editorial comment about the plight of homeless Aboriginal people in local parks. Someone had fire-bombed one of the camps but no-one in authority seem very worried about the incident.

I still have a copy headed 'Violation of human dignity', and reading it now, I find it hard to believe such balanced and moderate language caused a panic and also brought an Australian chapter of the Ku Klux Klan out of hiding and into my office.

Chris Mitchell, a young sports' sub at that time who later became editor-in-chief of the Australian, wrote in his memoir, *Making Headlines*, about the surprising criticism our paper received for simply publishing the facts and calling for action. The police, business leaders and the boss of the tourist bureau wanted me to 'stop publishing and exaggerating such negative stories'.

Editors get used to upsetting people, and I also received letters of support, but I was stunned when representatives of the Ku Klux Klan, an organisation I had previously dismissed as an urban myth in Australia, turned up in my office, not only to complain, but to seek my support in their struggle to stop black radicals from taking over the country.

The two Klansmen warned me about a dangerous bloke named Eddie Mabo, who was posing as a gardener out at James Cook University. He had to be stopped in his tracks before he ruined the country. According to them, Mabo had 'slipped under the radar', while everyone was watching that show pony Charlie Perkins.

The details of this encounter have remained unpublished all these years as I had reluctantly agreed that our discussion would be off the record.

However, with Mabo Day now celebrated nationally and racism still an issue in sport and in our public and political debates, I am writing about this unique experience now, in the hope that it will remind today's generations that bigots often find shelter under the banner of patriotism.

I have also heard echoes of the Klan in Senate debates and in divisive rallies promoting racism under the guise of nationalism. It would seem that the bigoted views I encountered almost 40 years ago have found new homes and new outlets in today's society.

I would also like to think that the families of the great land rights leaders I engaged with back then might take even more pride in what their people achieved. They probably didn't know there was a well-connected group of racists working behind the scenes to block Native Title.

The Ku Klux Klan, as a structured organisation in Australia, was considered to be something of a myth and not a political or social reality. That was certainly the impression I gained from my fellow journalists and editors.

My visitors didn't fit the usual bill for redneck racists or bigots. One was a returned serviceman and member of the Chamber of Commerce who also had a high-profile as a fundraiser for local charities. The younger man was building a public profile with political expectations for the next council elections.

I assumed they'd asked to meet me with me to either promote some worthy cause or to propose a publicity stunt to wrangle free press for the council candidate. The older bloke wore a coat and tie on a hot day, and I was surprised by how relaxed he seemed in my cramped office, which was poorly served by a single, ancient overhead fan that was set on the slowest speed, so copy paper wouldn't be blown away. The young man wore an open shirt, shorts and long socks, but seemed uncomfortable.

Then it happened. Straight out of the blue. The words Ku Klux Klan dropped smoothly into the polite opening exchange, with the civic elder/war veteran taking the lead. No preamble, no caution in delivery, just a statement of fact — up front and open.

'Look,' the older man said, 'some of my people didn't want me to do this, but I'm not the sort of bloke to go behind your back. Your editorials are way off the mark and if you want to keep faith with *Bulletin* readers you should do what we did and have a good look at the Ku Klux Klan. Put aside all the bullshit that the lefties and commos throw at it and you'll see there's nothing wrong with retaining your European identity and not having other races erode your values or beliefs. We're more interested in fighting behind the scenes than posing with bloody burning crosses and white hoods, but believe me, the problem with the blacks here is just as bad as in America.'

He paused, waited a moment, then turned to the younger man and smiled. 'See, he hasn't fainted or thrown us out of the building.'

So, these people were obviously upset by my editorial suggesting that Aborigines sleeping rough in the park should not be terrorised by firebombs, or that the community, as well as our civic leaders, should take a more active role in finding solutions.

I had expected some reaction, but certainly not a visit from Klan affiliates minus their hoods and Crusader white robes.

Maybe they were worried about the public support I'd received in letters to the editor, including one from the City Council's new social worker, Frank Hornby, who had also tipped me off that Townsville was about to appoint the first local government Aboriginal liaison officer in Queensland — not a white bloke in shorts and long socks, but a black person from either the Bindal or Wulgurukaba clans. I had to admit that, until Frank spoke to me, I didn't know that Townsville's Indigenous families still identified with their original tribal or clan structures.

It was clear that things were moving much too fast for the more conservative Townsville locals. There was concern that Perc Tucker, the former State Opposition Leader had taken Labor to total control of the City Council and had 'stacked' it with academics and intellectuals from James Cook University, as well as trade unionists and sporting personalities. The fact that electors had not only given Perc Tucker all of the ten seats on council but had also voted in four women, was still being absorbed at the 'men only' North Queensland Club over spilt brandy and much muttering.

It wasn't unusual for editors to deal with upset readers, but I'd joined a rather select group of my colleagues — a newspaper editor who had received an unexpected briefing from the Ku Klux Klan.

I desperately wanted to hear more and knew I had to let these blokes run without my losing control in my own office. I suspected they weren't here to be interviewed, but I badly wanted to get them on the record and into print. They had the confidence to identify themselves with the Klan, so I knew there was nothing I could offer that might change their views — besides, I was a journalist and that wasn't my job.

I was determined not to do anything that might terminate this exclusive insight into an organisation I didn't even know existed in my community. I recalled my first editor's advice 23 years earlier. 'Colt, I want my reporters to know what is under ever mossy rock in this town… who's up who and who's paying the rent.'

And in this case, these people had come out from under their rock. They hadn't been exposed by brilliant investigative reporting from one of my senior staff. I was intrigued but also felt pissed off. It was a smart move on their part, whether they realised it or not, because I was unlikely to get any copy out of this exchange unless I managed to get them onto the record.

I stopped staring, sat back in a more relaxed pose and gestured with both hands, as if I were opening a door. 'Gentlemen… please go on. I get paid to listen.'

The younger man still looked worried.,

'Before we say anything more, this is all confidential, right?'

Shit. There goes our *Townsville Bulletin* exclusive and probably the best story of my life, but I still wanted to learn more about these two.

The man in the brown suit took over again. 'Yes, no names, no pack drill.'

I nodded, hoping I might still get an opportunity if I showed enough interest in their cause.

'So, let me get this straight. We're talking about the Ku Klux Klan here? Southern states of America stuff?'

The young bloke looked suddenly worried, but the other man just smiled.

'We've been in contact with some of their people in the States. It's not against the law to associate with groups who have a common cause of free speech.'

'So, what do you want from me and my paper?'

'We just want to put you in the picture. You probably know I'm one of the backers of the new anti-socialist team in the next Council Elections?'

I nodded but didn't try to point out that his team wasn't actually carrying an anti-Labor tag but was campaigning as non-political independents. That would keep for another day — closer to the election.

He went on. 'You must know that our new Deputy Mayor, Margaret Reynolds, is even more of a leftie than her husband, Henry. Now they can infiltrate the city administration and James Cook University for their own ends. And what about that Islander bloke, Mabo? One minute he's cutting sugar cane, next they get him into the uni leaning on a rake as a gardener and now he's trying to take back the whole of the bloody Torres Strait.'

'So, you're saying that this paper shouldn't cover the big land rights conference at James Cook or Eddie Mabo's school for Aboriginal and Islander kids? They both helped put Townsville on the map.'

'It might be on some sort of media map, but it's not the map we want for our community. And, by the way, don't you realise your own newspaper ran an editorial slamming Mabo's school when it first kicked off? It was in the time of old Jim Gibbard. He called it apartheid in reverse. Now look what you're doing, writing about the so-called plight of coons being firebombed under Victoria Bridge.'

He must have seen my eyes flicker because he paused and then defensively leaned forward. I stiffened my back, held my ground and he continued.

'Believe me, coons is the right term for that lot. They've either been kicked off Palm Island by their own blackfellas or are out-of-towners who've done time at Stuart for violent crimes. They don't send the mongrels home, just dump them down by the creek. If the coppers won't move them, then someone will take on the job of cleaning up that part of town.'

This was interesting. I knew the police were investigating drunken soldiers looking for women and trouble in the park as the most likely culprits. Fights were common, but the fire-bombing under Victoria Bride was a dangerous escalation. It did more than set fire to the dry grass — it focused attention on a problem that most people tried to ignore and had been the peg for my editorial.

'Do you condone violence? Is that part of the Klan manifest?'

He just shrugged. 'You should realise the problem in the parks is not Townsville's fault. It's the Government and the shit-stirrers. We shouldn't have coons brawling and living in filth under the bridge in the first place. We should ship them all back to Palm Island and let nature take its course. The bloody Government's already given them the best piece of real estate on the east coast of Australia. Have you fished the shoals out there and seen North East Bay? It's like a scene from South Pacific.'

He sat back and they both looked to me for comment. I wanted to get off the park issue and probe them on land rights.

'What's wrong with the proposal to give Aborigines the same rights as white people to own real estate like Palm Island and other places?'

'Don't talk about land rights. It's a land grab, pure and simple. That's the problem with this Mabo fellow. Those two academics at the university Reynolds and Loos are stirring the bastard up — they should be run out of town.'

I hadn't had a lot to do with Eddie Mabo. Other activists such as Archie Smallwood and Monty Prior were more regular visitors to the *Bulletin*'s newsroom. Mabo did most of his campaigning through the university, and at Indigenous conferences and seminars. But from personal contacts, and from his published papers that I'd read, he seemed very inclusive, even with his strong advocacy for sovereignty in the Torres Strait.

'So, you're really worried about Mabo? He doesn't come across as radical or violent. I've had activists in this office who get much hotter under the collar than he has. Blokes like Shorty O'Neill thumping the table. Eddie's a lot quieter and talks about the law.'

'That's my point… he's coming in under the bloody radar. The Yanks have a saying that the law is an ass and you journalists should know that ours are full of holes. Word's come up the line that leftie lawyers from down south are rallying to the Mabo cause. They see a long and profitable legal fight. No one elects the bloody judges, so none of us will have a say in the outcome. We can only hope that Jo Bjelke-Petersen throws up a few roadblocks with new legislation to protect our property. That's where papers like the *Bulletin* should be throwing your weight.'

He waited for a response, but I wasn't about to give an opinion or show him any of the cards I might have up my editor's sleeve. I still hoped they might go on the record, even if it meant publishing their racist views it would still expose the Klan's existence. 'Any more observations you'd like to make?'

'For a start you can stop giving piss-ant activists like Smallwood a run, just because he's got a job in the bloody railways and has wormed his way into a union position.'

The younger man then chimed in. 'We tried to get the Minister to sack him, but he's protected by the unions.'

The older man seemed unhappy about the interruption and I guessed the young bloke wasn't supposed to talk about the Klan's contacts at Ministerial level in the State Government.

I wasn't surprised that Smallwood was also in their sights, because he was one of the most persistent and effective activists in the community. Archie had also focused on my newspaper as a potential source to get a balanced Indigenous message out, with letters to the editor and tips on issues and incidents that might make news but also help his cause.

'Any more observations you'd like to make?'

They looked at each other. It was the young bloke's turn to speak. This meeting was probably being used as a training session for his potential career in local government. He tried to sound assertive.

'Why do you give space for people like that radical Perkins? Freedom Bus touring New South Wales for God's sake… more like Promoting Violence Bus for my money. I hope they lock him up if he ever crosses the border in it. You even ran a story recently when he was up here advocating that more Abos should get involved in politics.'

I cut in. 'Perkins did say he didn't care whether they supported the left or the right of politics, they just needed to get involved. Like Neville Bonner in the Liberal Party. But is that still a problem for you?

The young fellow seemed lost for words. He hadn't expected a question.

His mentor quickly stepped in. 'Of course it's a problem. Bloody Bonner dressed up as a conservative in a safari suit. He's still a black radical infiltrating politics. None of them should even be allowed to vote. They didn't fight for their country… I never saw a blackfella in the any of the units I served in.'

I knew about the 'black diggers' and the struggle most of them had to even enlist in a system designed to debar Indigenous men from war service. 'I'm surprised you didn't read about Reg Saunders. He was at an Indigenous leadership conference here a while back. Made the rank of captain. Served in the Middle East and Borneo. Quite a few black men managed to buck the system that stopped them from enlisting.'

He shrugged, 'Well, I didn't come across any.'

I was interested to hear if he had any party-political support. 'I assume you're working through the conservative side of politics?'

He studied me for a moment and then smiled.

'Well, that's where the power base in Queensland is. but I told you we're working at all levels and have broader support than you realise. Even the conservative side of politics has been infiltrated by black supporters. Look at the Katters, started off as commos and jumped to the Country Party after the split in the ALP. Joh needs to pull that young Bob up on a short lead… talking about black and white mates playing rugby league together is no reason to hand over the bloody playing field and the rest of Charters Towers to the blackfellas, and that's what will happen.'

'So, you even have problems with some of the Country Party?'

'Carrying on about how blacks and whites are all good mates out in the bush and sharing a rugby league field with them in Charters Towers is one thing, but Katter doesn't seem to realise that land rights is all about handing that land back to the blacks… as well as the cattle stations and mines. I don't think that young fella will be around politics for much longer.'

They looked at each other and the older man nodded encouragingly to the young bloke. I suspected that our meeting was probably being used as a training session for his potential career in local government, so I tried to get him to loosen up. 'Will you be taking some of the Klan policies into the council if you're elected?'

'I don't want to talk about the election, I just want to know if you'll give us a run, stop writing editorials that focus on negative things. You shouldn't be covering people like Mabo, the Smallwoods and the Priors every time there's a rally or protest. We've got to form our own alliances and networks to get anything done. Young men like me are taking up the challenge and people like you in the media should be too.'

They both looked at me expectantly.

'Well, thanks for coming in gentlemen. Let me just say that the *Townsville Bulletin*'s current policy is to report the news fairly and without fear or favour. Our focus is on covering both sides of a story, which includes giving the striking unions a say, as well as the bosses and broadening the appeal of our newspaper.'

I opened my notebook and picked up a pen.

'So, in the interest of balance I'd be happy to publish anything you might want to say publicly about the issues you've raised… providing they carry the validity of authorship and aren't anonymous.'

The young Klansman looked puzzled. 'What do you mean by that?'

'What he means is that we won't get a bloody run on this unless someone is prepared to put his name to it… he's asking us to go on the record.'

'Shit, I can't do that.'

I could see the elements of a good story floating off into the ether but had one more crack at them.

'I've been off the rounds and editing for a few years now, but I'll try not to misquote you. This might take a while. I've got quite a few questions to ask as well.'

The older man, stood up, smiled at me and shrugged his shoulders.

He reached out his hand. 'Thanks for your time anyway. I half expected to find stony ground in here.'

I wasn't surprised that he'd parted with a Biblical reference. I was learning quickly that racists could present in many forms—some covert, some quite open.

Of course, I shook his offered hand, to do otherwise would have shown a lack of editorial impartiality. I suspected it was also a smart move by the Klansman to ensure confidentiality would be honoured and I would take their names to my grave.

When they were leaving, I was handed a note on a piece of paper. *A Multicultural Society for the Future. Al Grassby, Melbourne 1973...* they wanted me to look it up. Grassby was Minister for Immigration in the Whitlam Government and had championed multi-culturalism for Australia. I wasn't surprised he was included on the Klan's 'hit list'.

'It's the socialists' philosophy for Australia to the year 2000,' the older man explained in outrage. 'By then, all the government schools will be teaching Turkish, Arabic, Greek and Italian, immigration will be unchecked, and we'll have lost our Anglo-Saxon culture.'

After they left, I took some notes and thought about the circumstances that had led to this unexpected and unsettling encounter.

Maybe I shouldn't have been so surprised. Powerful voices were being raised across Australia in opposing land rights and refusing to address the glaring problems in Aboriginal and Torres Strait Islander communities.

Around that time, I also published a story accurately quoting veteran Senator Glen Sheil, who not only openly supported apartheid for Australia, but referred to 'city boongs' and 'bush boongs' in an interview with a senior journalist.

We ran it *sic erat scriptum*. Sic, that beautiful three-letter abbreviation that would tell the world our story was 'complete and with errors, colloquialisms and surprise assertions.'

However, Senator Sheil's assertions weren't as surprising as we expected. The story went national, but he was never reprimanded by his party and was re-endorsed for the next election.

I thought more about what had motivated these people to speak so openly to me — even off the record. Sure, the editorials had sparked them off, but from their comments about the university and the council I knew there was much more at play.

Considering the normal growth rate of Townsville over the past century, James Cook University had appeared on the city's outskirts 'overnight'. There weren't many home-grown professors or academics to staff it, so most of the people out there were newcomers — more specifically from 'Down South'.

The culture shock was being felt on both sides. A strong 'ivory tower' mentality was evident amongst many academics who feared they had arrived in the heart of red-neck Australia. For some of the locals it was as if highly intelligent but dangerous alien life forms had landed at Wulguru and the Army at Three Brigade had done nothing about it.

I had engaged Emeritus Professor Colin Roderick as our book reviewer. Colin, a former publisher and author, had recently established the Centre for Australian Literary Studies at JCU and I wasn't surprised when he told me that most of his colleagues read only *The Age*, with Brisbane's *Courier Mail* as the next best option. It was an intellectual status symbol not to read the local rag.

When Colin pointed out that the *Bulletin* was also being identified negatively with other publications in our stable across North Queensland, including a racy tabloid weekly *The Advertiser,* I knew what he was talking about. 'Poofs in the park' and 'Darkies make bad neighbours' were not the kind of headlines the folk out at James Cook were used to.

That's what made the last city council election results so interesting. This so-called racist red-neck community had voted overwhelming for a leftist administration. We now had councillors bulging with degrees, doctorates and international academic awards as well as the usual war ribbons and sports medals.

Even the *Bulletin* under the editorship of veteran newspaperman Jim Gibbard, had problems handing all this change in the Whitlam era during a new wave of women's issues and Indigenous land rights.

It was public knowledge, at least within *Bulletin* and City Council circles, that Margaret Reynolds and one of her officials from The Women's Electoral lobby, had approached Jim Gibbard, with a carefully crafted statement about the need for more women to take an active interest in politics and all the levels of government in Australia.

Old Jim, ever the gentleman, heard them out politely, and as he escorted them to his office door, ceremoniously tore their submission into several strips in front of them and dropped it from shoulder height into his wastepaper bin.

Margaret Reynolds went on to have a distinguished career, not only in local government, but as a Labor Senator and an Australian delegate to the United Nations.

I was still mulling over all this when I drove to my home in the suburb of Heatley where my children were swimming in our above-ground pool with the Prior kids from next door — little white and black children splashing and laughing in the water.

Clifford Prior worked as a welder on the industrial estate. When we talked over a beer, it was about barramundi, rugby league, kids, and the downturn in the metal trades.

The family over the back fence, the Kanais, cooked pigs, Island style, in a pit under a mango tree. When someone died, they played muffled drums quietly inside the house all night and every night for a full week. None of the neighbours complained. A few days earlier they'd shown off their new baby daughter and her gold christening brooch.

My wife Barbara was intrigued by the little girl's name, Niceone. 'How lovely. Niccie-onie, is that how you pronounce it?'

Both parents burst into smiles.

'No... she's so beautiful we called her Nice One'.

Neighbourly friendship, laughter and multi-culturalism, Townsville style, over the back fence.

Unsettled by my encounter with the Klan, I wondered if things would be better when these kids grew up. I hoped that despite a hidden chapter of the Klan lurking within our city's dynamics, the underlying community spirit of this colourful place might just be fertile enough to allow the seeds being planted by Eddie Mabo out at James Cook Uni to yield fruit in the years to come.

# CHAPTER 35.

# The end of the journalistic road?

*The holy grail slips out of reach.*

Things couldn't have been better. Barbara had given birth to Andrew, a healthy little brother for Emma, Richard and Vicki.

Our paper's circulation was also on the rise and the prolonged industrial action by journalists striking for more money in the new age of computers and cold type looked like being resolved.

But the highlight of my professional career, the trip to China, was about to resurface in the form of an erratic heartbeat. Far from being anything like a holy grail of journalism, it was taking new form as the death knell to my career in writing.

The specialist had just finished looking at the E.C.G. printout and I was still sweating from the exercise routine he'd put me though. What seemed like an eternity of repetitive stepping from the floor onto a small footstool had my heart pounding, but I was please there'd been no repeat of the frightening palpations.

What hours do editors work? He probably wasn't going to believe this, but I'd give it a try.

'I'm on call. My home phone number is in the phone book.'

He looked at me rather strangely and fiddled with his spotted bowtie.

'I mean my private number is in the after-hours list for the *Bulletin*. Obviously, I don't work 24 hours, but I've got to be available.'

He nodded. 'Do you get many work-related calls after five?'

'My hours can be anywhere from 9 a.m. to 2.30 in the morning, depending on what's happening. We report and publish the news.' I held up my hands in a gesture I hoped he'd understand.

'As editor, do you fire as well as hire?'

'Of course. I recently sacked two people. One a high-profile reporter who was making more embarrassing mistakes than a first-year cadet, the other a woman posing as a journalist.'

'How did you feel about that?'

'Pretty relieved, actually. I'm sure they'll probably look back in years to come and think it was the best thing that ever happened to them… parting company with me and the Townsville *Bulletin*.'

He nodded, but I doubted that he really understood. Of course, sacking people was usually unpleasant but sometimes it had to be done. I didn't tell him that on parting one of them told me there was a heart of pure malice beating beneath my calm exterior. It was meant as an insult, but I felt rather chuffed about it. This was the newspaper game for Christ's sake and editors were supposed to be like that.

The specialist turned a page on his notebook and continued.

'Do you get headaches?'

'No.'

'Nosebleeds?'

'No.'

'Short of breath?'

'No.'

'Lose your temper?'

'No… yes, maybe once or twice a year.'

'Wish you could lose your temper more often?'

'Do you mean, am I by nature, probably a violent man?'

He smiled again but didn't chuckle. 'Ok, you get my gist. Stress can show in many forms, but just because you don't show some of the symptoms doesn't mean you are stress-free.'

I didn't need a long lecture about stress because we'd just been through the Abe Saffron and corrupt copper months with the threat of millions of dollars in damages and the possibility of my ears being sent home as a warning. I thought I'd handled those stressful times pretty well and I was now anxious for this specialist to do his job and come up with a cure for an erratic heartbeat.

'So, what's the diagnosis?'

'Kim was right in referring you. He's been doing a good job of monitoring your condition for the past year but, as you know, the latest ECG troubled him. I won't be calling an ambulance on the basis of the one I just did, but it's something we need to watch closely.'

He flipped through some papers on his deck. 'He says a high-altitude experience last year might have been at play here. Jogging up near Tibet?'

I nodded.

He shook his head. 'I'm surprised the Chinese didn't either brief you about the risk of altitude sickness or stop you in your tracks.'

'All they told us was to ensure there was boiling water on the stoves in our yurts... to stop carbon monoxide poisoning when we were sleeping. A couple of us had been jogging every morning during the tour, because we were eating and drinking so much at all the official banquets.'

'How high were you?'

'I think it was around 3000 metres but some of the roads into there was just under 4000.'

He grimaced. 'That's better than 11,00 feet on the old scale.... didn't they supply you with oxygen as a precaution?'

'No.' I was feeling a bit stupid about this. 'We wouldn't have been out jogging if they had. I remember feeling puffed, out of breath, simply with the exertion of cleaning my teeth that morning. but everyone else seemed to be going about business as usual. Two of the delegation, including one of the girls went horse riding with the Tibetans.'

'Probably a better health option than jogging... did you collapse?'

'I don't think I blacked out, but I could hardly move after I got back from the run. We didn't go far, and both called it quits pretty quickly. I became dizzy and disoriented and had a terrible headache, like the world's worst hangover, until they got us down to a lower altitude.'

'What about the others?'

'The head of our delegation, an older man, had quite a bad turn and had to be taken straight down to Xining. My jogging mate, Garry, felt a bit crook. The Chinese were in a panic and a doctor checked all of us. I apparently had the highest blood pressure and they wanted to pack me off with poor old John. But I didn't feel I was sick enough to be rushed down like a casualty and stayed on the bus with the others. I know they put John on oxygen.'

'Did you recover fairy quickly at low altitude?'

'The monster hangover went, but I still felt crook. I didn't know anything was wrong until the palpations started in Hong Kong on the way home, a few weeks later.'

'Kim tells me you had one in front of him. During a consultation... how bad are they.'

'I don't have any control... it's not as if I can stop them by relaxing and taking deep breaths or anything. I try that, but I think they still just run their course.'

I didn't tell him one once racked me so much that my upper torso seemed to shake and rock. The sprung lounge chair I was sitting on started to rock as well. I'd been assuring Barbara that I was okay — it was nothing. But I saw her looking at me and tears were running down my beautiful pregnant wife's face.

'The best thing we can do, is get you to slow down.'

'What do you mean by slow down?'

'Your seven days a week on call every 24 hours approach won't help you get on top of this. I can't see why you can't take more time off… say a day in the middle of the week to play golf… and a proper weekend off as well.'

He looked at me for a response.

'That's what editors do. I'm not a special case. You can't time-manage news or newspaper production to suit the individual. We get holidays, that's how we unwind, and I do it with my family, but for the rest of the year we can't just switch on and off, like you're suggesting.'

He nodded, but I wasn't sure if he understood.

'Mr. Hannay let me be more specific. Your run on the top of the mountain has certainly contributed to your condition, but there's also an underlying problem with your heart. Your ECG results were showing an improvement at the start but they're showing more warning signs in recent months.'

I decided to interrupt 'We've had some industrial problems at the *Bulletin* during that time. We're the first regional newspaper in Australia to go fully with new computer technology from Canada. It's a massive change in technology.'

I had been storing this up for months and decided this was as good a time as any to let it all out.

'I'm copping it from all sides because editors are exempt, and I'm stuck between my staff and management. The journalists' union has convinced my people that radiation from computer screens will make them sterile or cause miscarriages. Changing from typewriters to computers will also send them all blind in a few years and journalists, who are being paid to sort through bullshit on a daily basis, are accepting everything the AJA tells them… without question. I had one of the screens tested by the physics department out at James Cook and it has less radiation than a bloody fluorescent light bulb, but I'm still copping black bans on news agency copy and rolling strikes. Last week when it looked like we might not get a paper out for the first time in our history I worked two days with only four hours' sleep.'

There, I'd got it all out, and I felt much better.

'So, you think when it all gets back to normal… I mean your version of normal hours… your health will somehow miraculously improve?'

I didn't know what to say. I sensed I was starting to piss him off

'Mr. Hannay, when you came through my door, I joked that you looked as fit as a scrub bull. But don't be fooled by your own appearance of general well-being. Listen to what I'm saying. Get regular ECG checks with Kim, don't argue if he wants them monthly, and take his prescriptions. But, if you do nothing about your lifestyle and continue as you are, I can't guarantee that we'll both still be having a discussion like this in five years' time. So, I hope you might reconsider how much of your life you allocate to work.'

I knew he was trying to soften the message, but I was finally getting it. I was in the wrong fucking job if I wanted to see my kids grow up.

Resign as editor? Leave journalism? What other work could I do?

A job that didn't involve crafting or using the written word was unthinkable.

# PART 3
# NO
# REGRETS

# CHAPTER 36.

# Engaging with words after newsroom journalism

My health was stabilised after leaving the *Bulletin* newsroom and sticking to doctor's orders and medication, but my work for the next 36 years still involved the management of words as a public servant, communicator, speech writer, author and free-lance journalist.

In later years, there was also the fun of words to make people laugh, with magazine satire and blokes' humour for the Packer Press under the penname of *J.P. Elliot*. I also helped a series of politicians and city administrations look much better than they probably were, but believe I was never involved in false narratives — now known as 'fake news'.

My work involved overseas travel and interchange with inter-esting people from many cultures and faiths under grand-sounding titles such as 'Townsville City Envoy' and 'Executive Director of the Pacific Asia Congress of Municipalities'.

I was a house guest of General Richard B. Myers, when he was Chairman of the US Joint Chiefs of Staff. Barbara and I shared several breakfasts with Dick and Mary Jo while the Americans were still clearing up the debris of the September 11 terrorist attack on the Pentagon. The general, who is now President of Kansas State University, said it was okay for me to drop his name if I ever needed to.

The relationship that started over 20 years ago between one of world's most powerful military leaders and a city council employee in a regional Australian city is, I believe, just another grassroot example of the USA Australia Alliance in its most basic and personal form.

The Americans call it an 'enduring' alliance, mainly to remind Presidents such as Donald Trump that political leaders aren't the only one who make decisions about such important matters — Aussie and Yanks decided several generations ago that they enjoyed each other's company and shared values that were worth fighting for.

I had retained a personal interest in the events of World War Two in the Pacific seeing I probably owed my life to the fact that Pop Sorrensen didn't have to proceed with his family suicide plans after the Japanese advance was stopped.

I was also living in Townsville, a frontline city that was bombed by the enemy and was quickly developed into the largest Allied base in the South West Pacific once the Americans and their 5th Air Force joined the battle after Pearl Harbour.

Many of the city's 20,000 residents were being evacuated, the Kennedy Regiment was fighting the King's enemies overseas, so the local militia had their bayonets sharpened by the armourer, were given ten rounds of ammunition and sent to the beaches to dig in and await the might of a Japanese fleet and their battle-hardened marines.

Then, pretty much overnight, an extra 80,000 snappily dressed and well-armed Americans started arriving to lend a hand. It might have been an alliance of shared values and culture but there was also a heady mix of flirtations, romances and fist fights with the locals — which I'm told just strengthened the bonds.

My father flew with the 5th USF before the Australian bomber squadrons were formed and I recall him coming to their defence when one of our younger extended family members who was big on 'Ban the Bomb' rallies, started sounding off about the Americans during the Cold War.

Dad wasn't particularly expressive, but I remember his words 'It's a free country so you can get stuck into the Yanks as much as you like, but just remember one thing — they're the only Americans we've got!'

When the US veterans came back as honoured guests for the 50th. Anniversary Celebrations of Victory in the Pacific Celebrations there were tears in their eyes as they marked through Townsville to a rapturous welcome from their Australian mates.

That's when the Colt and Dick Myers slipped into a friendship that just seemed appropriate, and probably inevitable considering the powerful emotional forces generated by a 100-year alliance that is still in play today.

My love of the written word has also kept me active in retirement and provided some unexpected challenges. More recently, I helped the 'outspoken maverick politician', The Hon. Bob Katter MP. write his memoir, *Conversations with Katter*, which was published in 2018. Because I'm a North Queenslander, I believe 'The Man Under the Hat' who actually has a keen and engaging sense of humour, probably thought I would translate it accurately, so it could also be read by people south of the border.

Many former colleagues asked why I would burden myself in my twilight years with such a challenging commission, considering that one of them had published an opinion piece stating that Katter, when debating in the House of Representatives, 'uses words like a cliff in Norway uses lemmings.' I just thought it was a great opportunity to sit down with the second longest serving politician in Australia's history, ask a lot of questions and try to quote him accurately. That's what the Colt was trained to do.

Barbara has been a far more successful writer than the young man who kissed her on Kelly's Beach all those years ago. She is one of Australia's leading authors of women's fiction and has had more than 12 million books published worldwide.

The Colt and Barb have four children and seven grandkids scattered across the state.

# CHAPTER 37.

## Maybe one regret

*The father who couldn't cuddle his little boy.*

In writing about my father, I now realise I should have sat down with him and asked why he obviously found it so difficult to embrace me when I was young. Maybe it would have helped.

Like many Australian war babies, I didn't have a conscious contact with my dad until aged three. There's a wartime photo of Mum and me with Dad on leave from active service proudly displaying his sergeant's stripes, but no protective arm or cuddle for the 'kid'.

It looks like a happy family, but I was terrified of him. I was my mother's miracle child, the one to survive after several miscarriages, so most of the photos with Mum have her protectively holding my hand — not so Dad. After this picture was taken, he went off to America to crew bombers back across the Pacific for the final push against the Japanese and was in San Francisco when peace was declared.

Because prisoners of war had transport priority, Dad and his crewmates were stuck there in 1945 and were among the last Australians to come home by sea.

I was cautious but also excited about having a father back in the family. So, when we headed off for a beach picnic and stopped the car on a bush track for Dad to have a leak behind some trees, I dashed out to join him in this new adventure as a four-year-old with very limited close contact with fellow males.

I didn't know he was a man with what we now call PTS as well as a hang-up about modesty and privacy. I copped a vicious slap across the side of my little face and ran back sobbing, in genuine shock and pain, to the safety of my mother's arms. I had known her all my life and had only been with this strange person called Daddy for about a week.

There were no repeat slaps when I was young, but no regular cuddles or hugs either. At an early age Dad taught me how to shake hands 'properly', just like his father had, but I never thought the clasping of hands was a particularly good gesture for a man to have emotional contact with his children. That's probably why I cuddled my own kids so much.

As a young adult I started to realise that my 'old man', although physically strong, was still reliving wartime experiences. He suffered headaches so severe that he'd have memory losses for several days and had to be left quietly curled up in a darkened bedroom. There were two periods of assessment in a repatriation hospital in Brisbane and he was eventually classified as a TPI, a Totally and Permanently Incapacitated ex-serviceman.

Mum confided with me that Dad was troubled by the realisation that he also been responsible for killing innocent civilians as well as his hated enemy during night-time carpet bombing of Indonesian cities and towns which also contained military targets towards the end of the war.

About the time of my father's 'breakdown' we had a visit from one of his old crewmates, Col Robinson, who'd swapped places with a sick navigator from another aircraft for one of the squadron's raids on Japanese positions in Borneo. It turned out to be a very unlucky transfer because Col's bomber was shot down and the crew suffered greatly at the hands of the Japanese.

An allied prisoner had been decapitated with a samurai sword in front of Col who was next in line. He had then been blindfolded and forced to kneel. The executioner had then struck the blind-folded Aussie across the back of the neck, not with the sword, but with a solid length of bamboo. It was all a great joke designed to break the spirit of the captured navigator who was being inter-rogated about the latest technical equipment recovered from the downed aircraft.

Col told us it left him with a firm belief that he knew exactly what it felt like, emotionally, to be decapitated. What baffled me was why he was so open about his experiences and actually put a humorous spin on such a horrific event — while my father was the one with the PTS and the mental and emotional problems.

Some years later when Dad was buying a new car, he'd selected a Ford rather than a much cheaper Mitsubishi. He openly refused to consider a 'Jap car'. When I suggested it was probably time to get over wartime prejudices, I copped a blast.

'On one of our raids over Rabaul, we'd developed such a defen-sive formation with our cones of machine-gun fire that the Jap fighters couldn't get close enough to us. So, one of them did this bloody kamikaze thing and flew straight into the nose of our leading Liberator and blew it and two of my best mates out of the sky.'

'Okay Dad, but the war's been over for 30 years now.'

'You don't understand, the Jap plane was an Oscar.'

I just shrugged.

'Oscars were made by Mitsubishi. You really think I'm going to buy one of them instead of a Yank car?'

When Dad died of kidney failure at the age of 91, our family discovered more about his war. One of his grand-daughters Emma, found a report among his papers written by Dad's commanding officer, the 'skipper' on the Liberator bomber which he'd crewed. It was full of praise for 'the heroism of our flight engineer air gunner, Sergeant Hannay, whose actions in freeing a bomb lodged in the bomb bay at great personal risk undoubtedly saved our aircraft and the lives of his fellow crew members.'

It seems there was a high risk that the bomb, which was hanging from the undercarriage, would have taken the impact of landing rather than the plane's wheels and of course, would have exploded. Dad had been held by the arms by two of his mates and lowered into the open bomb bay where he eventually kicked the bomb free.

He would have been partly exposed to the slipstream turbulence of an aircraft travelling at high speed while staring down at the Indian Ocean thousands of feet below. It was a desperate solution which was attempted several times. I can only wonder about the trust Dad had developed with two blokes bearing his full weight.

And, of course the war touched the families of all those who served. There is another wartime picture of my mother and me, a little toddler, in the tranquil setting of a beautiful garden. I cannot imagine what was going through her mind. A husband and four brothers at war across the globe, from the North Sea, Russia and the Mediterranean to the jungles of the South West Pacific and the memory of a terrible family suicide pact that would have taken both our lives if the Japanese had not been turned in the Battle of The Coral Sea and stopped at Milne Bay and Kokoda.

# CHAPTER 38.

# What happened to them?

### Tommy and the 'Spanish Dancer'

In my first year of marriage in Bundaberg, I was approached by the Queensland News Editor of the ABC, Graeme Irvine, on his annual tour of regional centres poaching graded staff. After training in Brisbane on radio and television production, I was posted to Townsville where Barbara and I bought our first home for $11,000 — cyclone damaged from Althea of course, but still habitable. And that's where I caught up with Tommy.

Tommy saw the end coming at the *News Mail* and resigned while I was overseas. He had moved to Townsville for a new start, was on top of the grog and had won respect and admiration though the excellence of his craft.

He was back at his peak when I met him again. I was with ABC News, covering a City Council meeting on my second day in Townsville and looking forward to catching up with my mate and mentor.

Tommy was at the Press table; fate had brought us together again. I hadn't seen him for six years. I was a married man now, and Barbara was expecting our first child. He tried to smile as I walked up, but half his face was covered with a medical mask. He looked like the Phantom of the Opera. I must have frowned.

'Good to see you again, Colt… don't look so worried, you can't catch it… it's just the Spanish Dancer.'

He was obviously very ill, but still on the job and stoic, as always. I hadn't heard about this. The larrikin spirit was still there, and he pushed an ashtray over to me with a smouldering cigarette balanced on the edge.

'Just my bloody luck, mate.'

'What an awful call, Tommy, how serious is it?'

'No, not the cancer.… it's my doctor. He's an alderman and he'll turn up any minute now and get right up me if he knows I've been smoking. Stick this fag in front of you and make out it's yours… take the odd drag on it, if you can, and I'll slip in a few puffs when the Doc is distracted by debate.'

That's exactly what we did on our reunion — covered the council meeting together, while fooling Tommy's eagle-eyed doctor Norm Scott-Young. We even stopped off for a quick drink afterwards and had a good laugh.

It was a hot night and the beer started to go flat quickly. Tommy asked the startled barmaid for a salt shaker and shook some into his beer. It immediately came to life and frothed up a new head. That's what he'd always done at The Imperial. I had been holding up okay until that happened. All the memories came flooding back.

My mate Tommy, the bloke who took me under his wing when I was sixteen, who diagnosed my poetic guts-ache, who taught me how to behave in a public bar, who had been through it all with me, with Myles, Bevan and Percy. Tommy saw me wiping my eyes and came to my rescue, a usual, with his keen sense of irony.

'Incurable skin cancer, can you believe it, mate? Me wearing a hat almost day and night. When my doctor up here asked me if I'd been exposed to much sun, I told him I'd been kept in the bloody dark most of my life and I needed major surgery to remove my hat…but that's how it goes, Colt… that's how it goes.'

Tommy, the cynic who believed that miracles might happen on the racecourse, seemed to know that his luck had finally run out. I had moved on by the time he died but took comfort in a vision I had created with my old mentor sitting down with St Peter at the Pearly Gates, pointing out how Genesis could indeed be improved with some judicious sub-editing.

## Mort Nash and editors who were appointed by God

'I don't want my reporters championing bloody causes and writing commentary instead of balanced news… writers must not intrude into their copy. So be careful about taking the high moral ground and making too many statements of so-called fact. Just because you might think it's important doesn't mean it has some inane right to be bloody published. That's why God created editors and why editors created editorials… we decide these things.'

I was instructed, verbally abused, mentored and traumatised by three editors in my formative years. The man whose voice still rings loudest in my ears is Mort Nash, one of the nation's great smokers, lawn bowlers and cynics. He was also my mentor and protector in the most vulnerable period of my young life.

It is this dominant memory my first editor that has probably resulted in the unintentional blending of his character with some of my experiences with Ron Harvey who was editor in my later years of training and even Alex Rainnie, the veteran ABC newsman of North Queensland.

I admit to probably extending Mort's tenure as editor of the *News Mail* and hope that despite the rough and tumble of these events and my use of muscular language, he comes through as a very decent and caring man. The memory of all my old colleagues is very dear to me.

## Percy Grey

Percy worked all his life at the *News Mail*. I don't believe he ever misquoted anyone or got a fact wrong in the many thousands of stories he wrote about his home town and the people in it. He was both proud and content to be a, 'working journalist and hack,' a writer who could tackle any reporting task.

I found the piece he wrote about the Russian Ambassador, Ivan Kurdivkov, from an old *News Mail* file. Being curious about what happened to the ambassador I also did an internet search and discovered that several sites spell his name as Kurdyukov. Sorry, but I'm sticking with Percy's — I just cannot imagine him making such a basic reporting error as that.

They named a street after Percy when he died. He would have liked that. Percy never sought praise or awards from his peers, but he would have been chuffed to know that the community he served so well wanted to honour him that way.

## Bevan and Mervyn

Bevan and Mervyn were returned men, colleagues and good mates to me as a younger man. I have tried to portray them as honestly as possible but admit that on occasions they get mixed up in the stories, the timing and the shared memories of others. I believe there were at least six ex-servicemen 'out the back'. None of them revelled in recounting war stories but, in my formative years, I picked up a common theme of larrikin humour at times bordering on the dark side, a readiness to help others, and strangely enough, an optimistic outlook about the future — even with another world war threatening on the horizon.

Bevan's dislike of the Vichy French was understandable. He had been captured by them in Syria and had seen a wounded mate tortured, by a medic of all people, before an exchange of prisoners had been organised.

Bevan was still there when I returned to Bundy as News Editor in the late '70s. He was always full of good advice. I never raised the question about the damage to my Holden ute.

When we of the younger generation complained about things — work, the weather, life in general, small injuries or flat beer — quiet little Mervyn would simply shake his head. 'Just remember, son… you're not stuck in the mud and no bastard is shooting at you.'

I cannot recall the circumstances in which it was delivered, but one of Bevan's homilies is etched into my brain. 'If your bayonet gets stuck in the sternum or pelvis it's best to fire off the round you have in the chamber. That will shatter the bone and four times out of five the recoil will pull it out anyway.' It was the 'four times out of five' that sent a shiver up my spine.

### Roy Theodore

Most journalists don't expect to learn much about their craft from someone in management, but my experience with Roy was different. We didn't know at the time, but he was probably the most experienced sub-editor who ever walked through the *News Mail*'s door, having worked in Sydney, Melbourne and Wellington, as well as on the Brisbane *Telegraph*.

In 1962, he launched and wrote the paper's first community column under the penname of Sam. It became the longest running column in the regional dailies of Australia.

The newspaper industry recognised his talents and elected him as president of the Regional Dailies Association of Australia and a delegate on the International Press Institute. Roy also served as a councillor on the Australian Press Council.

During an industrial dispute involving all the regional dailies of Australia in the early 1980s, the Australian Journalists Association said something nasty about the bosses. The aggrieved journos were led by two of my old colleagues, Quentin Dempster, who did his time on the *Maryborough Chronicle* and whose turf overlapped with mine on the *News Mail*, and Norm Harriden, a former ABC industrial rounds-man turned union official.

Roy, the spokesman for the regional dailies was offended by this attack on the integrity of management and responded by stating that if the AJA wanted a 'knuckle sandwich', he was prepared to accommodate them.

At the time, I was editor of the *Townsville Bulletin* and my staff, who saw this as blatant intimidation, threatened to walk out. I didn't think it would be much use arguing. Only someone who was with me when I was a young bloke and had seen Roy stand up and defend his editorial staff against the threat of physical violence in The Imperial, would have known what I was talking about.

## Senior Sergeant Arthur Pitts

The honest cop of Miriam Vale fame returned to Brisbane in the 1970s when newly appointed Commissioner Ray Whitrod tried to clean up corruption in the highest levels of the Police Force.

Arthur was a member of the Commissioner's new Criminal Intelligent Unit and went straight in as head of the most corrupt police unit in Queensland, the Licencing Branch. The Branch had only arrested two illegal SP bookmakers in the previous four years — Arthur Pitts nabbed 17 in his first three months. Maybe some coppers are just better at their jobs than others?

But things turned bad for Pitts when corrupt politicians, as well as bent policemen, eventually forced Whitrod out, and replaced him with the biggest crook of them all, Commissioner Terry Lewis.

In 1974 Pitts bugged his own home to record Terry Lewis' bagman, Jack Herbert, offering him $1,500 a month to give prior warning of any intended raids on SP bookies who were under Herbert's protection.

That should have been the end of it, but 'The Joke' or 'The Rat Pack', as the crooked network was known, was just too deeply entrenched and far too powerful. Jack Herbert was cleared of corruption and there was a concerted campaign to discredit Arthur Pitts.

The big, dedicated, respected and effective policeman, who gave me some life lessons as a young reporter in the bush, ended his career working in the Lost Property Office in Brisbane Police Headquarters.

I assume he took special pleasure in eventually seeing the Police Commissioner and his senior cronies doing jail time as a result of the Fitzgerald Inquiry. But I am sure he was pissed off about Jack Herbert.

Herbert did a runner to England when the Fitzgerald inquiry started but agreed to return and give evidence against his corrupt mates on the condition of indemnity. He told Commissioner Tony Fitzgerald that he had bagged $3 million for the Rat Pack and admitted that he had tried to bribe Arthur Pitts.

If you ever travel north on the Bruce Highway, the old Miriam Vale Police residence, where the Pitts' children kept a lookout for passing criminals and stolen cars, is on the left, just opposite the servo which has always been famous for its fresh mud crab sandwiches. Ask for a splash of vinegar and an extra sprinkle of pepper.

The pub looks just the same and I hope they still hold the Bushman's Carnival each year. I don't think coppers are allowed to kidnap young reporters now days — which is possibly a shame.

## Women in journalism

Mort Nash was right about the women. They soon entered the profession in increasing numbers. They were in senior positions in the ABC News when I joined in 1971 and were amongst my most valued staff members when I became an editor.

One of the later *News Mail* girls, Nancy Bates, was appointed editor of the Maryborough chronicle.

Of course, I saw all this from the male perspective and have no doubt that many women from my era might have differing views about their treatment in the so-called 'golden age of journalism'.

One of the most outstanding young journalists in my time was a girl. I call Margie McDonald, a girl because she seemed very young and probably was at the time I encountered her on the Townsville *Bulletin*. Young yes, but also feisty and talented.

Margie was working on sport, which surprised me because, despite equality in basic salaries for male and female journos, sport writers and subs on newspapers were always men — or at least that had been my experience.

But Margie was different. Leon 'Sharkey' Searle my chief sub described her as a bottle of champagne that had just been uncorked. She was bubbly, cheerful and celebratory, especially if she'd just filed an award-winning story about junior soccer, an informed critique of a Foley Shield rugby league final, or the struggle by 'associates' to be given equal status as men the Townsville Golf club.

She wrote sharp, clean copy and my sports' editor, Bruce McDonald, guarded her like a Rottweiler.

I feared she would be 'wasted' in sport. In my early years, veteran rounds-men described how sports writers still used the original copy that some ancient Greek has scribed into a clay tablet — and ever since then all they did was change the scores. I'll admit I was still carrying some of that bias at that time, but I also saw Margie had great potential for police or local government rounds, and she was obviously suited to feature writing.

I tried to exercise my God-given power as editor and move her from sport to general reporting, but of course, she would not budge. Sport was her life and sports journalism was her career.

I am pleased she resisted because Margie McDonald retired recently after a brilliant career as one of Australia's most respected and valued sport writers — described by her peers as 'journalism's most loved lady'.

## Better times for people like Myles

Myles Carruthers was replaced at the *News Mail* by a self-proclaimed Polynesian prince, Rodway Barnes, who had also served with one of the New Zealand Battalions in the bloody Monte Casino campaign in Italy during World War Two.

Offset printing was being embraced, newspapers were changing, and so too were attitudes towards gender and sexual preferences. The new word 'gay' seemed to be much more appropriate.

Rodway was quite open about his sexuality and his male partner was included in the *News Mail* mob's activities in The Imperial without comment. No one ever beat him up and he didn't have to leave town. Rodway spent the rest of his life in Bundy.

## The Laws of Libel and crooked coppers

*'Any imputation concerning any person by which the reputation of that person is likely to be injured'* was memorised by most young journalists of my era… we had to know about the Laws of Libel to avoid defaming someone with our printed words.

One should take care, even in an autobiography in which the most horrible character is given a false name. I used Boris because it has a certain dangerous, violent ring to it and reminds me of the black and white horror movie actor, Boris Karloff.

The bloke who everyone believed 'did poor Myles over', is the only character in this book who was given a pseudonym. The last time I checked he was still alive but had mellowed considerably in old age.

My experiences with the controversial Mervyn Stevenson, have been recorded accurately in the Colt's story, but I still mulled over whether I should go into such negative detail about a man who was never charged, let alone convicted of any of his rumoured crimes.

In balance it should be noted that Stevenson was given a police honour guard at his funeral and is listed in the Stockman's Hall of Fame in Winton as one of the Outback's heroes.

Publishers might be encouraged by the fact that the dead cannot be libelled, as least not legally, but my old school training in journalism also warned me to avoid inadvertently colouring this chapter with too much rumour and to stick to my own personal experiences. I was encouraged by old Townsville *Bulletin*, *Northern Miner* and ABC journalists who had also shared unsettling experiences with the stock squad boss towards the end of his career. 'Just set it down accurately and let others make up their own minds.'

In 2006 Katter raised the issue of stock squad corruption in Federal Parliament, referring to 'the crooked creek cattle company' as it was known to many northern bush people during the time of Stevenson. He also praised ABC broadcast journalist Steve Austin for his courage in pursuing the story while Stevenson was still alive.

Then in 2002, an inquest in Townsville into the disappearance of Perth Backpacker Tony Jones, heard that a suspect seen drinking in the same bar before the young man went missing in 1982, fitted the description of Stevenson. It received nation-wide publicity.

For my money, I'm much more comfortable about Sergeant Arthur Pitts being described as a heroic copper along with other honest and steadfast officers like Jack Sanderson and Warren Butterworth in NQ. He took on corrupt senior officers in the Queensland Police Force and they ruined his career. I don't think they gave him an honour guard when he died.

## What ever happened to the AJA?

I should point out that the AJA no longer exists. Journalists are now part of an alliance which is a very broad church covering, 'everyone who informs or entertains Australians'. I wish them well.

There is, of course, a code of ethics, a much amended and expanded one to cater for all the new industrial brothers and sisters who are also professionally engaged in informing and entertaining.

There is even a para which says that today's editors cannot require a journalist to do an 'intrusion'. Being required to intrude into personal privacy for the sake of a good headline, or a heat of the moment quote that might soon be regretted, caused me much angst as a young man — so I have some sympathy with the new code.

But I can also hear the voice of old Mort Nash: 'What do you bloody mean… intrusions are optional? Don't they realise God created editors to make these decisions?'

If only the Alliance had been around in my early years.

'No thanks, Mr. Nash, I'm only 16. I'd rather not go and talk to the grieving widow. I'm sorry but I'm too young and sensitive. Don't frown at me like that… you can't make me! You be careful, Mr. Nash, I've got all the actors, musicians, stunt men, film makers, rock stars, public relations people, special events organisers, marketing managers and pole-dancers right behind me.'

Under the new code journalists are also required to 'do their utmost' to have errors corrected. I had to read that several times.

'Colt, I don't want you making mistakes in the first bloody place, but when you do fuck up I need to know straight away, so I can correct them. Every time an error actually gets into print, all of us get dipped in shit. And there's only one thing worse than making mistakes… that's not correcting them in the next bloody edition.'

'Yes, Mr. Nash… I'll remember that.'

However, after more careful consideration, I have realised that in today's competitive media culture the Alliance didn't see the need to insist that journalists correct their mistakes. Featuring the errors of fellow journalists working on competing papers is all the go these days.

## The ABC in its heyday

It was probably that kiss on Kelly's beach that led to the next phase of my career as a journalist. A head-hunter from ABC News in Brisbane, none other than the new Queensland editor Graeme Irvine, had arrived in town and let it be known he was happy to meet experienced print journos who might be interested in converting to radio and television.

I'm sure I was influenced by my old editor, Mort Nash who had a low opinion of television. For him, even tabloid papers were the work of the Devil because he was convinced they packaged news too tightly and reduced a journalist's ability to tell the full story with adequate balance.

I mentioned the interviews to my lovely new wife and showed appropriate professional print journalist disdain in doing so. I was surprised — her response was part encouragement clothed in a serious challenge to my new-husband delicate ego.

'I think you'd be very good on television … but you'd have to dress and groom better for work and wear a neck tie correctly. Those ABC reporters all look great and they speak beautiful English.'

So, I got the message loud and clear, went and bought a pair of flared pants and a pink shirt, stopped pulling my tie to one side like newspaper journos and detectives and joined ABC News in 1971.

Much later Barbara told me she had hoped I'd once again have an opportunity to report from interesting places overseas, only this time with her and a lot of kids with dual citizenship and an international outlook on life.

When she was very little, my wife fantasised about touring the world when she grew up and having babies of various colours. Apparently, there were children from the four corners of the globe, but no fathers in the picture. That plan had been dropped after she reached puberty and learned about the baby-making process in a family strongly influenced by the High Church of England.

I regret that Barb's dreams of being stationed in places such as London, Paris or New York were never realised. However, we did have beautiful little kids in regional cities that were great places to bring up children. This lifestyle also allowed my talented wife to keep teaching at secondary school level and take the first steps to becoming a best-selling novelist.

I never regretted my five and a bit year with Aunty in Brisbane, Townsville and Mackay. It was a time of rapid expansion in regional news services and, for a while, money flowed from the Whitlam Government like the mighty Burdekin River in full flood.

Aunty was probably the best-informed media organisation in the country in the 1970s.

We had card-carrying 'official ABC correspondents' in every small town, fuel stop, fishing village or inhabited island across a great swathe of north and north-western Queensland. They were paid a pittance but had status in their communities and helped the working journalists in ABC News to stay well-grounded in terms of what regional Australians really cared about.

They ranged from CWA presidents and shopkeepers to town clerks and a bloke named Bob Katter senior out in Mount Isa who was soon to be appointed Minister for the Army.

Occasionally they made copy themselves — like the time I called Sergeant Butterworth on Magnetic Island and asked if there was any news.

'Well, I do have the ABC's Island correspondent in the lockup… disorderly conduct and resisting arrest. A political debate in the Arcadia Hotel that got over-heated.'

But they also produced leads for National news broadcasts. Like the time large groups of frightened Aboriginal people, men women and little kids, gathered around the police station in a small Gulf Country town. What was happening?

A kadaicha man, with the power of life or death, had been seen ghosting through the paperbarks, complete with ceremonial paint and emu feather shoes to cover his tracks. He had journeyed from the desert country many hundreds of kilometres to the south, to bring justice for a relative who had been killed in a fight.

All the locals knew the justice would be swift and deadly. A bone to be pointed or some other form of deadly charm and they believed it would be safer to camp in the sergeant's backyard until this secret business was settled.

It all got a run, along with the road reports, beef prices, council news, public meetings, crocodile attacks and rodeo results. *The*

*North-Western ABC News… compiled today by Elliot Hannay and read by Malcom Florence.*

Then, Whitlam imploded, and the Fraser budget razor gang took to Aunty like she was a prostitute in London's White Chapel who needed to be dispatched with as much mutilation as possible. Of course, the most painful cuts were in the regional centres where entire local news services disappeared, and regional editorial autonomy was threatened by constant review and policy advice from 'above'. Local office managers, most of them former casual announcers, started to override the journalists in charge.

I sensed the News Department was in trouble in the regional centres when a manager, whose main role was to sign chits and read our greatly reduced local news segments was advised by 'management' that he should ensure balance in the ABC's coverage of the State Election.

To this end he instructed me to list the political content of all our local news broadcasts. He had produced an exercise book with the names of the local candidates, with dates and space to record the amount of air time that each received in the course of our journalists' coverage of the news of the day. He also advised that it was his call as manager to continue this system as a matter of form after the elections.

Instead of journalists independently deciding what was fit to cover and broadcast, we had to consult the bloody check list and chase up candidates for a story, or for comment, just so the tally on the bottom of the manager's exercise book showed that everyone had been given equal time.

My job as journalist in charge, which was to present the news of the day in the most accurate and balanced form that I could achieve against deadlines, was about to be compromised by an inappropriate management tool that had the potential to force us to seek out and run tripe from wannabe politicians that wasn't actually news — even worse, pretend it was news and run it to ensure the sheet was balanced.

Fraser ordered the budget cuts, but it was ABC's aloof management who decided where and how the savings would be made and I don't believe Aunty ever recovered to full health as a result.

Mort Nash was wrong back in 1958 when he forecast that television would not function well as a disseminator of news, but he was dead set right when he said television's natural role is to entertain and combining news with entertainment and giving it the false clothing of 'current affairs', would be problematic.

Q&A is most certainly entertaining, but do viewers come away better informed about the important issues it covers or are opinions just further entrenched by its adversarial format?

In my time current affairs staffers were recruited from universities, not seconded from the ABC's own pool of news journalists. They all wanted to appear on camera and their management openly encouraged them to flout the editorial standards that applied to the news department.

I left when my colleagues were threating to strike over management's decision to allow current affairs staff to break news in competition with the highly regarded ABC News broadcasts.

But, even on a bad day Aunty can shine above all the commercial radio and television networks with its massive scope and content. However, ABC bosses should realise they've lost much of our trust because they've been acting too much like politicians, brawling internally, overly sensitive to criticism and often too busy promoting their brand.

In my day, ABC News had oversight from experienced editors for all its stories even the most urgent ones from the most trusted hands. Qualified journalists who stuffed up major stories by being unprofessional (undue emphasis, wrongful omission or errors of fact) were usually demoted or sacked. I'm not sure if that still happens.

That said, I am much more than *A Friend of the ABC* — professionally I fell deeply in love with Aunty fifty years ago and the passion remains to this day.

## Where are the printers and their Chapel Fathers?

Australia's two big printing unions amalgamated in 1966 to form the Printing and Kindred Industries Union (PKIU) and it served its members well during a period of painful change in the industry.

The boys 'out the back' had a much longer history of industrial action than the journalists and the AJA and, for my money, they were better prepared and better led when the time came to phase out hard copy and hot metal.

The AJA used black-bans and strike action to protect its interests, but the PKIU used its industrial muscle to hammer out more concessions from the employers. If the presses stopped, there were no papers on the streets — as simple as that.

The Chapel Fathers knew that change was inevitable and did some tough bargaining while they still had the power to make the transition period very painful for the employers. They wanted more than redundancy packages, they wanted as many of their brothers as possible to be accommodated in the new soft copy, cold metal era.

The retraining programmes they won, particularly for the younger printers who had many more years of expected employment ahead of them, were extensive and practical.

Many compositors, linotype operators, pressmen and other printing tradesmen were retrained as computer and IT specialists, photographers, advertising reps or managers, distribution managers, journalists and sub-editors.

In 1970, the PKIU had 60,000 members, but by 1995 it had ceased to exist and had amalgamated with the Manufacturing Workers Union.

Today I am reminded of my youthful experience with my printer mates and the slugs of hot type metal which emerged from the now extinct linotype machines. Asking me, the 16-year-old cadet reporter, about a heading and then slipping me the white-hot slug for closer inspection reinforced the printers' long held belief about journalists. It wasn't that they thought they had developed much lower pain thresholds — they were just a lot smarter than us.

## Young politicians who rocked the boat

At the time of my visit from the Ku Klux Klan in Townsville, young Bob Katter seemed to be the odd man out amongst conservative politicians in supporting the advancement of Aboriginal and Torres Strait Island people. He was very much a lone and vulnerable voice, but that soon changed.

Most people were surprised when he was appointed Minister for Aboriginal Affairs in Queensland in 1984 and then he did something to surprise them even more — he sat down and listened to the First Australians on reserves and isolated communities and worked with conviction and passion to improve their lot.

Between 1984 and 1992 the Katter Ministry helped deliver inalienable freehold title of one million hectares of land to the people who had occupied it for thousands of years.

Community councils were elected to act as trustees, 700 Indigenous workers were engaged and trained to construct more than 2000 houses, and 800 title deeds were issued.

Unfortunately, this progress was not sustained under successive new governments. Katter recently lamented: 'A lot of the legislation and initiatives from back then have been overridden, overturned and or reversed. The battle to win back the rights and freedoms of the First Australians will sadly have to be fought again.'

While persistent quality journalism from the *Courier Mail* and the ABC's *Four Corners* exposed corruption in Queensland, the Deputy Premier Bill Gunn, backed by Katter, were the two conservative politicians responsible for establishing the Fitzgerald Royal Commission while Premier Bjelke-Petersen was 'out of town' — a move that cost them government.

Writing in *The Australian* in 2011, Aboriginal activist and academic Noel Pearson, described Katter as 'the greatest Federal Minister for Aboriginal Affairs Australia never had' and regretted the fact that respect for Katter's deep personal involvement in indigenous issues was 'lost in translation south of the Queensland border'.

## Eddie Mabo and the KKK

After the Klan appeared in my office, I suffered professional frustration about not being able to tell their story which would have exposed the Klan's existence, not only in North Queensland but nationally.

However, I took some comfort with my old editor's mantra about knowing 'who's up who and who's paying the rent'. This information would have to keep for a rainy day.

If the Klan's threat to sack Aboriginal activist and railway unionist Archie Smallwood had succeeded, I had enough information about the perpetrators to make it a front-page lead and push for his rein-statement — knowing it had been racially and politically motivated.

But unless there was a trigger, I had to remain silent, even in later years when I had professional contacts or worked on commit-tees with Eddie Mabo, Charles Perkins, Chicka Dixon and Shorty O'Neill, and a much closer mateship with Townsville's first local government Aboriginal liaison officer, Alex Illin.

Was I hiding behind professional ethics or was I afraid these out-spoken champions of the First Australians would think less of me for not throwing the Klan out of my office and naming them publicly?

I was encouraged that Professor Gracelyn Smallwood, who like her late father, has always called it like she sees it, had no problems with my actions or my timing. She also understood that I had to use racially offensive language when quoting bigots and neo-Nazis and believed the message of the story was far more important.

At least the Klan helped strengthen my journalistic view that black voices also needed to be heard in this period of emotional and potentially violent debate in our society.

After I left *The Bulletin*, a new generation of journalists, including David Anthony kept the door open for people like Archie Smallwood who campaigned until the day he died, often with shared discussions and meals with local reporters in Zorba's Café or the Newmarket Hotel.

David, who was editor of the local Atherton Tableland news-papers while I was writing this memoir, told me that the last story he wrote about Archie Smallwood was in 1985 after the historic handover at Uluru where Archie had been a special guest at the ceremony performed by the Governor General Sir Ninian Stevens. The veteran Townsville activist who'd also been a target of the

KKK, had lived to see one of the most symbolic highlights for land rights in Australia, but died soon after.

Ten years after the Klan warned me about Mabo, the campaign for land rights on Murray Island was national news. Eddie Mabo's struggle for justice is well documented, so too is the opposition it received and the fear it generated for many non-indigenous land-holders at that time.

Eddie died in 1992, just five months before the High Court delivered its historic finding which overturned terra nullius, the long-standing and bizarre legal view that no-one owned land in this continent before the whitefellas arrived. And, no, cattlemen and farmers weren't turfed off their family properties and black-fellas didn't start claiming homes and suburban back yards.

It is significant that Eddie Mabo's funeral in Townsville was one of the biggest ever seen in the city, or in North Queensland for that matter. That public gesture of respect was not confined to out-of-towners travelling from across the country. At that time, the way our community honoured Eddie's memory and his achievements seemed to me to be a far more accurate reflection of Townsville's character than my encounter with a couple of wannabe Klansmen a decade earlier. After all, this was the birthplace of Mabo's land rights, this was the place where he received the encouragement and the support, not only to take up the fight, but to see it through.

Then, in 1995, Eddie's grave was vandalised on the night of his memorial service which in Islander culture was three years after his death. The city was shamed, reconciliation was questioned or challenged by even moderate local activists and there was fear that anger might spill over into violence.

The word 'Abo' had been scrawled across Eddie's memorial in red paint along with an incorrectly drawn Nazi swastika, so the spectre of the KKK was raised once again. Only a year before, there had been outrage over a photo of soldiers at Lavarack Barracks posing in Klan hoods, albeit with several of their black mates seated un-masked in the front row. It was dismissed by the authorities as a stupid stunt, but it also made the national news.

I would be the last person to defend the Klan, but I was close to the events of that time and was tasked with the job to keep communication flowing between the Mayor's office, the Mabo family representatives, the Police, State and Federal Governments up to Ministerial level, and local and national Indigenous representatives.

Unfortunately, the Police investigation failed to charge the suspected offenders after evidence was lost at the John Tonge Forensic Centre in Brisbane. But there was enough physical and circumstantial evidence to indicate this was most likely an act of juvenile vandalism by absconders from the nearby Cleveland Bay Youth Detention Centre. The red paint used on Eddie's memorial was believed to have come from the sexton's storeroom that had been broken and entered. It was claimed there were also traces of paint on the juvenile suspects.

Some people will be reluctant to accept this conclusion and that is understandable when one considers how often the Klan, or at least its fellow-travellers, have surfaced in North Queensland.

Eddie's remains were reinterred on his beloved Murray Island and things settled down in Townsville. Then, four years later another local ratbag claimed affiliation on the internet with the KKK, complete with images of a burning cross and the sinister white hood, to attack the pending national stolen generation apology to Australia's Indigenous people. More national negative publicity for Townsville.

Again, in 2003, racist pamphlets began appearing in the letter-boxes of black families. They carried the letters KKK and the Nazi swastika.

So, the Colt does have some regrets. I just wish this minority wasn't so bloody active in this wonderful part of Australia, in a community where there are also so many examples of inclusion and equality in the daily lives of its citizens. Take a look at the Jezzine Barracks redevelopment which is now a community asset that proudly features the indigenous and military histories of the site with world-class interpretive elements and public art developed by locals — a partnership between the Bindal and, Wulgurukaba traditional owners and the 200,000 other people who now call Townsville 'home'.

## A long wait for Indigenous justice

Fifty-eight years ago I wrote a single-column story about an Aboriginal man winning exemption from The Act in the Bundaberg Magistrate's Court. Some 13 years later, when I returned from a stint freelancing overseas, the legal age for drinking had been dropped to 18 and the coppers no longer arrested old ladies on witchcraft related laws, but Indigenous injustice was still alive and flourishing.

I accompanied a delegation of inquiry with the Whitlam Government's new Minister for Aboriginal Affairs, Gordon Bryant, and several members of the Canberra Press Gallery. We visited remote Queensland regional centres and town camps, including Boulia, Camooweal and Mt Isa. Here we learned that not only were Indigenous people still being deprived of their wages, their impounded savings were being stolen by their State 'guard-ians' and a police sergeant had been charged.

Bryant believed the theft was widespread. He challenged the State Government and acted to have the Commonwealth Bank divest itself of all trust funds linked to the Protection Acts. I broke the story nationally on ABC radio that day and, once again, waited for a positive outcome.

Almost half a century later, in March 2018, I saw an advertisement in our weekly newspaper on the Atherton Tablelands calling for claimants to join the latest Stolen Indigenous Wages Class Action against the Queensland Government.

I suspect it was only of passing interest to most of the paper's readers, but the term 'stolen wages' sent a shudder through me. If I was unsettled, how must the surviving victims of this crime and their families feel? I decided to wait no longer.

I was the only white face in a large gathering at the public meeting and informed the lawyers that I had some personal history in the case. While I no longer had editorial space or television and radio bulletins at my disposal, I was willing to help promote their cause — pro bono.

I am now on call, to spread the word or give evidence. Around 30 elders have died since the claim was mounted. Our courts are slow in dispensing justice, but the moving stories of the departed have all been recorded. Historians have estimated that the outstanding payments in Queensland alone could amount to $500 million and involve thousands of recipients.

When the Klan delegation came into my office in Townsville in 1980, they most certainly walked past a young sports' sub named Chris Mitchell who worked from a desk just outside my office door. My encounter was never shared, but the editorial staff were well aware that our coverage of Indigenous affairs and racist incidents caused panic in some quarters. We copped complains just because we accurately reported the news of the day.

This apparently made a lasting impression on Mitchell who, in 2016, wrote *Making Headlines* after retiring as Editor in Chief of

*The Australian.* In his chapter on Aboriginal Australia he mentions his old Townsville editor as being 'a campaigner on Aboriginal issues'. At the time I'd assumed I was just being balanced in opening the editorial door to accommodate the black as well as the white view on issues facing our community. But now, I'm happy to wear the tag. If my staff saw me as a 'campaigner' all those years ago maybe I should start acting like one?

Old Mort Nash told me I'd be so busy as a reporter, even in a country town just covering the news rounds, that there wouldn't be much time left at the end of the shift to 'right wrongs and expose injustice'. I sensed that to achieve such high ideals, I'd also have to use adjectives and the boss had threatened to kick my arse all the way down the stairs if I ever used an adjective outside a direct quote. It could lead to 'opinionated copy'.

Now that I have time to spare in my old age, I might just have a good crack at this Stolen Wages issue. I have some very strong opinions about it, and I've been waiting for years to use all those adjectives.

*Footnote:* July 2019. An opinion piece I wrote was published in *The Australian*. *'It's as significant as the Mabo Decision. One of the biggest class action settlements in our legal history with $190 million compensation for wages stolen by earlier Queensland Governments and their agents. Good news for all Australians who aspire to a Fair Go, but why did it take so long?'*

The story carried a heading that included 'The Wages of Sin'. I was chuffed. The Colt had lived long enough to see one of the wrongs of his youth being righted in his old age.

## Lessons from The Imperial Hotel

In retrospect, I can probably thank the old hands at the *News Mail* for preparing me for some of life's more dangerous situations — the ones most often encountered far from home, comfort or help.

I am convinced that drinking in The Imperial as a young bloke and listening to the advice of Bevan, Mervyn, Tommy and Myles, helped me survive when I inadvertently wandered into the 'Toughest Bar in the World'.

It's official, Quinn's Bar in Papeete, Tahiti, was given that title in a published survey by one Randolph Wolfe in 1968 — almost two years after my experience there.

People who had been knifed, beaten up, or horribly disfigured by sexually transmitted diseases in the toughest ports around the world were quoted as saying: 'A man has never tasted the full extravagance of descent until he enters Quinn's.'

Quinn's, a large corrugated-iron beach hut on a beautiful tropical island, was staffed with gorgeous Polynesian dancing girls and sold glasses of rum for ten cents, and ice-cold beer for five cents.

What made it interesting was the fact that it had somehow been hidden from the eyes of morality and all forms of government control. The liquor and sanitation laws had been lost or ignored many years previously. There was only one toilet and it had no door.

Brutal in-house fist fights were not just tolerated… chairs were rearranged to accommodate the spectators. Knife fights were frowned upon during daylight hours but at night they were simply relegated outside onto the street, where passing island busses could stop and use their high-beam headlights to provide better illumination for combatants, cheering spectators and curious passengers.

It was the drinking hole for French Foreign Legionnaires and sailors stationed on Tahiti to keep order while France tested nuclear bombs in the atmosphere. These tough characters were drawn like moths to bright lights — bright lights in the form of smiling bar girls who introduced themselves with names like 'Nancy Nopants', 'Susie Surething', and 'Betty Buy Me A New Dress'.

The local colour was provided by massive, tattooed men with frangipani flowers stuck behind their ears, their long hair done up in buns with brightly coloured ribbons. The fact that many of these men also wore eye shadow and lipstick didn't seem out of place in such an exotic setting.

The bar operated at such a depraved level of acceptable conduct that you knew things were really out of hand when the French authorities arrived to close the place down in the early hours of the morning. The only way this could be achieved was by sending in the gendarmes and military police. These blokes, in their spiffy uniforms and Charles de Gaulle caps, seemed to take sadistic delight in beating drunk legionnaires and sailors senseless with their batons and throwing them bodily into prison vans.

In their state of drunken frenzy, the crowds became deaf as beetles, because police gunfire into the air didn't seem to register with anyone. I saw one gendarme empty a ten-shot semi-automatic pistol into the overhead canopy of a huge breadfruit tree, showering the brawlers outside with foliage and a few decent size branches. No one took any notice.

It was only when one copper lowered his shots onto the bitumen in front of him, sending sparks flying and ricochets howling and humming just over people's heads, that the crowds start to thin out.

I then realised that my Scottish drinking mate from earlier in the evening was being dragged into the back of a police car. Jack had stupidly worn his best shirt into Quinn's bar and, while heavily imbibing with several of the bar girls, had been quickly and publicly stripped to his shorts. His expensive silk shirt was now being worn by one of the bar staff.

Jack looked tough as nails, a man of few words. He had been raised in Glasgow and worked as a welder in the shipyards, but he also had a broken heart after being dumped by his Australian fiancée and was working his way back home to his widowed mother.

He'd spilled all this to me on our third night in Quinn's. It was that sort of place and had a strange magnetic attraction for young men of an age when the thirst for adventure and exotic experience is strong in their blood. It was also said about Quinn's that hard men would often cry like babies, realising that they had somehow ended up in the world's deepest den of depravity and they were so far from home they could only cry out for their mothers — like dying soldiers on the battlefield.

I had caught a glimpse of two large girls in floral dresses hurling the semi-conscious half-naked Scot off the front veranda and onto the road near the feet of the policemen. Against the backdrop of terror and violence and the smell of cordite, it looked like they had made some ancient Polynesian sacrifice to appease the angry gods, and the coppers gladly accepted him.

I cautiously walked towards the police, taking care to show I wasn't armed and unlike most of the others in the crowd, I had no immediate plans to crack their skulls with a big stick. I was still clutching a half-filled glass of beer, having quickly put my back to the nearest wall when the big brawl started.

I deliberately took a sip as I walked towards them, hoping it would give the impression of being an observer rather than an active participant, a man of the world displaying casual indifference to spilled blood, broken glass and baton charges.

I went into journalist mode, tried to sound confident and engaged in some quick, but polite talking to the head gendarme. Jack had been robbed. He was my mate. They probably spiked his drinks. He was an innocent abroad. I'd look after him.

The policeman couldn't understand me. I tried my limited schoolboy French 'Jack est ivre… Jack est mon ami…Jack est Scottish… Je suis journalist.' Still no reaction. These blokes were French, maybe they'd understand if I told them Jack had been jilted — he was a victim of an affair of the heart.

No way. The words just wouldn't come out. Too much time wasted ten years ago staring out the Bundy High School window dreaming about exotic locations.

Then, as a last resort, I ceremoniously raised my glass, drank a deep toast and held the empty beer glass over my left breast. 'Je suis Australien… Mon Oncle Geoffrey est mort dans Francais la premiere guerre… Vivre la France!'

I wanted to continue with this blatant patriotic blackmail but couldn't find the words to explain that Geoffrey was really my mother's uncle who got knocked in the First World War while defending a French village at the age of 19. Shit, I remember now it was probably a village in Belgium and not France. Where the fuck is Messines Ridge? Still, my middle name was Geoffrey and that would be a good one to throw into my appeal — if only I could.

The gendarme, who up until the patriotic toast to Uncle Geoffrey had seemed totally disinterested — busily reloading new rounds into his magazine with an occasional look at me that I assumed was Gallic distain — suddenly broke into a broad smile.

He slapped me on my shoulder, stood up straight, saluted, clicked his heels and loudly replied. 'Vivre Australie… jamais oublier Australie.'

I half expected a manly kiss on both cheeks, but it didn't happen. They simply dumped Jack face down in the filthy gutter and drove off.

I felt like writing to Bevan to tell him something amazing and uplifting had happened on my travels. I had met a decent Frenchman who had also publicly beaten the crap out of a squad of drunken legionnaires, the same bastard mob he had encountered in Syria.

*Footnote:* I returned many years later as part of a delegation planning for Australia to host the International Festival of Pacific Arts. I couldn't find Quinn's. There was a shopping centre where that wonderful den of inequity once stood, and someone had cut down the beautiful breadfruit tree that had shaded its entrance. I was saddened to hear that Quinn's had been burnt to the ground some years before in an act that many of the more devout locals said was retribution from Heaven. After all, hadn't God turned all the decadent people in Sodom and Gomorrah into salt for similar sins against decency?

I just thought that Tahiti, even with all its natural beauty, had lost some of its colour.

## Errors and omissions

I am in debt to Rory Gibson one of my young reporters on the *Townsville Daily Bulletin* who later returned to his old newspaper as the editor, after working in Fleet Street and also editing the *Fiji Times*. As I expected from an old-school journo, Rory corrected a serious error in my manuscript that would have caused embarrassment to the author and the publishers.

One of the most dramatic chapters in this story is about corrupt coppers in my time as editor of the *Bulletin*. To ensure the veracity of this piece I contacted Rory so the text could be verified independently by someone else who was there at the time.

His response: 'You need to correct the bit where you have me and the boys renting at Pallarenda when the coppers raided us. That's not correct. We were living at Rowes Bay.' They are both neighbouring bayside suburbs of Townsville, but hard-copy journos from the days of hot metal know you must get the facts right.

Jon Woodworth, the courageous 19-year-old who ran foul of the sinister Queensland Special Branch and also upset the big end of town, stopped me from misleading readers of this book. I was convinced that his informant was silenced by having one of his legs broken with an iron bar, but Jon tells me it was the threat of broken legs to be followed by a slow death that sent our terrified whistle-blower into hiding.

My wife Barbara also took me to task about the Sea Nymph on Kelly's Beach piece. 'I was not wearing a white bikini when you kissed me. I have never owned a white bikini in my life. It was a greenish colour.'

It is so vividly white in my memory that I cannot change it. However, in the interests of historical accuracy, I'll also admit it could have been a greenish colour.

## Do characters somehow speak to us from the past?

I can think of no better way to end the Colt's story than to relate an unusual incident that occurred very recently when I was doing a final check on some of the characters. Many of my older colleagues have passed away, but I wanted to see if others were still alive.

I typed in Bevan Waldock into a search on the internet and was stunned — there was a symbolic message from my old mate, and its source was only a few kilometres away from my home on the Atherton Tablelands.

A keen military historian with a metal detector had discovered Bevan's World War Two dog-tag, the metal coin-size disk with his AIF number stamped on it. The one he wore around his neck through the tough campaigns of North Africa and Syria. He had it when he was captured by the Vichy French all those years ago.

I was sad to learn that Bevan had died some years earlier but delighted that his long-lost dog-tag had been returned to his family.

This revelation triggered emotions in me that I didn't expect because of the unusual nature of my chance discovery and the timing.

The site on the internet is hidden away in what I understand is a 'forum' for people with a specialist interest in using metal detectors to unearth memorabilia from old wartime camps and training areas. But, for some strange reason, it jumped up on the top of the list when I first typed Bevan's name into Google. Strangely, it hasn't done that in any of my repeat searches — it's quite hard to find.

It also gave me comfort about the extensive dialogue that seemed to come from the very voices of my old mates when I was writing this story. Maybe there were some other emotional forces at work that were deeper than my fading memory?

There were over 80,000 Australian soldiers encamped on the Tablelands before they went into battle with the Japanese, but only one lost dog-tag has been discovered and it belonged to my mate and mentor Bevan, the man who could hold his own in an intellectual pub debate with the legendary Myles Carruthers. The same gentle bloke who knew five different ways to kill a man with his bare hands, and the colleague who saw that justice was metered out to the brute who bashed poor old Myles.

In wrapping up the Colt's story, I believe it is fitting that one of the great pub debaters of my youth should be given the final word. I know Bevan would have liked that.

*'You know it's synchronicity, don't you Bevan... this dog-tag thing and the Colt?'*

*'Ok, Myles, you've got me there... what in God's name is a synchronic city?'*

*'What in God's name indeed. It's from Jung... a causal principle as a basis for the apparent random, simultaneous occurrence of phenomena. He said it was linked to mystical reality.'*

*'I don't know who this Jung bloke is, but all I can say is that you've mixed with some pretty bloody strange people in your travels. To put it bluntly mate, you are once more frothing at the mouth with intellectual frog-shit, even though it may sound articulate. I lost my dog-tag swimming in the Barron River, the GSM got right up me, the armourer stamped out a new one, I went up into the islands and did terrible things to some terrible people and 75 years later some bloke finds the lost one close to where the Colt is living. That's the reality Myles... there is no such bloody thing as mystical reality... and talking about another reality that you're so obviously trying to avoid... it's your shout old mate.'*

# ACKNOWLEDGEMENTS

The Colt's story would never have been written without the support of my wife.

I started the memoir just over 20 years ago when Barbara had her first novel accepted after four years of rejections. While I struggled with my own narrative and dialogue, Barb not only raised kids and ran a household, but also had 52 books published and won several literary awards.

Encouraged by such commitment to writing by my life partner, I also persevered through times of frustration when I doubted that the right words would ever appear on the pages of my constantly reworked manuscripts.

The Colt's story would never have been published if Michael Wilkinson hadn't sent me a flurry of late night and early morning emails over Easter 2018 following my premature and widespread pitch to publishers. He thought there was a 'ripping yarn' in the Colt's story, but in its current form was too wordy and needed changes to smooth out the narrative sequence. I realised I would have to drop over 30,000 precious words, and the rejig would take months, but Barbara was delighted when I told her. Apparently she'd been saying that all along, but it wasn't registering with me — it's a blokes' thing?

So, thank you Michael and Wilkinson editor Jess Lomas.

Chris Mitchell encouraged me to share the KKK story, while Rory Gibson, John Gagliardi, Jon Woodworth and Max Tomlinson helped to confirm unreliable memories from the '80s. Reaching even further back in the mists of time, Mike Bingham,

John Mikkelsen, Roy Theodore, Terry Ryan and Gerry O'Connor generously shared experiences about our encounters with the unforgettable Myles Harrington Caruthers and the 'boys out the back'.

Courtesy *Townsville Bulletin.*

## ABOUT THE AUTHOR

Elliot Hannay is an author and veteran journalist. His career started in 1958 at the age of sixteen and he worked in newspapers, ABC radio and television, the public service and media consultancy for 60 years.

He edited one weekly and two daily newspapers in Queensland, toured China in 1980 on its first exchange with journalists from a Western nation and freelanced as a foreign correspondent in the Asia Pacific region, Central America and Europe.

Elliot lives in Townsville with his novelist wife Barbara who has written 57 more books than he has. They have four children and seven grandchildren.

## *'I laughed until I cried.'*

'The Colt's book should be read by anyone starting out in journalism today. We may have jumped from typewriters to iPads, but the craft of journalism has some basic rules which can only be learned on the job-most times the hard way.

'The days when young journalists would learn from old hands in the pub how to get stories, ask questions, develop contacts, retain a deadly fear of errors and approach their work with the right mixture of enthusiasm, honesty, shoe leather, scepticism and compassion, are long gone. But the rules for good journalists are still the same.

'I laughed until I cried at Hannay's description of some of the characters in his early days in journalism and his frank admission of his own painful naivety as he started out as a 16-year-old on his local paper in Bundaberg and shared his fears as editor of the *Townsville Daily Bulletin* when under pressure from dark forces.

'As he says, for years past and years to come, the essential challenge for any journalist remains the same – finding out who's up who and who's paying the rent.'

*Glenda Korporaal OAM.*
*Glenda Korporaal received the Order of Australia Medal on Australia Day 2019 for her services to print media journalism. A long-serving foreign correspondent, she was The Australian newspaper's China correspondent and former associate business editor. She has lived and worked in Canberra and Washington DC and has a Masters of Arts (Economics) from the George Washington University*

## 'The Monster of Racism had been let out of the cage.'

'In the 1970s–80s there was a rising between First Australians and the European newcomers (who are now 95% of the population). Serious confrontation, rioting, jailings and ongoing soul-destroying court battles were constantly occurring.

'There was, inevitably, the rise of the extremist groups which Elliot Hannay not only was threatened by, but rather courageously confronted. He makes light of this in his book, but it was a dangerous time.

'To quote but two examples — in my hometown Cloncurry and nearby Mt Isa, there were three First Australians bashed to death in jail cells. Two water police who were regulating fishing and the environment vanished without a trace when they were working between two First Australian settlements. The violence was real, these were registered deaths. In neither case were the probable culprits investigated. That is both the alleged white and black culprits. No-one in the three arms of Government was prepared to further inflame the monster of racism that had been let out of the cage.

'Hannay, one of his northern colleagues Max Tomlinson and the ABCs Steve Austin were three journalists who threw their great personal courage and extraordinary strong sense of justice into the cause and made Australia a much better place than it was. They are, like so many others of the truly courageous history makers – destined to go unheralded.

'It should anger us that these journalists, as a result of their natural humility, at that time failed to communicate the fear and rage which they had to confront and the inspirational heroism they exemplified. But, those of us that were close to the action could see this so very clearly.'

*Bob Katter*
*Hon. Bob Katter MLA, MP. Former Minister Aboriginal Affairs,*
*Northern Development, Heritage, Mines and Energy. He is the second*
*longest serving politician in the history of Australia.*

## 'Finally, the truth can be told… the Ku Klux Klan was a reality.'

'This is a book that should be read by all Australians: black, white, young and old. Not just because it features my late activist father Archie Smallwood in one of the most powerful chapters of the Colt's story, but because we all need to confront the insidious racism and bigotry from the land rights' era which is still with us today in new forms, hidden in false agendas of nationalism.

'The author has been known to our family for almost 40 years as the newspaper editor who opened the door to our courageous father and other high-profile northern Indigenous activists. He writes in this memoir that he was just trying to do his job as an old-school journalist committed to providing his readers with both sides of an issue that had the potential to divide our nation. But not all editors were doing that in the 1970s and 1980s and I'm just glad that a young man like Elliot Hannay was in the chair at that time and was prepared to put the voices of my people into print.

'Finally, the full story can be told about how the Ku Klux Klan was a reality. Our homegrown white supremacists not only tried to block my father and other activists seeking justice for their people but were also out to destroy them.'

*Gracelyn Smallwood*
*Professor Smallwood PhD 'First Australians' Human Rights', MSc.*
*Public Health, RN/midwife and activist of 50 years identifies as*
*a Birrigubba, Kalkadoon and South Sea Islander woman and received*
*the Order of Australia in 1992 for services to public health and*
*HIV AIDS education. She was a guest of the South African President,*
*Nelson Mandela at his African AIDS Summit in 1997, and won the*
*Deadly Award for Outstanding Lifetime Achievements in Australian*
*Indigenous Health in 2007. Professor Smallwood is also a member of*
*the Harvard University FXB and Human Rights Consortium.*